IN THE
SHADOW
of the
GREAT WALL

Megan Lewis

IN THE
SHADOW
of the
GREAT WALL

MEGAN KNOYLE LEWIS

Gomer

First published in 2019 by Gomer Press,
Llandysul, Ceredigion SA44 4JL

ISBN 978 1 78562 289 2

A CIP record for this title is available from the British Library.

This book is published with the financial support of the
Welsh Books Council.

Printed and bound in Wales at
Gomer Press, Llandysul, Ceredigion
www.gomer.co.uk

In memory of my mother
Eluned Lewis (nee Knoyle) who always encouraged me
to look beyond the horizon.

ACKNOWEDGEMENTS

The ride could never have even started without a kaleidoscope of people.

At a time when many doubted me, I was especially grateful for the initial encouragement of my family – husband Iestyn Thomas, children Gethin, Gwenllian and Iona (even though they thought I was mad), sister Rhiannon Lewis, cousin Rowena Gulland, and Drs Peter Bourne and Mary King, not forgetting my cousin Sir David Lewis, Lord Mayor of London at the time, who not only provided a letter of support but enabled another from Sir William Ehrmann, British ambassador to China.

At varying times on the Great Wall journey, my little team consisted of Rowena, who provided both moral and financial support; Mr Ren, who guided us conscientiously; and He Guo Sheng, who steered us through the tricky waters of local bureaucracy. Li May made a mean morning coffee, and for all his foibles, in a strange way the mercurial Li Jing had the horses' best interests at heart. The argumentative Hua and steadfast Peng Wenchao provided irreplaceable back-up and became my valued companions.

Thanks go to our main sponsors, the Shandan Military Horse Stud for our wonderful horses, the Jiazhuo Special Trailer Co for our very special trailer, Les Spark of FnE saddles for our two indispensable adjustable saddles, and last but certainly not least, old friend Frank Hodal for backing the ride from the very start with his extremely generous financial sponsorship of a horse (Zorbee) all the way across Eurasia. Charles Owen supplied the helmet which saved me from possible fatal injury; Kanteq, the body protector which gave me the confidence to ride when I was recovering; Cutana Hats, hat brims which kept off sun and rain; Lansdowne, lightweight rugs; Just Chaps, natty and functional half-chaps; Plas Equestrian, endurance bridles; and Shires Equestrian, reflective gear. All of these companies I approached specifically for sponsorship due to their existing and well-deserved high reputation for quality products, and I am proud to say several of them are based in Wales.

On my initial recce to China, I was hosted by Sarah Noble Hua. Xu Bing and Shi Junmin of the China Children and Teenagers Fund, Mr Chu Wen and Mr Zhao of the Yihe stud, farrier Mr Ji Yongshi and my Chinese teacher Liu Xinlian all helped to get me on my way. I will be ever grateful to Kath Naday and Ed Jocelyn for coming to my rescue and providing a bolt-hole after my accident, and to Andy McEwan for enabling me to conquer the Great Firewall of China.

The subsequent success of the China ride was almost entirely due to Chinese Equestrian Association members Li Kening (Kenny Li or Kubi) who promoted our cause, Wu Gangfang (Wutzala) who got things organised, and Harry Tse who acquired official approval from the Chinese authorities. Irish lawyer David McNeill stepped in to smooth out legal concerns.

The Zunhua Women's Federation, Mr Zhang of the Brother Win stables, and the horsey communities in Hohhot and Yinchuan, all helped us on our way and hosted us with splendid banquets. I would like to single out the Joy Hotel in Guyuan, who looked after the horses free of charge for three months after my accident, and organised a tremendous re-launch.

Other people who deserve a mention include my long distance riding vet Lisa Adshead for her advice and medical supplies, and the people who kept things ticking over at home – in particular Iestyn, who looked after my affairs; Rob Jones, who kept an eye on the ponies; and good neighbour Marina Thomas.

And of course there are many, many other people not mentioned here who directly or indirectly contributed to the success of the ride with advice and support. Thank you all.

On the book front, Meirion Davies at Gomer Press was kind enough to take on my script, my talented young editor Rebecca John moulded my modest efforts into some sort of order, Gary Evans refined my rough maps and Qin Chuan checked my Chinese. Thanks to Chris Saunders for his valuable input, as well as Rhiannon, Iona, Rowena, and Julia for their comments.

On behalf of the City of London may I extend my best wishes to you and your team in its endeavour to ride from China to UK over the 4 years 2008-12 between the two Olympic Games in Beijing and London. This is a wonderful idea and I feel sure it will further improve the excellent relations between out two great countries.

All good fortune to you on your exciting and enjoyable long journey.

Sir David Lewis
Lord Mayor of London 2007-8

PROLOGUE

'Please accept my warmest wishes as you begin such a spectacular journey. The Olympic motto "*Citius, Altius, Fortius*" does not include "*Longius*", but all four apply to your endeavour! I wish you a safe, enjoyable and successful journey.'

Sir William Ehrmann, British Ambassador to China 2000-2010

It was a cold autumn day in 2006 when I took my courage in both hands, turned to my husband Iestyn and said, 'What would you say if I told you that I wanted to ride from Beijing to London by horse?'

Such an easy thing to say, but I might not have been so quick to blurt it out if I had realised quite how much of a challenge I had set myself. The logistics were immense. Even as the crow flies the distance measures over 8,000 kilometres, or around five thousand miles, but the route on the ground would be much longer. Struggling through difficult terrain and adverse weather conditions would test to the limit my ability to maintain the condition of the horses, let alone negotiate rivers, roads, tricky border crossings and unhelpful officials. Even in the planning stage I would face huge disappointments and setbacks, and many times over the years I tossed and turned in bed, racked with sickening self-doubts. But always in the end the driving fear of not realising a long-held dream proved far greater than the struggle of achieving it.

One of the most common questions interviewers asked during my journey was what my family thought of what I was doing, and the answer I most often gave was, 'Well, my children think I am crazy, but are not surprised!'

Crazy I may have been, but ever since I was a young girl and read Aime Tschiffely's account of his ride from Buenos Aires to New York in the 1920s on two Criollo horses, I knew deep down that at some point in my life I would do a long ride. In fact, I had a sneaking ambition to ride right round the world. Perhaps what I did not foresee was that it would not be until I was an old age pensioner.

The lure of travelling through China and Central Asia was undoubtedly inspired by an idyllic Far Eastern childhood, mostly spent in Malaya (now Malaysia), where my father Dr Gerwyn Lewis was in the education service. After his retirement when I was thirteen, the family settled in London, but started to spend more time in Wales, our country of origin. It was while holidaying at our cottage in Cwrt-y-cadno, Carmarthenshire, that I began to ride bareback on my uncle Dai Brynteg's shepherding pony Dick ('Richard on Sundays' said Dai with a twinkle in his eye). I was totally hooked, and it was not long before my father bought my sister Rhiannon and I a fat little bay pony called Cariad from Llanybydder horse market. She regularly bucked me off, but failed to dent my passion for riding. Other ponies and horses followed over the years, and my great delight was the freedom to explore the moorland hills and forested valleys of north Carmarthenshire on horseback, a joyful release from the frantic pace of life in London. Sometimes I would stay overnight at a local youth hostel, and a couple of times I took off for a week round Mid Wales with only my pony for company. In the meantime, I continued to pursue my interest in Asia, taking degrees in Southeast Asian Studies and doing eight months research in Malaysia, before ending up as head of geography at a girls' school in Knightsbridge. But the seed of an idea had been born.

Nowadays it is an easy matter to sit down in front of a computer at home to research and plan an expedition in a distant country; contacts are only an email, text, or internet chat away. People easily forget that in those pre-internet days reliable up-to-date information could be excessively difficult to access, international phone calls were prohibitively expensive, and communication by letter a slow, tedious process with no guarantee that letters would actually reach their destination. The cost of travel abroad was also high compared with today. I was enjoying my life in London and Wales and it was somehow never the right time to take the plunge. In fact, I remember thinking that I really needed some unhappy upheaval in my life to propel me into action. Instead came a huge life change with marriage to husband Iestyn and the arrival of our children Gethin,

Gwenllian, and Iona. The dream faded into the background. When my father generously offered to let us take over his Carmarthenshire sheep farm, we jumped at the chance and within the year had moved lock, stock and barrel down to Ffrwdfal. While I coped with lambing and built up a small but successful Welsh pony stud, Iestyn ran a sportswear business, taught, and coached rugby before starting Challenge Aid, a charity raising money for disadvantaged children through fitness challenges. I also tried my hand at endurance riding with a series of Arabian horses, winning several races and being selected for the British Intermediate Team. But for over twenty years my travel abroad was confined to a couple of short trips across the Channel.

By the end of 2006 all our children had left home and I found myself if not with unlimited free time, at least with more freedom to travel. The idea of my long horse ride started to resurface. China was opening up to foreigners, and Iestyn had recently developed connections with a charity based in Beijing. A fever of excitement was building up towards the imminent Beijing and London Olympics. It seemed an obvious challenge to carry a message of goodwill from one to the other.

I realised that life was passing me by and I still had not done my long ride. It was now or never!

And Iestyn's response? He had long been aware of my secret ambitions and hardly batted an eyelid at my rash pronouncement. Not all reactions were quite so phlegmatic and although my immediate family had no doubt I could pull it off, some people obviously regarded my bold statement of intention as the ramblings of an elderly woman in a late-life crisis. I determined to prove them wrong.

So this is the story of how I started my Long Horse Ride, and in doing so, became the first person on record to ride by horse from one end of the Ming Great Wall of China to the other.

CHAPTER ONE

A HORSE IS NOT A BICYCLE

老骥伏枥, 志在千里
lǎo jì fú lì, zhì zài qiān lǐ
An old warhorse in the stable still longs to gallop a thousand li.

Friday, October 2, 2008. Gusts of warm air buffeted in through the cab windows as the truck rattled along the Jingzang Expressway north of Beijing. Beside me the Chinese driver sucked slowly on the cheap cigarette he held in one hand and manoeuvred the steering wheel with the other. In the side mirror I could just see two large brown hairy rumps and a smaller grey one shifting and swaying with the motion of the vehicle as they braced themselves against the rails surrounding the truck bed. A strand of black tail poking out through a gap whipped in the wind created by our passage. The horses' bodies were out of sight behind a load of hay bales piled in front of them and tucked firmly under a faded canvas tarpaulin. I knew it also hid sacks of grain, saddles and bridles, and a few holdalls of equipment and personal items.

Curving steadily round a bend on the steep valley side, we plunged into a tunnel, ceiling lights flicking across the windscreen and over the horses' backsides, which continued to sway rhythmically as we shot out into the bright sun on the other side. Nothing seemed to faze them, and I breathed a contented sigh of relief. After two years of interminable struggle, I was finally on my way to start riding from the eastern end of the Great Wall of China where it reached the Bohai Sea.

The challenge that lay ahead was not just one of distance, but of the practicalities of travelling by horse. 'Oh I know someone who has done that,' people often commented when I told them I was riding across Eurasia.

'What, they are riding by horse?' I would raise my eyebrows

quizzically. Only a handful of people had ridden sizeable parts of the continent on horseback, and I thought I knew just about all of them.

'Oh no, by bicycle,' they would reply brightly. Or by motorbike, or Land Rover, or tuk-tuk, or pogo stick – substitute whichever applies.

At this point I would sigh to myself and resist the temptation to make the glaringly obvious statement: 'A horse is not a bicycle.' Without in any way denigrating the immense achievement of those who have pedalled their way relentlessly across burning deserts and up countless steep mountainsides while I sat back and let four legs do all the work, I found the majority of people had no appreciation of the vast logistics and unique problems involved in globetrotting by horse. Having said which, I would be pretty damn impressed by anyone who did it on a pogo stick.

Although thoroughbred racehorses can gallop at speeds of up to 70 kph (c45mph) over short distances, and supremely fit endurance horses cover substantial distances during races, the average horse can travel only relatively slowly on extended journeys. I calculated my average travel distances would probably be around 30 kilometres (c20 miles) a day, meaning I could realistically aim for distances of around 160 kilometres (c100 miles) a week, allowing leeway for days off and the like. A fit cyclist on favourable terrain might comfortably cover in a day what I would expect to cover in a week.

Horses need constant daily feeding and watering, and they drink a lot of water. And I mean a lot of water. Compared with the 1 to 3 litres a day drunk by humans, a horse can knock back 30 to 50 litres a day, and that is just lazing around in cool weather. They are also 'trickle feeders' which means they are not designed to go without feeding for more than a few hours at a time.

At night they cannot be stashed away under the stairs in a hostel like a bicycle, and, particularly in more populated areas, it can be a challenge to find somewhere safe to overnight them, assuming the owners are willing to cope with the mess. After taking the saddle and bridle off at the end of the day they need to be checked over, groomed, watered and fed before the rider can even begin to think of their own needs, and the same palaver must be repeated in the morning and often during the day.

Horses are prone to mysterious lameness which may require days, if not weeks, of rest. Getting out the repair kit and slapping on a puncture patch is not an option. It is certain they will need medical attention at some point, whether for cuts, bruises, sores, rashes, coughs or something more serious. They suffer from a variety of unpleasant diseases with alarming names such as swamp fever, strangles, lockjaw, contagious equine metritis, and West Nile virus. Crossing borders is always a total nightmare as some of these require long quarantine periods and courses of injections backed up by copious amounts of paperwork (sometimes in several different languages), which must be signed by veterinarians on both sides of the border. After which, if you are lucky, permission might be given to allow the horse to cross into the specified country.

Riding a horse is irritatingly high profile when you are trying to avoid the attention of local officials in some countries. This is not helped by their social repertoire, which can include kicking, biting, bucking, rearing, spooking, escaping and running away, farting and leaving droppings in public places.

Not like a bicycle then.

'So why on earth would you ever voluntarily choose to travel by horse?' you may ask – a question I have asked myself at times. But in fact, for me the positives overwhelmingly outstrip the negatives.

Appreciating different environments and lifestyles is surely one of the main reasons for travel. With its slow pace and quiet, non-invasive progress across country, the horse allows you to open up your senses fully to drink in the surrounding environment, whether wild soaring mountains or noisy street markets. Wildlife may be startled by humans on foot, but graciously accept the presence of a horse. In steep terrain, the horse does all the hard work, allowing you to sit back and enjoy the scenery in a way that walkers are unable to do. A horse can scramble along steep mountain goat tracks or across sandy desert and muddy swampland, clamber over embankments and low walls and squeeze through narrow gaps. In other words, it can access places difficult or impossible for mechanical forms of travel.

Then there is the unique connection the horse provides with people you encounter on the way. Horse people already share common ground and are only too willing to chat with, help out, or host a fellow horse owner. But even in urban areas people are eager to engage with a horse and its rider, and children run up in excitement. Questions come thick and fast. 'Can I stroke him? Can I give him a carrot/apple/sugar lump? Does he need water? Can I take my photo with him? Is there anything I can do for you?' and, most plaintively, 'I have never touched a horse before.'

But perhaps most important is the bond that is built up with a living creature who becomes a valued journey companion. No mechanical contraption can substitute for the feeling of picking your way across country with a horse beneath you, a partnership facing and overcoming together the challenges of river crossings, rocky tracks, snow storms, and busy roads. To fully understand this bond, you need to have experienced the moment a hesitant horse trusts you enough to wade through a deep pool or step behind you onto a shaky bridge, the moment when it whickers gently at you in the morning, rubs its head companionably against your back, and puts its soft muzzle into your hand.

Planning had begun in earnest at the beginning of 2007, and the first major decision to be made was which route to take. I had considered a northerly route via Mongolia to take advantage of the grassy Eurasian steppe which runs in an almost unbroken belt from Manchuria to Hungary. It was along this path that the Mongol armies of Genghis Khan swept on their bloody invasions of Central Asia and Europe. But travelling further south through China presented the more interesting option of following the Great Wall of China and the ancient Silk Road across the Gobi Desert, and it was this idea that captivated me.

I decided to break up the enormous distance from Beijing to London into about six more manageable stages of roughly 2,000 kilometres (c1000 - 1500 miles), a distance I felt I could achieve in three to four months for each. The time allotted for stages was dictated by several factors. Visas for most countries were limited to periods of three months, though an extension was sometimes possible. I could not abandon my responsibilities at home for too long at a time, and the breaks in between would give time to regroup and concentrate on planning the next leg. By confining travel to the milder spring and autumn periods, I hoped to avoid the scorching summers and icy winters of Central Eurasia, when temperatures could soar above 40C before plunging to minus 40C, making travel by horse all but impossible. Finally, the breaks allowed some leeway within the time schedule should setbacks occur during the ride, a significant consideration as I had committed myself to arriving in London by the 2012 Olympics.

First, I needed to concentrate on tackling the Ming Great Wall of China. Riding by horse from one end to the other presented a whole challenge in itself, which I was keen to try. As far as I was aware this had not been done before, although explorer Robin Hanbury-Tenison and his wife Louella had ridden sections in the 1980s. If I was successful, I would be the first person on record to achieve this feat. I could use the first stretch to Beijing as a trial leg to test the water and build up contacts. Starting from the eastern end of the Great Wall on the coast at Shanhaiguan, this leg ran about 500 kilometres (300 miles) to the Great Wall at Badaling in Beijing municipality. The first full stage would then extend nearly 2,500 kilometres (around 1,500 miles) from Badaling, the official start for the Beijing to London ride, to the western end of the Great Wall at Jiayuguan. I planned to complete the trial leg in early summer 2008, just before the Olympics, and start the main stage in the autumn.

Should I use a packhorse or a support vehicle? Ideally, I favoured a ride without vehicle support which would be cheaper and more in the spirit of adventure I hoped to foster. However, it rapidly became evident that the seriously inhospitable terrain I would be encountering in places would make some form of vehicle back-up unavoidable. There would be no inns providing water and fodder for travelling animals on desert roads as there would have been a hundred years previously, and these essentials would have to be transported by vehicle. The wellbeing of the horses was of paramount importance to me, and something I was not prepared to gamble with.

There was also the thorny issue of Chinese bureaucracy which had more potential to scupper the venture than anything else. I hoped to surf the Chinese wave of enthusiasm for the Olympics, but knew they might not be so sympathetic to a lone foreigner trying to ride a horse across China with no apparent support. While staying in a backpackers' hostel in Lahore the year before, I had met Steve McCutcheon, who was endeavouring to ride on horseback from Delhi to Beijing. In spite of doing all he could to make sure he had acquired the relevant permissions, only two weeks into China the police clamped down and put the kibosh on his trek. I determined to go through official channels as much as I could, and if that necessitated vehicle support, so be it.

Hours researching on the internet threw up much useful information. Among other things I discovered that the equine department at Hartpury College in Gloucestershire had links with the Chinese Equestrian Association. Through them I contacted their British liaison officer, Sarah Noble Hua. A slim, dark British woman married to a mainland Chinese businessman, she spoke fluent Mandarin and was acting as a consultant to the CEA. Their son Alex Hua Tian was an accomplished young event rider bidding to become the first Chinese citizen to compete in this discipline at the 2008 Olympics. She was keen to be involved and I arranged to go out to China in the autumn of 2007 to meet up and look into logistics.

In October 2007 I arrived in bustling Beijing. Sarah and husband Hua Shan had a spacious flat in one of the former diplomatic compounds on a quiet road where persimmon trees were dropping their soft orange fruit to splat on the pavement below. This was my base for the next three weeks while we went for meetings with everyone from the chief vet for China to the editor of the magazine *China National Geography*. Everyone seemed to want to come along, and at one point I began to fear it might turn into something akin to the invasion of the Mongol hordes. Among others, I met up with Ed Jocelyn, a Brit who had walked the route of Mao Zedong's Long March and trekked with pack mules.

The highpoint was a trip out to the Shandan Military Horse Stud in Gansu, as they had offered to supply horses. After a long train journey, I was picked up at a little station in the middle of nowhere by representatives from the stud, including Wu Shuli who had ridden almost all the way round China on Shandan horses. The stud headquarters were situated an hour's drive away at the centre of a small military settlement located on grassy foothills with a stunning backdrop of the snow-capped Qilian mountains to the south. The stud traditionally supplied horses to the Chinese army, but with the demise of the Soviet bloc, they had reduced numbers dramatically from thousands down to a few hundred. Several geldings had been put aside, and I was able to try out a willing little chestnut on a test ride over the hills, down gorges and across rushing rivers.

I returned to Wales feeling highly motivated and buoyant. I had already done a short evening course in Mandarin Chinese, but now I set out to study it more seriously. I marched into the Chinese Studies Department at St. David's University College, just down the road in Lampeter, and persuaded them to let me sit in on first year Chinese degree classes in return for purchasing a full Chinese lion dancing costume for them to use at Chinese New Year. Things looked rosy and I could not wait to crack on with preparations for a tentative start and trial run the following summer.

However, things very rarely run to plan and in February 2008 I had a severe knock-back. Sarah's son Alex Hua Tian had qualified to compete in the Olympics, and Sarah admitted she could not spare the time to help organise the ride. It was a blow after all the effort that had been expended over the year, but I had learnt a lot which would stand me in good stead. I started organising from scratch once again, this time using my contacts in the China Children and Teenagers Fund (CCTF), the charity Iestyn had connected with in Beijing. In March I flew out to China to meet up with Ben Xu, a quietly intelligent and sympathetic representative of the charity. My top priority was to identify one or two suitable mounts. A horsey contact of Ben's knew the manager of the Yihe stud on the Kangxi grasslands just to the north of Beijing, a popular area for Beijingers to hire out horses for a gallop across the plain. Ben Xu had kindly earmarked Shi Junmin, a young English-speaking trainee, to help me.

It may be helpful here to give a short explanation regarding Chinese names. The most important thing to remember is that the Chinese always put their family name first, so Shi Junmin's family name was Shi and his personal given name Junmin. Many Chinese also choose to have a nickname, which may be Chinese and/or another language. Junmin had chosen the English nickname Larry, so he could introduce himself in English as Larry Shi. Ben Xu's Chinese name was Xu Bing, from his family name Xu and his given name Bing, which he translated to Ben in English. As an older man, he would usually be formally addressed as *Xu Xiansheng* or Mr Xu, and more informally but still respectfully as *Lao Xu* or Old Xu. Age does not have the same negative connotations in China as in the West. Given names are normally only used by close friends or family, but it is now acceptable among the younger set to be more casual in conversation, particularly when mixing with foreigners. I called Junmin by his given Chinese name Junmin, or nickname Larry, and he called me by my given name Megan.

Junmin and I pushed our way through the Beijing crowds to board a bus for the hour's drive to Kangzhuang, where we were met by stud manager Mr Zhao Wenxing, who drove us to a neat, well run yard bordering on the Jingzang Expressway. Two long stable buildings with loose boxes and outside pens overlooked a large outdoor sand school, a round pen, an empty swim pool for the horses and a couple of fields of brood mares. Owned by wealthy Chinese Mr Chu Wen, who had made his money in the booming construction industry, it mainly accommodated Arabian horses. These included a couple of glamorous stallions that the *lao ban* or boss used for barrel racing – an American cowboy competition involving a timed clover-leaf run round three barrels. This was an increasingly popular sport among the nouveau riche of the Chinese horsey set. Over a cup of *cha* in his room in the stable block, Mr Zhao proved to be a fount of good advice. Yes, he could help sort us out with horses. But it would be better to leave horse purchase until later as horses were likely to be expensive now when they were due to be used for the summer holiday trade. I thought again and discussed it with Ben Xu later.

'I think it would be better if you left everything until after the Olympics,' he advised.

I had to agree with him. It seemed more sensible to postpone everything until the autumn when the Olympics were over. Quite apart from the cost of horses, it should ease visa worries as I had heard that people were encountering difficulties with longer stay visas in the run-up to the Games. It would give me more time to plan following the last minute change of circumstances, and with the Olympics out of the way people should hopefully have more time to help. The weather would also be more pleasant with the oppressive heat of summer over. With the promise of help to find horses when I returned in September secured, I returned home with confidence restored.

I also had another ally on board as my younger cousin Rowena Gulland had immediately been enthused by the idea of the ride, and her engineer husband Matt had just been offered an oil job in Atyrau, Kazakhstan. Situated on the northern shore of the Caspian Sea, it was bang on my route, and if Matt had not accepted the post, I suspect his life would not have been worth living. Their two demanding young children presented a slight handicap as we did not think it feasible to strap them to the front of our saddles, but Matt prudently volunteered to take charge of them while Rowena joined me on the first leg in China. She had been brought up in Hong Kong and had travelled widely, including a solo trip to China in the 1980s, a honeymoon through the 'stans' (Kazakhstan, Uzbekistan, Kyrgyzstan), and two years living on the North West Frontier of Pakistan. I knew she would be unfazed by any situation we might meet, and would be the perfect companion for the trial stage.

It is always handy to have a Lord Mayor of London knocking around in the family at such times, and another cousin, Sir David Lewis, was prevailed upon to provide a message of support. Not only that but he contacted his old friend Sir William Ehrmann, who fortuitously was the incumbent British Ambassador to China. Sir William was not in a position to officially endorse the ride, but he kindly wrote and signed a letter of encouragement. I quietly hoped Chinese officials would focus on the headed notepaper and signature so I could use it to persuade them I had official British sanction.

It was all systems go. But the event that really made me feel I had sealed my commitment to the ride came in early summer. Although I had been able to sort out helpers to keep a careful eye on my Welsh ponies while I was abroad, I realised that it was not really feasible to continue actively breeding, as I was likely to be absent in the spring when the foals arrived. It seemed a shame to let lovely broodmares with such good bloodlines go to waste, so I decided to offer some of my best mares on loan to selected studs for the duration of the ride. Consequently, in June I watched Cwrtycadno Perlen and Cwrtycadno Glain being loaded onto a lorry for the long haul up to the Waxwing stud in Scotland. It was not without a tear in my eye, though I knew they could not have landed in a better home. If anything made me realise the dream was becoming a reality, that moment did!

Planning a detailed route from Shanhaiguan to Badaling proved almost impossible, as the only maps I had been able to acquire in China were very small scale and limited to main roads, with virtually no topographical details. Matt managed to find a source of old 1:250,000 US relief maps of China dating from the 1940s on the internet, so I tried downloading and resizing them, printing out sections and sticking them together again to make workable maps, and then trying to mark on the new roads. But it was an almost hopeless task, and the situation on the ground when we actually rode this section was so completely changed that my efforts turned out to be worse than useless. It was apparent that a good guide would be essential.

By July 2008 a ride website was up and running, and I was sending out endless letters and emails to selected companies asking for sponsorship, though only to firms in whose products I had complete faith. I wanted to be sure I could stand by the brands that I promoted through the ride.

One of my prime concerns was finding suitable saddles. As a former endurance rider, I was acutely aware that a badly fitting saddle could cause saddle sores, muscle wastage, and even lameness. Unfortunately, I had no idea what size or shape of horse I was likely to end up with in China, and knew a qualified fitting service en route would be out of the question. I had written to Les Spark of the Free 'n' Easy Saddle company, whose saddles I had greatly admired on the endurance circuit, to see if he would be willing to donate or reduce the cost of a saddle. So I was delighted when I had a phone call from Les.

'We would like to sponsor you with two customised saddles,' he said, 'and we can also provide you with numnahs to go with them.'

This was fabulous news. FnE saddles have two wide weight-spreading panels that can be adjusted to the shape of the horse's back with a few turns of a screw, and they also flex as the horse moves. Almost all saddles have a gullet or tunnel under the saddle seat which keeps the saddle from pressing on the horse's spine. Each saddle panel on the FnE saddles had its own separate numnah or saddle pad, leaving the space down the gullet and over the horse's spine open to the air. Les had experimented by adding pockets in the numnahs where they hung down behind the saddle flaps. It was a great excitement to see the saddles, complete with extra D rings for attaching saddle bags, tying jackets, etc. when I visited the workshop to learn how to adjust them.

Local Welsh company Plas Equestrian made up a couple of bridles in my chosen colours of red and green. They had the added advantage of being fitted with clips to attach the bit and reins. This allowed for easy removal of the bit when grazing or feeding the horses, and it was a matter of a moment to reclip the reins onto the headcollar for leading or tying the horse. Another local company,

Lansdowne, sponsored me with weatherproof horse rugs made to my specifications, with the minimum of straps to cut down on weight.

And last, but most certainly not least, I was immensely grateful to receive regular financial backing from Frank Hodal of the American probiotics company Vidazorb to cover running costs of a horse to be called Zorbee after their busy bee mascot. I opened a Long Horse Ride bank account, and Frank's first payment formed the opening deposit.

The travel agency were astonished when my passport came back from the Chinese embassy with the sixty-day visa I had applied for, and it was a relief to know I had ample time to prepare and carry out the trial run.

My flight to Beijing was booked for August 31, 2008, and it was now a rush to make sure I had all my equipment sorted and packed. Rowena and I were taking a saddle each out to China, and I spent the last couple of days carefully calculating how to keep within the baggage limit, several times repacking the cardboard box which had to serve as a suitcase, and using a pocket scales strung up from the banisters in the hall.

My centre of operations for a month in Beijing was a rather musty Chinese hotel in Hepingli, an older residential suburb with low rise blocks of flats on either side of tree-lined streets. The electrics and plumbing were slightly dodgy, but it was only six minutes' walk from the subway and at 168 yuan a night (about £14) it was affordable on my limited budget. In fact, since food and travel were also very cheap in China, I probably spent less on living expenses than I would have at home. The receptionist looked horrified at the copious amounts of luggage that kept emerging from the taxi, but my room was spacious enough to accommodate everything, and had an en suite shower room, television (Chinese channel only), kettle, air con, and most importantly internet connection, so it was almost a little home from home. I loved being in a non-tourist part of the city, lulled to sleep by crickets in the trees at night, and woken by voluble Chinese street conversations in the morning. The downside was the fact that no one spoke a syllable of English, a challenge for my still distinctly wobbly command of Chinese. My mantra became 'When in doubt, phone Ben Xu'.

The first thing to do was sort out horses, and Junmin and I spent an hour and a half on a crowded bus to Kangzhuang, where we were picked up by Mr Zhao. We first drove out to a small Chinese village to meet horse dealer Mr Xi Jian Chuang at his traditional rural courtyard house, where he had a couple of horses tied up in the yard. He produced the first candidate, a small, plain, grey Mongolian gelding with a thick neck and a hogged mane – the equine version of a crew cut. His legs and feet were strong and his temperament seemed quiet. Most horses trot by moving diagonal pairs of legs simultaneously, but this gelding could pace, a lateral gait in which the pairs of legs on the same side move together. It is common among Mongolian horses and is very comfortable. I also tried a bigger horse, about fifteen hands high (a hand is four inches). She was a bit on the lean side but her legs looked OK and she went amenably, so she was put on the shortlist with the gelding.

A Mr Tuo showed us three fifteen-hand horses at a pre-arranged meeting place: two chestnuts with scrawny back ends and dreadful hocks, and a nice five-year-old bay mare. She was unshod and a little sore on the stony track, which unfortunately meant we could not trot her, but she seemed quiet and comfortable. We spent another hour driving round the Kangxi grasslands in case anything else caught my eye, but most were too finely built, and the only other likely ones we saw either had horrendous sores or behaved atrociously.

I ended up negotiating for Mr Xi's two horses. However, the bay mare haunted me and I later decided to buy her as well, as we would need three horses if we had a guide.

The official currency of China is renminbi (RMB), commonly referred to as *yuan*. At 29000 yuan, or around £2,500, the bill for the three horses was one of my main outlays, but we were a long way from the steppes where horses would be cheaper. Arranging payment proved surprisingly tricky. Realising that withdrawing money from British banks was difficult in major Chinese cities and impossible in the back country, I opened a Bank of China account. I then had unprecedented difficulty transferring money into it, only to discover some time later that the money was not registering in my Chinese branch as it had not been changed from sterling into Chinese yuan. Not realising this, I was forced to trawl round half the ATMs in Beijing with all my bank cards to withdraw enough money to pay for the horses, but eventually I was able to return to Kangzhuang carrying the cash. The bay mares were called Bei Bei and Jing Jing after the Beijing Olympic mascots, and the Mongolian pony was called Zorbee after the mascot of our sponsor Vidazorb.

Horses were now in place, but everything else continued to be an uphill struggle, not helped by my poor command of Chinese. I was having difficulty editing my website and a frustrating amount of time was spent kicking my heels and waiting for responses from various contacts. Kath Naday, a friend of Ed Jocelyn's, interviewed me for *Beijing This Month* and I managed to lose my mobile with all my vital phone numbers at our meeting. Kath had promised to put me in touch with Chinese tourist guide Richard Chen, who knew the region along the Great Wall to the east of Beijing, but it was some time before I managed to hunt down her phone number again. Richard and I eventually met and he was able to give me valuable information with regard to routes and terrain as a result of which I changed my route plan and schedule.

I met up with Liu Xinlian, my Chinese teacher from Lampeter who lived in Beijing.

'Be careful. You must wear plenty of warm clothes,' she warned.

'I'm sure we'll be OK.'

'You don't understand. It is very cold to the north of Beijing in autumn. It can be freezing.'

She was not the only one of my Chinese friends who were deeply concerned about the arctic conditions they were convinced gripped the countryside to the north. I took their warnings with a pinch of salt, but made sure I packed my thermal underwear.

With only a week to go I did not have a guide or back-up vehicle and was tearing my hair out, when Junmin phoned me.

'My neighbour may be able to come with you as a guide. He is retired and knows how to ride horses.'

I instantly grabbed at this opportunity.

'How about meeting up at the hotel this evening?'

Mr Ren Hong was a wiry and matter-of-fact ex-military man with close-cropped grey hair and round glasses who was apparently experienced with horses, but spoke no English. Through Junmin he grilled me penetratingly on the nuts and bolts of the ride, being particularly concerned as to whether it was officially sanctioned. I showed him my letter from the British ambassador, kept my answers vague, and crossed my fingers. It seemed to do the trick, as he announced that subject to the horses being up to scratch, he could see his way to accompanying us. We agreed on a payment of 375 yuan a day (£30) plus expenses, which would add up to a total of 9,375 yuan, or £750, for the twenty-five days I had allowed for the trial stage. We had also been joined by a tall, well-built young Chinese with an earnest face and broken English. This was He Guo Sheng, a friend of a contact of Rowena's who had just got in touch with me.

'Yes. I think I can get car,' he said haltingly. I breathed a sigh of relief and we all repaired to a nearby restaurant where I treated them to supper. Mr Ren beamed and spoke to Junmin, who turned to me.

'Mr Ren wants you to know he likes to sing when he is riding.'

Two days later, Guo Sheng drove us out to Kangzhuang, where Mr Ren pronounced himself satisfied with the horses. We spent some time wrangling over logistics with Mr Zhao and booked a truck to Shanhaiguan for 2000 yuan before visiting the feed yard. It was fascinating to see the different feeds that horses ate in China. As well as rather dusty looking oats, they also fed ground maize and beans, and some small couscous-like peas. There were no compound feeds and I was quite glad when Mr Zhao took the initiative in calculating and ordering what we needed. It came to 1500 yuan, or about £120, for three horses for a month including hay, which was pretty impressive after British prices! We decided that the truck taking the horses to Shanhaiguan should make a couple of feed drops along our route as our back-up car would not be able to carry all the feed at one go. Mr Zhao agreed to get the horses shod by the stud farrier before they left. Guo Sheng organised a hired four-wheel drive SUV (Sports Utility Vehicle) at 12,000 yuan or £960. Then he suddenly announced that he would like to come along as a volunteer driver, so the last piece of the jigsaw was fitted in. Between his English and my Chinese, we should be able to get by.

There was just time to dash around sorting out finances for various payments and stocking up at Dongjiao market with basics such as water containers, feed buckets and tethering ropes. My ride fund was haemorrhaging but I knew Rowena would be contributing, and some capital costs, such as for horses, would be rolled over. Ben Xu contacted the Zunhua Women's Federation, who said they could find somewhere to store a feed drop in Zunhua on our route. I met up with David Shaw, head of media at the British Embassy, who was very encouraging and enthusiastic in his mission to describe me as a crazy Brit.

Rowena flew in on Thursday, October 1 to stay with her friend Blom, who was letting us store all our surplus kit in her garage, and we spent a productive afternoon organising our various bags into some sort of order. On Saturday morning Guo Sheng would pick up the SUV and drive to Shanhaiguan with Rowena. But I would not be with them.

'Friday you must go with horses,' he had told me a few days before. They were being transported to Shanhaiguan then, and someone needed to be with them when they arrived. So on Friday morning Xinlian and husband Michael drove me to meet the truck in the square in Kangzhuang. The show was on the road.

CHAPTER TWO

THE DRAGON'S HEAD

千里之行始于足下

qiān lǐ zhī háng shǐ yú zú xià

A journey of a thousand miles begins with a single step.

Laozi, Daoist philosopher (Sixth century BC)

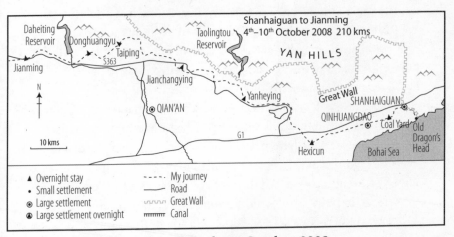

Saturday, 4 October – Monday, 6 October, 2008.
Shanhaiguan to Yanheying.
85 km. Daily average 28 km.

Agrey autumn day on the Chinese coast near Shanhaiguan. Behind us on a stony outcrop at the edge of the beach rose a massive square crenellated bastion dating from the Ming dynasty, solid blocks of pale stone topped by weathered grey bricks. A few hundred yards away along a sweep of rocky coastline topped by ancient wall, the bulky tower and bulwark at Laolongtou, or Old Dragon's Head, butted into the leaden expanse of the Bohai Sea like the snout of a dormant dragon. Day-trippers dotted the beach where a couple of patient hireling horses swished their tails and a

rious camel shifted from foot to foot. Small waves slipped up
nd, leaving a lacy fringe of foam as they retreated, and causing
Jing to skitter nervously. I dismounted and led her down to the
er's edge. I had no intention of being unceremoniously dumped
fore I had even set off. Rowena and Mr Ren urged their horses Bei
ei and Zorbee forward to join me. Besides the mounted contingent,
the small send-off group included our indispensable driver and
factotum Guo Sheng, a television crew from Shanhaiguan, and a
rather bemused German tourist.

'What are you doing here with the horses?' he had asked.

'Riding to London,' we replied to his incredulous surprise.

I could scarcely believe it was actually happening at last. All the
doubts and fears of the previous months melted away to be overcome
by an overwhelming sense of anticipation.

After a brief television interview we all lined up for media photos,
and I made sure to brandish the Welsh flag I had brought with me.
In the spirit of international cooperation I felt it apt to display a
Welsh dragon at Old Dragon's Head. This was particularly so as I
hoped to eventually ride all the way across Eurasia to Worm's Head
('wurm' is an old Viking word for dragon) on the Welsh coast.

'Ahoy,' hollered Mr Ren suddenly, although there was not a ship
in sight. He wheeled his horse round and pounded up the sloping
beach as if re-living his army days with a military charge. It seemed
we were off at last! But instead of battle-hardened troops at his
heels, Mr Ren was lumbered with two British matrons of uncertain
age. Over the next three weeks our ladylike progress and often
insubordinate attitude severely tested his patience, but he took his
role as our guide and protector very seriously. Through the ancient
archway in the wall we clattered, and up the road past startled faces
in cars that slowed down to let us pass. 'Ahoy,' cried Mr Ren again
as we hung a sharp right onto a small earth lane running along the
foot of the great embankment that marked the remains of the Great
Wall. We had hacked down to the sea along the top of it only an hour
previously, but at a more dignified pace. Chinese villagers turned to
stare at our flying forms as we dashed at a spanking trot past the

guesthouse where we had stayed the previous night. I was beginning to hope this energetic riding style was not indicative of our progress in the future or the horses would be worn out within the week. Little earth brick houses and market gardens with farmers bending over neat rows of vegetables flashed by. Thankfully we started to get into more unfamiliar territory. Mr Ren began to lose steam and the pace began to slow. We reached a main road and milled around aimlessly for a few minutes until Mr Ren spotted the wall once more. But tranquillity descended under a gloomy sky, and we now marched soberly into Shanhaiguan town with uncomprehending traffic speeding past.

We entered a large paved square overshadowed to the east by a great stone and brick tower. Above a narrow arched gateway a large sign in black Chinese characters was prominently displayed on a double-tiered roof: 'Di Yi Guan Xia Tian First Pass Under Heaven'. This East Gate is all that is left of the Ming period Shanhaiguan fort which guarded the eastern end of the Great Wall, but it has a particular resonance in Chinese history for the part it played in the downfall of the Ming, the last native Han Chinese dynasty. We reined in our horses and looked up at it in awe. It was through this gate that the mounted hordes of the nomadic Manchu poured in 1644 to take control of Beijing and establish the Qing dynasty. But incredibly the gate was opened for them by Ming general Wu Sangui. What on earth prompted this extraordinary act that was seemingly a betrayal of the highest order?

Essentially, he had found himself stuck between a rock and a hard place. To the north of the wall the nomadic Manchu were seeking to expand their power base, but within China the last Ming emperor Chongzhen was also facing a serious internal threat from Chinese rebel chief Li Zicheng. While the main forces of the Ming army were fully engaged against the Manchus to the northeast, the rebels overran Beijing. Tourists now flock to the site on Coal Hill to the north of the Forbidden City where a despairing emperor Chongzhen fled to commit suicide, having tried to stab his screaming concubines to death. With the Ming

*forces in a desperate situation Wu Sangui might have been expected
to choose to throw in his lot with the Chinese rebels rather than the
Manchu invaders. But then he heard that Li Zicheng had butchered
thirty-eight members of his household in Beijing, including his father,
whose head was hung from the city wall. And another story relates
how Wu Sangui was infuriated when Li Zicheng stole his beautiful
concubine Chen Yuan, although this is generally acknowledged to be
a romantic fairy tale. Whatever the truth, it seems the Ming generals
believed it was better to take a gamble on saving their own skins through
an alliance with the Manchu. Two days later Wu Sangui opened the
East Gate and welcomed the Manchu into China. Of course, once
within the Great Wall the Manchu quickly took advantage of this
golden opportunity to conquer China and bring in the Qing dynasty.
Wu Sangui was rewarded with a fief in Yunnan (whether he got the
girl or not is another story), but the Manchu Qing ruled for nearly 300
years until the last emperor Pu Yi was deposed by nationalists at the
beginning of the twentieth century. As conquerors from outside the wall,
they had no need to maintain it, and the wall fell into disrepair.*

It was a little ironic that we had started riding from the location of the
event which led to the demise of the Great Wall we were following.

We turned our horses' heads to the west. Where Manchu warriors
had once galloped there was now a new brick-paved passageway
lined with souvenir shops. A fine drizzle set in and Mr Ren seemed
uncertain of which direction to take, so we huddled disconsolately
under the main gate while he determined our next move. Passing
Chinese stared at us curiously, something I was to get very used to
in the months ahead. After consulting a couple of passers-by Mr Ren
seemed to come to a decision and we were off again.

I had hoped to follow the Ming Great Wall where possible, but
after crossing the narrow plain at Shanhaiguan, the wall scrambles
up the steep slopes of Mount Jiao and switchbacks along the
precipitous mountain range flanking the north China lowlands. For
the moment we would have to tramp through urban sprawl on the
narrow coastal strip.

Shanhaiguan Television had treated us to an unexpected slap-up Chinese meal at midday, and as a result we had started out much later than anticipated. It was disconcerting to find that night was rapidly falling as we plodded along the highway out of town, competing with the pedestrians, bicycles and motor scooters crowding the slow lane. As pitch dark descended on the unlit road, rattling lorries continued to hurtle past within inches, headlights flashing over our trudging figures. Jing Jing seemed a little lame and I got off and led her: hopefully it was just from a knock while travelling in the truck. After what seemed an age, we arrived at a coal yard on the edge of neighbouring town Qinhuangdao. Guo Sheng had already parked up the SUV which carried our bags and horse feed, including several bales of hay secured under a tarpaulin on the roof rack. The horses were watered, fed and tied to the pillars of a grimy weighing shed in the sooty yard with a slab of hay each, and we walked a short way down the street to rooms in a low one-storey building. This was fairly typical of the type of accommodation we would soon expect to stay in, with two drab rooms leading off a small dingy entrance hall. Sparsely furnished in dormitory style, they each contained four metal beds equipped with hard mattresses, folded quilts, and bean bag pillows. Rowena and I lugged our sleeping bags and backpacks into one room while Mr Ren and Guo Sheng settled into the other. Washing facilities consisted of a plastic bowl set in a tripod frame in the passageway. There were no toilets, but Rowena and I snuck into the relatively clean washroom with squat toilets belonging to a petrol garage across the street, remembering to take our own supply of toilet paper.

It was a dispiriting start to the following day. Rain greeted us on waking and we could not get into the coal yard to feed the horses until 7am. The young women attendants at the garage forestalled our attempt to creep into their washroom, and desperation forced us to resort to a roofless semi-abandoned public toilet along the street. As people had basically added their contributions to a pile in the corner of the earth floor, it was not a very salutary experience, particularly with rain dripping down one's neck.

It took the whole day to negotiate the industrial port town of Qinhuangdao along a north ring road cacophonous with rowdy traffic. In Chinese, a foreigner is called '*waiguoren*' or 'outside country person', but the slang term is '*laowai*' or 'old outsider'. It seemed that honking and klaxoning was the most appropriate expression of greeting when faced with *laowai* on horseback. Thankfully horses in China are accustomed to being treated like vehicles and ours were completely unflappable. Any horse owner can tell you that umbrellas might just as well be flesh-eating monsters as far as most self-respecting nags are concerned, but Jing Jing strode with total unconcern past a woman brandishing an open umbrella in her face while lorries rattled past a couple of feet away.

Crossroads were especially daunting as they seemed to be a general free-for-all of every variety of transport. As the lights changed a charge would ensue from one direction which became caught up with the tail end of the charge from traffic crossing in the other direction. This resulted in a whirlpool of intermingled vehicles, bicycles and mopeds, not to mention handcarts, at the centre of the crossroads. Adding to the confusion, red lights in China do not prevent road users from turning right, and one could still be wiped out by vehicles surging round the corner. But we had reckoned without Mr Ren, who relished his new self-appointed role as traffic policeman for the *laowai*, striding theatrically ahead to block the oncoming traffic with an upward sweep of the hand, and marshalling Rowena and me across the road to safety like a couple of hesitant schoolgirls.

Our progress elicited considerable interest, and cyclists wobbled precariously as they craned round to gawp at us.

'It's only a matter of time before someone falls off their bike,' Rowena commented wryly.

A steady drizzle dampened our spirits, not improved when Rowena and I spent nearly half an hour loitering outside a police station in the rain while Mr Ren disappeared inside to pick their brains for routes.

'I expect he's really just gone in for a cup of tea.'

Rowena always did have a dry sense of humour.

The only bright side was that Jing Jing was no longer lame. But morale was fully restored when we stopped for lunch at an eating house on a busy street where trains rumbled across a railway bridge overhead. Tying the horses to a lorry in the courtyard, we retreated inside to eat hot bowls of steaming dumplings washed down with copious amounts of Chinese tea from a metal teapot.

As the rain thinned to a faint spitting and then stopped, we finally branched off the ring road and left the madness behind. The reflection of light breaking through rosy-edged clouds glinted in the puddles of a pot-holed road leading out into open country. A lone cyclist swished by, his upside-down image mirrored in the wet surface so it seemed to be flying through a mottled peach sky. In the western glow ahead lay the promise of immersing ourselves in a real experience of China and our spirits lifted.

A couple of miles further on, Guo Sheng had found us accommodation at a small inn at the centre of Yuguanzhen, a typical small country town with untidy rows of two-storey shophouses lining a narrow main street. Rowena and I had an upstairs room with double bed and television overlooking a confined central courtyard where we managed with difficulty to find places to tie the horses. There was the standard slit-in-the-concrete-floor toilet, and even a tepid solar shower set up at one end of a dingy storeroom. Rowena braved it to wash her hair before we ventured out to eat.

A few lights glimmered in the dark empty street as we strolled out to find supper. There is always somewhere to eat in China, and we were soon scrutinising a menu solely written in Chinese characters or hanzi. But though I had tried to learn the hanzi for various food items, it was still unintelligible to me.

'Guo Sheng, can you choose for us?'

'What do you like to eat?'

'I can try almost anything, but no heads or feet.'

I have never gone a bundle on chicken's feet and fish eyes, but leaving our Chinese colleagues to order gave us the chance to try different dishes without mistakenly opting for something too outlandish. The Chinese style of dining, whereby all the dishes are placed in the middle of the table to be shared by everyone, has the advantage that we could sample everything and focus on the dishes we liked. Guo Sheng and my other Chinese colleagues soon sussed out the foods I was particularly partial to, and aubergine or *quiezi* became a regular choice. I learnt two new things that night. Firstly, that rice is not a fundamental part of the meal in North China, and secondly that the Chinese say '*Quiezi!*' (roughly pronounced 'chee-eh-dze') instead of 'Cheese!' for the camera.

A waitress laid a plastic cover over the white tablecloth, then placed plates and bowls in front of us. Rowena and I were presented with spoons.

'*Bu yao, tamen yao kuaizi.* They don't want them, they want chopsticks,' said Guo Sheng firmly, and the waitress scuttled away to fetch two more pairs. Mr Ren and Guo Sheng had been under the impression that all foreigners were incapable of using chopsticks, so they were pleasantly surprised to find that both Rowena and I, with our Oriental upbringing, were completely at home with them. The reason for the plastic table cover soon became clear, as in China it is perfectly acceptable to put any gristle or rejected food straight onto the table. At the end of a banquet the table sometimes looked like a war zone, but the residue would just be folded up in the plastic cover and taken away, leaving the white tablecloth underneath clean. This meal set the pattern for eating in China, as eating houses were so ubiquitous and cheap and the food so delicious that it was pointless to prepare our own.

It was only now as we started travelling through backwater areas that I realised quite how essential it was to have knowledge of at least a smattering of hanzi or Chinese characters. In areas unfrequented by foreigners, all shop fronts, information signs, road signs, menus, in fact everything, is written in hanzi. It was only in large towns and tourist spots that we encountered pinyin or Romanised phonetic writing, and if nothing else I made sure I knew the characters for male and female toilets. But to acquire even a basic knowledge of Chinese characters can be a daunting task as they are symbols originally based on pictographs, each one portraying a different meaning. Even in modern simplified Chinese there are over 80,000 characters, and for a basic working level of literacy in Chinese you would probably need to know around 2,000-3,000 characters. When Roman script only requires learning 26 alphabet letters, you might ask why bother using hanzi at all?

The secret of its significance and success lies in the huge size of China, a country which encompasses people speaking very different languages and dialects. The main Chinese dialect is Mandarin, widely spoken in the north where the power base generally lay, and used as the court and official language since the fourteenth century. In the early twentieth century it became the official Chinese lingua franca, and when we talk about learning Chinese, we are most certainly referring to Mandarin Chinese. But besides Mandarin there are many other Chinese dialects which are very different. When I was a child growing up in Malaya, the Chinese I heard spoken on the streets and in the shophouses was Cantonese, Hokkien, or Hakka, dialects of emigrants from the southern provinces of Guangdong, Guangxi, Fujian, and Jiangxi. They are as different from Mandarin and each other as European languages such as French, English, and Russian. But although Chinese characters may represent a different spoken word in each language/dialect, the meaning they denote remains the same, in the same way people speaking different languages can understand the numeric symbols 1,2,3. Different Chinese dialect groups may not be able to understand each other speaking, but all literate Chinese can read the same newspapers, books and official documents. The use of Chinese script goes a long way to explaining how such an enormous and unwieldy nation was able to develop a homogeneous identity and stay unified over the centuries.

I felt the adventure had really begun the next day when we started to strike out into the countryside of Hebei province. In the distance to the north we could see the line of the Yan hills along which ran the Great Wall. I was hoping that we would be able to use earth tracks which would be easier on the horses, so I was a little disappointed to find that almost all the small country roads in this part of China were now surfaced in concrete. But we began to enjoy some strikingly picturesque scenery. It was the harvest season. Maize stalks with crinkled leaves like brown paper littered the fields untidily or were piled into bulky heaps ready to be carried away in huge trembling loads on hidden carts drawn by oxen. Women in headscarves bending over green rows of lettuces straightened their backs to watch us pass, and a couple of resigned cows tethered to an electricity pole chewed the cud philosophically. The ground swelled into low undulating hills coated with dry feathery grass where a herd of white goats drifted through rippling shadows beneath a stand of fluttering poplar. Traditional courtyard farmhouses lined the streets of the small villages we rode through. Simple brick gateways were often embellished with gaily coloured tiles or topped by a curved tiled roof beneath which double doors opened onto a courtyard with a low farmhouse on the far side. The homely smell of woodsmoke drifted into our nostrils. Over the next couple of weeks, we caught tantalising glimpses of courtyard interiors through open doorways, some with a laden fruit tree or neat vegetable garden, some with fat golden maize cobs spread out to dry. There might be a tethered goat or cow, or puppies rolling in the dust, or an elderly couple enjoying the sun. Occasionally, as with homes all over the world, there were piles of clutter and weeds. Being on horseback was a plus, as if the doors were closed, we could sometimes peep over the walls!

Mr Ren was in cheerful mood, singing out loud as he led his charges over the hills, stopping to fashion leafy circlets of willow for us to wear on our heads. We looked like a bevy of equestrian wood nymphs, and if the locals were not staring strangely at us before, they certainly were then. The response to our passage through eastern Hebei over the next few days was generally one of amazement and occasionally suspicion at the sight of these strange mounted barbarians. Determined to keep the side up, we paraded through the villages with fixed smiles, waving to right and left like royalty and greeting all and sundry with a '*Ni hao*', the standard Chinese greeting which literally means 'you good' or 'how are you'. But it was worth it to be rewarded when a startled face dissolved into a beaming smile.

'*Tamen hen youhao!* They're friendly!' exclaimed one woman in surprise to her companion.

Guo Sheng had made a concerted effort to find somewhere a bit more suitable for the horses on the third evening, and led us to a low farmhouse on the outskirts of the small town of Yanheying. It had a sizeable yard in front, containing piles of bricks and a flatbed trailer to which we were able to tie the horses. Most Chinese peasant farmers' houses in the north traditionally only have three rooms: a central entrance hall acting as a kitchen and containing a built-in wood fired stove, and two rooms leading off to either side which are used for sleeping, eating, or storage. At least one, traditionally to the right of the kitchen, will contain a *kang*, or brick sleeping platform, heated in winter by hot air flowing through the wall from the stove. Our host family was relatively well-off as the husband was a steelworker, so they had a fairly sizeable house which had been extended to include several extra rooms. I expected to find the largest being used as a modern living room, but it was in fact functioning as a store for agricultural produce. In spite of all this extra space, the kitchen and eating area were still in the narrow entrance passageway, with a white-tiled brick stove in its traditional place immediately to the right of the front door. A large wok fitted into the top of the stove over the fire, which the lady of the house stoked up with wood, poked through an opening at the front.

Soon the metallic scraping of a ladle and the smell of frying noodles, vegetables and flatbread heralded the arrival of supper. A couple of bottles of beer and a shot of vodka later, Mr Ren was demonstrating the exercises he had been teaching Rowena for her bad back and inducing Guo Shen to perform ballet stretches on the door frame amid much jollity.

'I think we should start every morning with exercises by Mr Ren,' Rowena was saying cheerfully, when a visitor entered. The mood quietened down considerably when he turned out to be a local government official who had heard that *waiguoren* had landed in town. After some polite discussion, all was apparently sorted amicably, and he left. Rowena and I retired to bed and looked forward to a sound night's sleep, but it appeared that the attraction of *waiguoren* had encouraged a string of social visits, as people came and went during the night, and their voices rose and fell in endless discussion. Eventually the visitors left, but we did not get our beauty sleep in any case as the guard dog chained up by the horses barked all night.

Bleary eyed, we arose the next morning to the smell of breakfast noodles. It was only then that Guo Sheng admitted that the nocturnal visitors had been the *jingcha* or police, insisting that we be taken to a 'foreigners' hotel' in Lulong, about thirty miles away. Funnily enough I had read that the Hanbury-Tenisons also had difficulties trying to stay in Yanheying over twenty years earlier. They were told it was a security area and actually ended up in the Lulong hotel. So little change in attitude after so much time! But our guardian angel Guo Sheng was made of sterner stuff. He had valiantly argued that it was crazy to throw us out of town in the middle of the night, and eventually the *jingcha* begrudgingly capitulated.

Hot water for our morning wash in a plastic bowl was provided in a thermos, and cold water came from the well outside. The family were fortunate to have their own well and had installed a pump which worked by pulling down a lever on the outside wall – this resulted in a sudden gush of water from a huge hose more suited to a fire engine. It must have been freezing in winter, but it seemed the concept of arranging tap water inside the house was still a novelty. As we rode out of the yard accompanied by smiling farewells from our hosts, we were faced with a sombre line-up of dour local officials silently checking up on our departure. We opted to omit the regal wave and 'Ni hao' and marched round the corner in what we hoped was a suitably dignified fashion. I was sorely tempted to sneak a photo, but decided it was not worth the risk of having my camera confiscated. Guo Sheng had succeeded in keeping the officials at bay this time, but I could not help worrying. Was this going to be a regular occurrence, and what if the police stopped us completely?

CHAPTER THREE

WHY AREN'T YOU RIDING YOUR HORSE?

万事开头难
wàn shì kāi tóu nán -
All things are difficult before they are easy.

Tuesday, 7 October – Friday, 10 October, 2008.
Yanheying to Jianming.
120 km. Daily average 30 km.

'Women *bixu yong xiao lu*. We must use small roads,' I said firmly to Mr Ren once again as he pored over a tattered map. Rowena and I had continually impressed on him our horror of main roads, and he had gone to a lot of effort to identify *xiao lu* or small roads or tracks. In crowded Hebei, it was not always an easy task to find these, but over the next two days Mr Ren came up trumps, although it resulted in a couple of long days in the saddle. We headed north towards the hills along country lanes through small villages, the peace only broken by the noisy three-wheeled agricultural trucks which are used to carry everything in China from harvested crops to large rocks. Once we even saw a couple of Mongolian horses crammed in the back. They chugged slowly along, making an incredibly loud explosive 'phut phut', and I sometimes turned round to discover that the ancient lorry I could hear bearing noisily down on us from behind was actually a modest three-wheeler truck. Traders used them to buy and sell their wares, and we could hear coal and agricultural merchants calling out over a loudspeaker as they trundled through the villages, reminding me of the rag-and-bone man with his horse and cart that used to clop up the street where I lived in London when I was a child.

After a couple of hours we came through a cutting in a small hill where an elderly graffiti artist was painting large Chinese characters onto the rock sides and a couple of cows wandered across the stony track.

'*Chang Cheng!*' Mr Ren suddenly called out.

And there indeed high up ahead we could see the Great Wall again, or Long Wall as it is called in Chinese, snaking along the ridge tops of the Yan hills. These present a formidable physical barrier even without the man-made barrier on top. Contrary to popular belief, there is no way anyone could ride a horse along or even beside this section of the Great Wall where it traces the length of jagged ridges, twisting and turning before plunging into valleys and clambering up precipitous hillsides. So it was a thrill to catch distant glimpses of the wall even when it was only identifiable by the tiny square pimples of watchtowers on the far skyline. It led us forward on our journey, every new sighting providing evidence that we were making headway and prompting a feeling of satisfaction mixed with excited anticipation.

There have been many misconceptions about the Great Wall of China, one being that it can be seen from space with the naked eye. It has also often been regarded as a single unbroken entity thousands of years old. In fact, the Chinese have built a whole series of fortifications at different periods to control or ward off incursions by various nomadic groups from the northern grasslands. The Yuezhi, Mongols, and Manchu have all been hemmed out by Chinese walls, not to mention the Xiongnu or Hunnu, who are considered by some to be ancestors of the Huns. Construction of these long defensive walls has been an almost continual process since the Spring and Autumn dynastic period over 2,300 years ago.

The first wall of any length is thought to have been built between 215-210BC in by Qin Shihuangdi, the Qin dynasty emperor who unified China and was famously buried with his terracotta warriors near Xian. The western name 'China' derives from Qin, the Chinese themselves referring to their country as Zhongguo or the Middle Kingdom. Qin Shihuangdi's Great Wall consisted of a tamped earth barrier, probably fairly quickly thrown up, which was thought to link pre-existing sections of wall from previous smaller states. The fragmentary sections which still remain visible may suggest it was not one continuous wall. Han dynasty historian Sima Qian wrote, 'It started at Lintao, and extended to Liaodong, reaching a distance of more than ten thousand li.' The Great Wall is in fact often referred to by Chinese as Wanli Chang Cheng or Ten Thousand Li Long Wall. As a li is roughly half a kilometre or a third of a mile, this wall would have been around 3,300 kilometres in length. But this Qin wall lay 200 kilometres to the north of us, roughly following the border of Inner Mongolia.

The Qin wall was a very different structure to the stone and brick Ming wall we were now looking at, but has often mistakenly been confused with it. In 1793, Lord Macartney led the first British trade mission to China, famously refusing to kowtow or prostrate himself in a gesture of submission to the Qing emperor Qianlong. Neither Qianlong or Macartney were at all impressed by their meeting, but en route Macartney stopped at the Ming Great Wall in the Gubeikou pass and was blown away by the immense structure snaking away over 'the steepest highest and craggiest mountains'. He not only assumed it was the much older Qin wall, but confidently stated that it continued in this form for the rest of its 'one thousand and five hundred miles'. Even as late as 1909, American William Geil, who journeyed along the Ming Wall in the early twentieth century, perpetuated the myth that it had been built by Shihuangdi. It was commentaries such as this that entrenched the idea of a single ancient Great Wall of China in western perception.

It is important to understand that when we refer to the Great Wall of China today, we are not referring to the Qin wall but to the latest and most substantial wall system built mainly after 1449 during the Ming dynasty (1368-1644). It is certainly not a single continuous wall, being broken up into different sections interspersed by gaps where the terrain provides a natural barrier, and overlapping in places. The sections stretch from Old Dragon's Head in the east to the western fort of Jiayuguan in Gansu province, a distance of around 1,500 miles, so at least Macartney got something right. In the east it takes the classic *form we know so well, a formidable crenellated stone-and-brick structure clambering up and down precipitous hills and interspersed with watchtowers. But as I was to find out, it takes a very different form further west.*

The Ming wall continued to dart in and out of view above us as we rode along the edge of the cultivated land stretching up to the base of the bare range. Clumps of bright red chilli peppers lent an occasional splash of colour to the scene, and in a field of bushes dotted with white cotton, a couple of donkeys flicked their long ears inquisitively forward. White ducks dabbled in the shallows as we came down to a wide, shingled riverbed braided with river channels. Mr Ren scouted up the side and found a place where we could splash safely across before scrambling up the riverbank and through a little alleyway to the road. The apple orchards were loaded with fruit, and like a naughty schoolboy Mr Ren was tempted to disappear on surreptitious scrumping forays for rather worm-eaten apples. For those who are not familiar with this very British term, 'scrumping' means the stealing of fruit from orchards, particularly apples, by mischievous boys.

'Windfalls,' he mimed, but still disappeared behind a tree when a car went past, and looked a little shame-faced when we were offered apples by the cheerful lady owner of an orchard he had just been scrumping in. Chinese farmers were busily occupied in the villages, perhaps driving a flock of sheep or goats, making rush mats in the yard outside their house, or scraping the bristles off a dead pig strung upside-down by a hind leg.

We stopped for a rest on a patch of littered waste land in Liujiaying Xiang and Guo Sheng appeared with a delicious *jian bing* each for us: these are a kind of Chinese crêpe made with egg, chopped vegetables, hoisin sauce, and a crispy waffle filling, generally eaten as a breakfast street food. A boisterous gang of small children gathered to try out their English on us, but meaningful conversation was difficult as the span of their vocabulary seemed to be limited to 'Hello'. No matter that we shouted out 'Goodbye' as we rode off up the road towards the hills, we could still hear a little chorus of 'hello' fading into the distance behind us.

By late afternoon we had been riding for some time and were wondering when we would reach our destination.

'*Duo yuan*, Mr Ren? How far is it, Mr Ren?'

'*Shi gongli*. Ten *gongli*,' came the confident reply. A *gongli* is a kilometre.

Several *gongli* further on and we had still not arrived.

'*Duo yuan*, Mr Ren?'

'*Shi gongli*.'

It was considerably more than *shi gongli* and dark had fallen by the time we reached the small town of Jianchenying. The crowded main street was lined with welding shops, creating an infernal atmosphere as sparks from the welding equipment lit up the faces of people bent over their work.

Guo Sheng had received a negative response when he phoned the local police to check if it was alright for us to stay in town, so we sneaked surreptitiously up a back alley to lodgings he had found at the far side. Our hosts ran a restaurant, so we were able to have a furtive evening meal glancing nervously through the window for the *jingcha*, while fluffy Pekingese lapdog Mao Mao came to beg at our table, sitting up on his haunches and praying with his two front feet together. Our spotless rooms overlooked a tiny yard lined with rose beds, but the accommodation for the horses was not quite so appropriate. Jing Jing managed to squeeze through the narrow entrance to a kind of pig pen by the toilets which two of the horses were expected to share, but when Mr Ren led Zorbee in, he immediately jumped out and demolished half the wall in the process, which cost us 200 yuan (about £20).

This was probably why Zorbee was distinctly unlevel first thing the next morning, so we took it slowly to start with. It was a long but delightful day on little gravel roads winding along the flanks of the Yan hills with steep bushy slopes up to the Great Wall on one side and terraced fields and orchards stretching away on the other. We passed a couple of gleaming lakes nestled in the hills, but being

China it was not long before the scenery was marred by an eyesore, such as a quarry slashing open a hillside or a cement factory pouring out grey dust. At the top of one climb stood a tall, colourfully painted roofed gateway framing the Wall on the ridge behind. Opposite were a couple of stalls selling baskets of apples and what looked like tiny red crab apples.

'*Zhe shi shenme, Mr Ren?* What are these, Mr Ren?'

'*Shan zha.*'

We were none the wiser, but later identified them as Chinese hawthorn or Crataegus pinnatifida. I became a huge fan of *shan zha* sweets, dark reddish-brown jelly-like strips with a sweet taste somewhere between plum and apple, and we always carried a supply in our pockets as snacks.

At midday we stopped at a village and fed the horses out of borrowed bowls. The local feed store only stocked pig food, but Mr Ren managed to track down some ground maize piled up in one of the village houses. It was not long before we attracted an audience and an elderly man bravely attempted to strike up a conversation. To my disappointment, I could hardly understand a word. I cheered up when a sprightly woman then subjected me to a penetrating interview within my vocabulary range and relayed my halting answers to a fascinated crowd of onlookers amid a chorus of appreciative 'aahs' and nodding of heads.

'*Duo da le?* How old are you?'

This inevitable question was of great import to the Chinese. The Confucian virtue of respect for one's elders is still highly valued, and no one is ever shy to ask a woman how old she is. The older you are, the more respect you earn.

'*Wu shi sui.* Fifty-nine,' prompted even more approving noises.

Further down the road we stopped to admire a huge shining new school in the process of being built and were surprised when a smartly dressed Chinese standing at the entrance addressed us in fluent English – by coincidence he was the English teacher.

One of the most diverting features of the villages in this part of China was the crude propaganda paintings on many of the walls.

As my grasp of Chinese characters was still very limited, Rowena and I spent some happy times guessing the civic or moral messages depicted in the pictures. Exhorting children to help blind people across the road seemed to be a common theme, but others warned against flying kites near electric lines, riding bikes with no hands, or plugging in equipment with wet hands (most electric fittings were extremely dodgy). There was sometimes an environmental theme (don't steal birds' eggs, catch butterflies, or chop down trees) or a moral tone. Rowena was particularly adept at guessing. A fat Chinese swigging from a bottle sat on a large wad of money, with a house and car in the background. Could it mean enjoy life while you can?

'Don't drink your possessions away,' chanted Rowena happily.

As the sun sank in the sky, we rode tired but content into a small village at the base of the hills.

'*Duo yuan, Mr Ren?*'

'*Shi gongli.*'

This village had more than its fair share of crude propaganda paintings. One showed an overweight *laowai*, evidently American, flaunting dollars in front of a Chinese.

'Don't accept black market money from the running dogs of capitalism,' surmised Rowena.

In view of this it was perhaps a little unwise to trust the bunch of villagers from whom Mr Ren subsequently asked directions. They pointed to a track which apparently led over the hills to our destination of Taipingzhen. Climbing up a rough road on the side of a small valley filled with apple trees, we came out onto a bare hillside. The evening sun bathed the stony slopes in a bright light, and dusky blue lowlands spread out to the south. Mr Ren sang merrily and renewed his naval calls of 'ahoy' to test an echo bouncing off the rocky valley side. A sense of well-being spread over us at the thought of supper and bed waiting only a short ride away.

Then, rounding a corner, we came abruptly to a locked gateway, incongruously adorned with an enormous concrete teapot. It was the entrance to some sort of dreadful themed leisure park in the middle of nowhere. Mr Ren interrogated the guard. No, we could not enter and no, there was no way through to Taipingzhen. It was a dead end. Our faces fell, and Mr Ren's mood changed dramatically from sunny to thunderous. He flounced back down the hill with Rowena and I plodding meekly behind. Through the village he stormed, venting his anger on anyone he deemed remotely culpable of misdirecting us. Even the village dogs looked cowed. I did not dare ask, 'Duo yuan, Mr Ren?' but I knew it was a long trudge ahead of us, and due to the encroaching darkness we were unable to enjoy a particularly pretty stretch of countryside. To cap it all, when we trotted on a bit to make up time, Jing Jing tripped and crashed onto the concrete track. I suffered minor grazes, but Jing Jing skinned her knees, so Rowena and I took turns to lead her the rest of the way. At times it was so dark we could hardly see where we were going as we stumbled along a sunken track, but eventually the lights of cars flashing past on the main road came into sight. A frustrating end to an otherwise beautiful day, and it was with relief that we led the weary horses across the main bridge into Taipingzhen where Guo Sheng was waiting to guide us into a hotel yard. We had covered about forty kilometres that day. I cleaned up Jing Jing's knees, but there was nowhere to tie the horses, and we ended up attaching their lead ropes to the iron rafters of the shed.

That night, the sound of the horses clattering around woke me. When I went down to investigate, all was quiet and three innocent faces stared in my direction, but the moment I returned to my room the clattering started again. In the morning a wheelbarrow had been knocked over, some glass broken, and the proprietors complained they had been kept awake all night and demanded extra money. Even more frustratingly we found that Zorbee was sore on the withers and would not let anyone touch him there. Riding him was out of the question, but Rowena and I offered to take turns to lead and ride the horses with Mr Ren. Unfortunately, Chinese masculine pride took precedence and Mr Ren resolutely refused our offer and insisted on walking the whole way. For a while we registered a protest by walking with him. It was totally beyond the comprehension of most Chinese as to why anyone would want to walk while leading a perfectly good horse. '*Weishenme bu qi ma?* Why aren't you riding your horse?' every other person queried, and after half an hour of this we gave up and got back on. Mr Ren had to endure the barrage and became increasingly tetchy.

The horses were tired, and that, together with all the setbacks, led us to opt for a short day of under twenty kilometres, and find somewhere we could graze them. Guo Sheng located a litter strewn area of waste ground with scattered trees and some meagre grazing at the small town of Donghuangyu. I pulled off Jing Jing's saddle and discovered to my despair that she had a small sore on her spine and one developing on her side. I put it down to pressure caused by a too tight crupper (a leather strap going under the horse's tail which stops the saddle shifting forward) as I had only fitted it the day before. It was only several days later that I realised that the saddle gullet was slightly too low on her unusually protruding spine, but the advantage of my FnE saddle was that it took a matter of minutes to adjust the saddle so it fitted properly. This was the only saddle fitting issue I had the whole way across Eurasia, but for now I would have to lead Jing Jing until the sore healed.

Rowena settled under a tree with her journal while Mr Ren scratched maps in the dust and discussed routes with a small group of spectators. There did not seem to be anywhere willing to accommodate us, so we deliberated at length about whether to move on and find a hotel further away, camp on the waste ground and gamble that the *jingcha* would not turn up, or split forces. Mr Ren took a firm 'all for one and one for all' stance and wanted us to stay together. We eventually decided to camp surreptitiously on the waste ground after nightfall, at which point Mr Ren disappeared and returned having negotiated rooms across the road. The proprietor was evidently unsure about the taking us in, as we had to sneak the horses into the yard under cover of darkness. But there was no problem eating at the restaurant next door, where we shared dishes of dumplings, salted whitebait, green beans, peanut salad, and spare ribs, plus bottles of beer, before retiring to bed. Rowena and I stood at the doorway to our room, which gave onto the dark yard, and watched flashes of lightning throwing up the black silhouette of the Yan hills and illuminating the outlines of the horses tied to the iron fence palings. Thunder rumbled and sheets of rain swept in. It seemed we had made a good decision not to camp.

But whether it was due to the electricity in the air, or anxiety about the constant problems we were facing, I could not sleep properly for worrying. How long would the horses continue to suffer sore backs and lameness? Would the whole project grind to a halt due to intervention by the police? If against all the odds I managed to reach Badaling this year, could I afford to pay for the horses over the winter, or should I start with new horses in the spring? Where would I find someone daft enough to drive a support vehicle across China for months, and how the dickens would I finance it? Logistical questions buzzed around in my head like angry bees. In the middle of the night even minor niggles balloon into insurmountable obstacles, and it was not long before I was asking myself once again why on earth I had committed myself to this hare-brained scheme that was obviously doomed to failure.

The following morning the rain clouds had cleared, and I pushed my qualms into the background. I could not afford to let them weaken my resolve. We left early to find the waste ground had been transformed into a bustling open air market, another reason I was glad we had not chosen to camp. Rowena and I took turns to ride Bei Bei and lead Jing Jing, and Guo Sheng took over leading Zorbee from Mr Ren, who drove off in the SUV. It was becoming more like the Long Horse Lead than the Long Horse Ride. We had left the foothills and found ourselves tramping along the noisy main road to Santunying, where I hoped to stay. Mr Ren had other plans, and when we arrived he turned up in the SUV looking very pleased with himself and accompanied by a Mr Lu who had kindly asked us for lunch. We discovered that not only was Mr Lu's place several kilometres back the way we had come from, but that Mr Ren's planned destination for the day was Jianming, several kilometres further on. It was unreasonable to expect weary horses to retrace their steps before continuing even further.

'*Ma lei le.* The horses are tired,' I complained.

Rowena and I put our joint feet down and said we would stop a little further on to let the horses rest and graze.

We waited in vain as Mr Ren disappeared for lunch with his new friend, leaving us without tethering ropes, water, or feed for the horses. Evidently he felt he had lost face, but equally on our part there was no way we were going to ignore the welfare of the horses. Eventually, after about two hours, he turned up and apologised to Rowena, but the honeymoon period was over. With only one horse rideable we stomped grumpily in single file along the busy main road towards Jianming, which according to Mr Ren was only '*shi gongli*' away. Of course, it was a lot further, and traffic roared past, spewing fumes over us. I thought wistfully of Robin Hanbury-Tenison's descriptions of cantering happily hand-in-hand with wife Louella along earth tracks through scenic Hebei countryside.

My heart sank again when we found our SUV parked outside a police station. Had Guo Sheng been arrested for aiding aliens? Thankfully, it was only a relatively minor problem. We were due to meet up with the Zunhua Women's Federation and were under the impression that they had phoned Jianming to sort out permission for us to stay there. This gave Guo Sheng the confidence to go to the police station and ask for advice regarding accommodation, but it appeared they were completely unaware of our arrival. Having advertised our presence, the usual dilemma reared its head. The police wanted us to stay in a 'foreigners' hotel' but none of the more upmarket hotels which qualified as such would take horses. Eventually the ever-resourceful Guo Sheng managed not only to find a yard where we could tie them overnight, but a hotel nearby that could accept *waiguoren*. Spirits were revived by a hot shower in the hotel and a meal of sweet and sour aubergines, beef and potato stew, and a pile of potato twiglets, not to mention the couple of bottles of Qingdao beer which were increasingly becoming a morale-boosting necessity.

It was the last time Guo Sheng went to the police, as he decided it was better in the future to act first and argue afterwards. As a staunchly law-abiding citizen, I had been a little concerned about our brushes with authority, but I now began to realise that rules were flexible in China. Officials were mainly scared of being held responsible if any harm came to us and were generally prepared to turn a blind eye so long as we kept a low profile. In fact, we had no further trouble with bureaucracy in Hebei and people became more relaxed about our presence as we neared Beijing, where locals are more used to foreigners.

But I had begun to feel disconsolate at all our setbacks and frustrations. Surely we were not going to continue hobbling along like this the rest of the way across China?

CHAPTER FOUR

MR PENG TO THE RESCUE

老马识途

lǎo mǎ shí tú

An old horse knows the way.

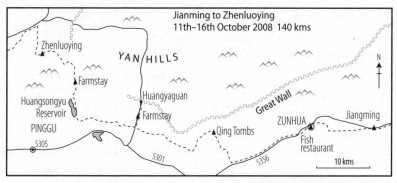

Saturday, 11 October – Thursday, 16 October, 2008.
Jianming to Zhenluoying.
140 km. Daily average 32 km.

'*Weishenme bu qi ma*,' queried a man standing at a shop door.
Mr Ren glowered and the *laowai* grimaced.

We were tramping up the main road towards Zunhua to the usual cacophony of sound: rumbling, honking and klaxoning of cars and lorries, chugging of three-wheeler trucks, put-putting of mopeds, wailing of police car sirens and the sharp crack of fireworks from a Chinese wedding. Mr Ren muttered resentfully as he towed a reluctant Zorbee up the dusty verge and occasionally barked orders at us. It seemed neither Zorbee nor the *laowai* could do anything right.

A couple of enormous grimy factories spewing smoke loomed up beyond a scrapyard, and the Great Wall rose above us: unfortunately, it was on an advertisement on a hoarding by the side of the road. A bed overtook us, strapped to a bicycle-drawn cart. We stopped at a roadside animal medical store to buy medicine for Zorbee and wormers for Jing Jing who was still looking lean.

But things were about to look up. At midday we turned down a lane and tied the horses to a log in a maize field. Guo Sheng had apparently been in contact with the Chinese Equestrian Association and representatives were due to rendezvous here with us. It was not long before a shiny new SUV pulled up, and a smartly dressed young Chinese introduced himself in English as Mr Wu Gang Fang, otherwise known as Wutzala. He ran the CEA website and also had an interest in promoting endurance riding in China.

I had in fact emailed him in March but had received no reply. I mentioned it to him.

'Yes, I remember,' he said with no further explanation. I still had a lot to learn about the Chinese.

A pretty young woman was introduced as Wutzala's wife and a tall lean man as Kenny Li, nickname Kubi, who had taken an interest in the venture and persuaded the others to come and meet us. Last but not least was Mr Peng, sturdy, with a round open face and a ready smile. Apparently, he had just spent eight months riding and driving round China with three Mongolian horses and a cart. Although I did not know it at the time, Wutzala, Kubi and most importantly Mr Peng were to play a huge part in my life over the months ahead.

We all retired to a restaurant round the corner to discuss the ride, and it was apparent that they were keen to be involved. Wutzala had heard of the ride plan before from a different source, but seemed surprised that it was my project. He knew Mr Li at the Shandan stud and immediately phoned him. It transpired Mr Li had been a little annoyed when the ride had seemingly fizzled out but was still keen to supply horses. There were plans for an FEI endurance ride at Shandan in summer of the following year, and it was suggested it might tie up with the ride. Most satisfyingly, and as a solution to our current problems, Mr Peng offered to lend us a horse to replace Zorbee.

'Come and join us,' persuaded Rowena.

The arrangement was to meet up with Mr Peng the following day at the Eastern Qing tombs, where the Zunhua Women's Federation had booked accommodation for us. That night our little team celebrated with a feast on the outskirts of Zunhua. A formidable woman had waved us into one of our more unusual stopovers, a fish restaurant. Little curved Chinese bridges led to brick eating pavilions perched on pillars in one of three large water lily-covered fish ponds. Reflections from festoons of coloured lights twinkled in the still water as dark fell. The horses were tied to trees on a narrow strip of land next to the sheer unguarded sides of the furthest pond and I prayed they wouldn't escape and fall in during the night.

A round turntable was placed on a heated *kang* in a private eating room, and we were served with a variety of dishes, the highlight being a whole steamed fish in a fragrant sauce, artistically decorated with cucumber slices and a carved pink vegetable rose. Replete, Rowena and I bedded down in our sleeping bags on either side of the table to sleep on the warm *kang*. Unfortunately, it was a bit too warm, as the *kang* developed 'hot spots' which did not make for the best night's sleep.

Mr Ren was in a foul mood again the next day, although we had now hit on the obvious solution of leading Zorbee from the back of one of the mares (Jing Jing's sore was better) and letting Mr Ren ride in the SUV with Guo Sheng. Why had we not thought of it before? They would follow us closely to make sure we were properly supervised in case of confrontation with local officials. Zorbee led easily along the busy road and it did not seem long before we were at the entrance to the Qing tombs twenty-two kilometres away. It was only another three kilometres to the tombs according to a sign at the gate, and we set off happily at a trot along a grassy strip of land through a belt of conifers beside the Spirit Way. This worn and degraded ancient stone roadway leads to the cluster of imperial tombs at the foot of the Yan hills, which formed a low blue silhouette ahead of us. We were still trotting along several great arched gateways later, not to mention a couple of elegant stone bridges and a paved pathway lined with guardian figures, where we paused to take photos by a stone horse. It was now well over six kilometres since we had left the entrance.

'We'll need some spirits if we ever get to the end of this Spirit way,' Rowena muttered.

But at last we came to our turn-off.

The Zunhua ladies had booked us into airy en suite rooms at a one-storey hotel right in the middle of the scattered Qing tombs complex. Leafy creepers climbed over trellises in a pretty central courtyard garden. A smiling Mr Peng arrived, followed by two young women from the Zunhua Women's Federation, a brace of Mrs Lius who ushered us into a private room for lunch. The table groaned with a display of mouth-watering meat and vegetable dishes, including sweet and sour pork, spicy beef and onion, omelette, and soup, as well as local specialities crunchy bees (I think it must have been the larvae, but they were very tasty) and chestnuts in toffee (to die for). One Mrs Liu spoke passable English, certainly better than my Chinese, so we chatted away amicably over our chopsticks, and discovered that the Federation had most generously paid for our overnight accommodation.

After waving off the Mrs Lius, we turned our attention to our new mounts. Mr Peng had arrived in what appeared to be a large furniture removal van, but emerging from its depths came two skinny Mongolian geldings, a small grey called Qing Qing and a little black imaginatively called Xiao Hei or Little Black. I was amazed to see they were shod with thick pieces of rubber, apparently cut from tyres. We led them over to be tied near Bei Bei and Jing Jing in the woods by the hotel, while the removal van removed Zorbee to Mr Peng's. This was sadly the last we saw of him as he was sold on. I knew that I could not afford to become too attached to any of our mounts in China, as I would not be allowed to take them across the border.

After all our tribulations, it was time for a day off. Mr Peng and Rowena sorted out the feed drop we had collected the evening before and Mr Ren cleaned saddles in the warm sun. I wrote my diary and attempted to let people know we were progressing slowly but surely. I had had an intensely frustrating experience the day before, wasting a rare opportunity to use the internet. Dropping into a *wang ba,* or internet café, in Zunhua while Peng fetched the feed, I had just finished a long email to David Shaw when the computer suddenly turned off before I sent it. Apparently, I had used up the hour I had paid for and that was that, my email had disappeared into the ether. So I was intrigued to see Mr Peng on the internet on his laptop although there was no wifi at the hotel. It seemed it was a must to get a dongle when I returned to China.

A text arrived from Ben Xu. 'Great, very cold, dress more.'

Still in our shirt sleeves we forayed out to do the tourist thing.

It was notable how quickly conquering nomads from outside the Great Wall became sinicised, and the Manchu of the Qing dynasty were no exception. The luxury and cultured lifestyle of the Chinese court must have seemed infinitely preferable to existing on boiled sheep and hard cheese in a tent on the howling steppes, and the Manchu emperors assimilated easily into Chinese society. Though never forgetting their steppe origins, they were educated leaders who encouraged the arts and sciences, and are thought of as Chinese by most Westerners. Their tomb complexes copy the pattern of the Ming imperial tombs.

The Eastern Qing tombs complex is one of two locations where Qing emperors were buried near Beijing. Some of the most prominent have their mausoleums here, including the first emperor Sunzhi, the able governor Kangxi, and the great scholar Qianlong (who spurned Macartney), not to mention the infamous Dowager Empress Cixi. As the tombs are a couple of hours drive from Beijing, they are less frequented and more peaceful than the Ming dynasty tombs near the capital, which bustle with tourists. In accordance with Chinese principles of geomancy or feng shui, they are scattered in a rough semi-circle among fields and woods on a south-facing slope with hills behind and to either side, though ironically just to the south of the Great Wall built by the Ming to keep out the very ancestors of the Manchu imperial family buried here.

With minor differences, the Ming and Qing imperial mausoleums followed much the same basic pattern. Within a high red wall a series of stone-paved courtyards gave on onto another through imposing gateways. Multi-eaved, red-tiled roofs proliferated, the curved ridge ends flicked up to support an uneven number of small pottery guardian figures, including dragon, phoenix, lion, and often the horned and hoofed scaly qilin. They would number nine on the imperial tombs but fewer on lesser buildings. Located in the first courtyard stood a 'Changing Hall' where the emperor changed into his ceremonial garments, and a kitchen where sacrificial food was prepared. The second courtyard contained an immense Hall of Eminent Favour where sacrificial offerings were made, with smaller halls to either side where monks recited scriptures, and ceremonial items were stored. Through a double-pillared gate in the back courtyard lay the Soul Tower which held a memorial stele, or stone slab, with the name of the tomb occupant. Straight up the middle of the whole complex ran the 'spirit way' along which only the emperor or empress could walk or be carried. The imperial retinue had to keep to paths at the side, and this explains why three graceful white marble bridges curve over lily ponds at the front, three doorways with heavy carved wooden doors open from one courtyard to another and three marble staircases lead up to the Hall of Eminent Favour. Here the middle staircase traditionally displays a rectangular marble slab depicting a dragon (representing the emperor) over a phoenix (representing the empress). After all this splendour it can be an anti-climax to find that the huge nondescript mound of earth behind all these magnificent structures is what actually covers the tomb vault, although it is accessed from the Soul Tower. All the tombs have specific names including the word 'ling' or tomb.

I was particularly drawn to the Dingdongling, the nursery rhyme sounding tomb of the infamous Dowager Empress Ci Xi. A highly ambitious and clever woman, she manipulated her way from a role as one of the lesser concubines of the Emperor Xianfeng to a position of considerable power following the accession of her young son Tongzhi onto the throne after Xianfeng's death. She effectively controlled the

Qing dynasty for forty-seven years between 1861 and the year of her death in 1908. Historically she has been portrayed as ruthless and cruel, backing the Boxer rebellion and notoriously ordering her son's favourite consort, the Pearl concubine, to be pushed to her death down a narrow well in the Forbidden City. In fact, she has probably received a lot of bad press and was no worse and in fact a lot better than many of China's rulers. She opened up China to foreign trade, and, among other advancements, banned foot binding and inhumane punishments such as 'death by a thousand cuts'. After Xianfeng's death, she worked alongside his widow Empress Chen, and their mausoleums lie side by side and are identical in plan. With their nomadic backgrounds Manchu women were forceful and independent, and Ci Xi struck a blow for women's lib by unusually having the phoenix placed above the dragon on the carvings in her tomb! Sadly, many of the riches of the Qing tombs have been looted over the years, leaving artefacts of historic interest rather depleted. This was possibly why exhibits displayed in Ci Xi's Hall of Eminent Favour included a strange tableau in a glass case captioned 'How To Ci Xi Keep Young' in which six-inch high wax figures depicted Ci Xi sipping her morning bowl of breast milk provided by a wet nurse.

Hidden behind a long wall next to the hotel was an equine complex with race track and stable blocks, owned by a *lao ban* or big boss who had made his money in iron mining. *Lao ban* quite literally means Old Plank in Chinese. The stud manager was keen to give us the grand tour and proudly guided us round a range of mainly imported horses, including a chestnut Arabian stallion and a big grey German Warmblood. Then the stable lads led out a couple of exquisite greyhound-like creatures, a gleaming ebony stallion, and an elegant filly whose burnished copper coat glowed with a strange ethereal sheen. She had reportedly been bought from Central Asia for a couple of million dollars. They gazed regally over our heads, exuding nobility and an easy arrogance.

'Akhal-Teke,' announced the manager.

An ancient breed of horse from Turkmenistan, the Akhal Teke

is characterised by its distinctive metallic lustre, and renowned for its speed and endurance. Famously, in 1935 a group of riders rode around 4,300 kilometres from Ashgabat in Turkmenistan to Moscow in eighty-four days, an average of around fifty kilometres a day, and this extraordinary feat has never been equalled. Their significance for the Chinese is that they are believed by many to be descendants of the fabled blood sweating 'heavenly horses' from the Ferghana valley in present day Uzbekistan which were so prized by Chinese two thousand years ago in the Han dynasty. After hearing report of them, the Han emperor Wudi sent an expedition to bring back some of these 'heavenly horses' to China, and it is thought that they are represented in the iconic Tang dynasty 'Flying Horse of Gansu' statue which has become the official Chinese symbol of tourism. As a result, they have become something of a status symbol for wealthy Chinese businessmen.

For such a costly import, I was surprised and a bit sceptical to see the million dollar filly had large white patches on her thighs – a colour anomaly which would be highly frowned on in some breeds. I pointed it out to Guo Sheng who spoke to the manager.

'No problem. He say all colour OK.'

I hoped so for the Old Plank's sake.

I had been agog to learn about Mr Peng's horse trip round China, and that evening I was rewarded when he brought out his laptop to show me some photos. Formerly a Beijing taxi driver, he had dropped everything a year previously to join forces with friend Yan Kecheng and embark on an ambitious challenge in the run up to the Beijing Olympics. In support of the Olympic spirit, they planned to visit every province in China by horse. My spoken Chinese was too limited to extricate the finer details, but the photos told the story. Mr Yan appeared in camouflage gear driving a four-wheeled box wagon with rubber tyres, pulled by three bony horses: a bay and two greys. On the green plastic tarpaulin cover was a large map of the route and the Chinese characters 'Zhong Guo Ma Zou' or 'China Horse Walk'. The roof was laden with what appeared to be sacks of grain. Another photo showed Mr Peng bundled up in an enormous olive-green army greatcoat and hat with ear flaps, astride a hairy, chestnut Mongolian gelding with a bucket head. The little caravan took about two months to reach Guangdong province in South China, where Mr Yan dropped out.

Nothing daunted, Mr Peng continued with a one-axle cart and two of the horses, plus new addition Qing Qing. Over the next six months he slowly made his way northwards through the rest of the provinces, finishing up in northernmost Heilongjiang. An odyssey of photos followed their progress through steaming southern forests, over icy western passes, and across hot, dusty northern deserts. Sometimes the wagon or cart and horses were laid up in six inches of snow, at other times they struggled through swamps of red mud on rutted tracks or rattled over a pontoon or suspension bridge. All the way he gathered appreciative fans.

Occasionally he bumped into fellow travellers. A young man with wild hair and beard, dressed in khaki shorts and shirt and humping a heavy rucksack, grinned at the camera.

'*Ta shi Deguoren. Ta zoulu dao Deguo.* He is German. He is walking to Germany,' said Mr Peng.

The photos demonstrated more clearly than anything else the enormity of Mr Peng's achievement. I felt humbled, but encouraged that we had someone of his experience on the team.

One photo towards the beginning included a petite woman with a pretty face.

'*Na shi shei?* Who is that?' I queried.

'*Wo furen.* My wife.' He was silent for a moment.

'*Women xianzai li hunle.* We are divorced now,' he said quietly. A breath of sadness hung in the air.

As we rode west across the Spirit Road and past Emperor Qianlong's tomb the following morning, the two mares were in buoyant spirits and even placid Bei Bei threw in a couple of bucks. Mr Ren scuttled ahead on Xiao Hei and Mr Peng hung back to bring up the rear on Qing Qing. Having been a little concerned at first as to whether the two skinny little horses would cut the mustard, we soon found that they set the pace with their fast running walk, and it was the two larger horses that lagged behind. We were now leaving behind the flat fields of the Hebei plain with its apple orchards, chestnut groves and neat stacks of maize stalks. The country grew increasingly hilly and wooded as we started to cross the craggy Yan hills to Miyun, five days away. We pottered along quiet roads twisting up leafy valleys scattered with brick farm buildings and pocket-sized plots of maize. Bright orange persimmons hung soft and round from trees on the hillsides, or were piled up in trailers at the edges of the orchards.

From here on we had no trouble finding accommodation, as local people within driving distance of Beijing were much more relaxed about welcoming tourists into their *nong jia yuan* or farm family courtyard houses. These homestays generally provided a clean room with sleeping space on a bed or *kang* with quilts supplied, a thermos of hot water for washing, very occasionally a shower, and a simple but tasty Chinese supper. Arrangements for the horses were not always so comfortable, and on one occasion they spent the night tied to various items of agricultural machinery, one of them over a rather dodgy manhole cover. I was rapidly finding that Chinese horses were expected to take in their stride situations which would appal my equestrian friends at home.

Arriving at a *nong jia yuan* tucked beneath rocky bluffs at the head of the long Huangsongyu reservoir two days later, we realised we had another problem. I had expected the mares' shoes to last the whole three weeks, but it was now evident that after only ten days riding the shoes were quite literally paper thin, and one of Jing Jing's front shoes had broken completely through in the middle. It was even more aggravating to find that the spare sets of horseshoes that I had asked for had not been put on the truck to Shanhaiguan. But where to find a *ti tie jia* or farrier? Mr Peng suggested putting on rubber tyre shoes but did not have the right nails, and I rapidly baulked when the farmer helpfully dug out some bog standard thick ones. Mr Peng drove off in the SUV and eventually returned with the news that he had found someone who was prepared to shoe them the following morning.

In Britain, it requires four years of training to legally qualify as a farrier but, as I was to find, this is not so in the rest of the world, and China was no exception.

'Guo Sheng, are you quite sure this man can shoe horses?'

'Yes, yes. He say thirty year he put shoe on donkey.'

My fears were borne out when the old man who had shod donkeys for thirty years turned up in the morning with some unusual tools and rather flimsy looking home-made donkey shoes. But needs must, and we decided to go ahead with Jing Jing who was the more amenable of the two mares. Chinese shoeing was a whole new experience for me, although I was to get used to some startling differences in the art of farriery as I progressed across Asia. For a start, most horses in Britain are hot shod, which means that their shoes are initially heated until red hot and carefully applied to the hoof to ensure a tight fit before being cooled down and nailed on, but right across Asia our horses were only ever cold shod. Jing Jing's foot was placed on a support and after the remains of the old shoe had been pulled off, the excess hoof growth was shaved off with a large chisel. The too-small donkey shoes were nailed onto her wide hooves and I winced when they were rasped severely back to fit the shoe. At home it is drummed into us that the shoe should always fit the hoof.

Bulky Bei Bei decided to be awkward and used her substantial weight to passively resist shoeing. I resigned myself to fighting a losing battle, but I had reckoned without Mr Peng's Chinese equanimity. Any Chinese village worth its salt has a fitness park like a playground for adults with a variety of fixed workout equipment in bright primary colours. Bei Bei was marched off and trussed up firmly like a turkey with our tethering ropes between two pieces of exercise apparatus.

'Yu, Yu,' Mr Peng calmed her with the Chinese version of 'whoa', and as the Big Brother-style official announcements over the village loudspeakers overhead exhorted the villagers to tidy up the village in preparation for a visit by the mayor of Beijing the following day, the shoes were nailed on.

Shoes fitted, we set off up a narrow wooded gorge rather

incongruously lined with solar street lights. Soon we were zig-zagging up the steep slope at the head of the valley. Guard dogs barked furiously behind the wall of a luxurious mansion, no doubt the weekend retreat of a powerful party official or wealthy businessman based in Beijing. The scenery was stunning and almost straight out of a Chinese landscape painting. Woods crept up to the base of soaring crags where bushes clung tortuously to crevices in the precipitous rock faces. One could almost imagine the curling clouds one sees in Chinese art. It seemed incredible that the Ming even bothered to build a wall across such seemingly impenetrable terrain, but there is evidence of at least one fatal attack when a Mongol raiding party sneaked through existing defences on the jagged ridges.

We passed a temple and plunged into a long tunnel through a high ridge. After the street lights on the valley road outside, it was ironic that the tunnel was completely unlit and pitch dark. We aimed at the circle of daylight at the far end and hoped a random lorry would not mow us down. As the sound of the horses' shoes bounced back off the walls and echoed around us, I reflected that the growing glimmer ahead seemed to symbolise the light at the end of another tunnel. I was feeling considerably more upbeat about the ride. We had sound horses, CEA support, and our new team member Mr Peng was proving to be a gem. Surely it would be plain sailing from now on.

CHAPTER FIVE

BADALING GREAT WALL

不到长城非好汉

bú dào Chángchéng fēi hǎohàn

He who has never been to the Great Wall is not a true man.

Friday, 17 October – Saturday, 25 October, 2008.

Zhenluoying to Kangzhuang.

179 km. Daily average 26 km.

'I think Bei Bei is lame,' said Rowena gloomily as we set out the next morning. I groaned as I watched Bei Bei's large rump waddling away. She definitely looked uneven. It seemed we were fated never to go far before we hit another setback. Rowena and I were in no doubt it was because of the donkey shoes, although everyone else disagreed, including a vet down the road. We decided to make it a short day and walk slowly over the ridge to the next valley, while Guo Sheng phoned Mr Zhao in Kangzhuang to plead with him to bring a proper farrier over.

On foot once more, Rowena trudged stoically up the hill out of town with Bei Bei plodding behind. In spite of the dull, grey backdrop, it was a beautiful road lined by trees flaunting flaming red autumn leaves. On the other side of the hill it descended gradually to a narrow valley floor brightened by the occasional green splash of a vegetable patch. Steep scrubby hills loomed out of the haze on either side, and on a thin sliver of terraced field clinging to the slope, a woman in jeans toiled, raking up walnut-coloured sweet potatoes from the moist soil. Yellow stacks of beaded corn cobs were piled high in the courtyards, and plump persimmons lit up leafless branches like tiny orange lanterns. We passed a white-bearded old gentleman leading a donkey loaded with mysterious wicker barrels, and a cheerful woman hawking creamy white tofu wrapped in a damp cloth from the back of a bicycle.

Twenty kilometres further down the road Mr Peng waved us down in front of a large restaurant which had guest rooms at the back. We led the horses across a kitchen passageway to an inner courtyard, providing the unforgettable sight of Bei Bei's hefty backside squeezing through two sets of fly-flaps to the inner recesses of the compound. Mr Peng had been busy on his mobile, and to everyone's relief, Mr Zhao turned up with the stud farrier, Mr Ji Yongshi, as we were having lunch. Mr Peng had persuaded them to make the round trip of well over 200 kilometres to help us out. Mr Ji was one of the handful of qualified Hong Kong-trained farriers in Beijing and in no time he had nailed a strong set of shoes onto Jing Jing. Bei Bei proved less amenable and had to be led down the road to a nearby vet to be sedated and restrained in the cattle crush. The vet also examined her feet and gave me some little enclosed glass vials containing a colourless liquid drug that I had to inject for the next few days. I was familiar with injecting sheep and horses, but assigned the job of smashing off the top of the vials to the steady hand of Guo Sheng. Whether it was the new shoes or the drugs, Bei Bei strode out sound again, and we had no further trouble for the rest of the week.

It was time to pick up our final feed drop in Miyun before meeting up with Mr Ren's *gege*, or elder brother, for dinner at a fish restaurant. A stout middle-aged man with receding slicked-back hair and dressed entirely in black, Mr Ren senior was an unsettling imitation of an underworld boss. Perhaps he was one. At his side was a nervous young interpreter he had thoughtfully employed to help conversation along, and his two henchmen included a shifty-looking gentleman with close-cropped hair who announced he ran a pit bull terrier stud. The glass turntable at the centre of the table in the private dining room was laden with a cornucopia of Chinese dishes, the centrepiece of which was a huge fish from the Miyun reservoir simmering in sauce on a brazier. The *laowai* were given the dubious privilege of being served the head and eye – or at least I got something inedible which Rowena claimed was the highly prized delicacy. The flesh at any rate was delicious. Bottles of beer were opened and Mr Ren beamed in satisfaction. Honour had been restored by the tremendous show his brother had put on, and he was a bit more civil to us from then on.

There was much talk of *Menggu ma*, or Mongolian horses, of which both Mr Ren and his brother were firm fans. Mr Ren senior had a friend with many good *Menggu ma* and I was invited to try them out when I returned the following year. A tray was brought round with several shot glasses and a bottle of *maotai,* a famous Chinese brand of *baijiu* or 'white spirit' made from sorghum, and one of Mao Zedong's favourite tipples.

'*Ganbei!*'

Raising his shot glass, pit bull terrier man was attempting to engage us in a drinking competition. *Ganbei* quite literally means empty cup, signifying 'Bottoms up!'. I had previously had my head nearly blown off emptying my cup of *baijiu* at Chinese dinners to cries of '*Ganbei*' and I knew what was in store. I sipped my drink primly, but Rowena proved stiffer opposition. As she matched pit bull man glass for glass, his admiration and interest increased, and I hoped he was not thinking of whisking her away to his stud.

Bei Bei was back to her old self in the morning, but we had only ridden a short way down the road before a car came screeching to a halt beside us and the restaurant proprietor jumped out. The horses had slightly gnawed a rather sorry specimen of a tree in the courtyard and he claimed it was some rare foreign variety he had imported at vast expense. In spite of our scepticism, Rowena forked out 400 yuan, which was much more than our hotel bill, and he drove off no doubt rubbing his hands in glee at his good fortune.

The landscape flattened out as we entered the valley of the Chao Bai river, where the hills and the Great Wall swung away from us in a great northward loop around the Miyun reservoir. A horrible narrow road with rushing traffic led into Miyun and it was a relief to stop for lunch at a restaurant where a huge poster outside depicted a donkey next to a smiling Labrador eyeing a large plate of food. Did they also cater for pets? But I knew enough hanzi to understand the meaning. It was a dog and donkey restaurant and the dog would soon be on the plate. Rowena and I stuck to our regular less exotic choices.

Tramping round Miyun on a ring road honking with traffic, we were met on the other side by a delegation from the Chinese Equestrian Association, including the now familiar faces of Kubi and Wutzala. They had arranged for us all to stay at the small town of Xitiangezhuang a couple of miles further on. The horses were accommodated in a large storage yard nearby and we were treated to yet another Chinese banquet perked up by liberal quantities of *maotai*. From there it was an easy day's ride to the tourist hot spot of Mutianyu, where we would rejoin the Great Wall. Providentially, for most of the way we were able to avoid the busy roads again by following the wide concrete lined canal which carries water from the Miyun reservoir southwards to supply Beijing. A small quiet gravel track ran along the bank for miles, at one point crossing the dry pebbly bed of the Bai river. In the distance far ahead, a pale blue band of hills came into view again, and I knew that the Great Wall twisted somewhere over them. There was a hint of winter in the clear crisp October air, and leaves flittered down in showers from poplar groves on either side. A cool breeze brushed across our faces while the weak autumn sun warmed our backs and our hearts. Guo Sheng found an idyllic spot among trees for lunch. We sat on the edge of the empty canal drinking beer and eating left over breakfast buns, hard-boiled eggs, and fruit, while the tethered horses foraged among the undergrowth and little swallows swooped over the trickle of water flowing along the paved canal floor.

We were now entering an area frequented by sightseers, and that night we stayed down the road from the Great Wall at Mutianyu, in a tourist-approved *nong jia yuan* fairly characteristic of rural courtyard houses near Beijing. On riding into Beijing municipality, we had also entered a 'Chinglish' zone, which added an even more surreal tone to the journey than we had already experienced. The menu at the restaurant where we ate that evening offered 'Stir fried dishcloth ground with meat,' which we chose to pass over.

Riding up to Mutianyu Great Wall the next morning, we passed an advert for a new lake resort. Above a caption proclaiming 'Reside by the side of the lake and live like a recluse in the mountains' was a bacchanalian picture of merrymakers waving glasses of champagne aloft at an alfresco picnic.

It seemed a must to do the tourist thing and visit the Great Wall at Mutianyu as we set out the following morning. Leaving the horses with Mr Ren, Rowena and I braved the stallholders lining the passageway up to the cable car, accompanied by Mr Peng. It was strange to be mingling suddenly with tourists and to encounter the first *waiguoren* we had seen since leaving Shanhaiguan. None of them would have the slightest conception that these two middle-aged women had arrived not in a tour bus or taxi, but on horseback.

We threaded our way through the crowds and browsed half-heartedly among the tatty souvenirs.

'*Duo shao qian?* How much is it?'

The stallholder quoted an exorbitant figure and Mr Peng sprang to our defence.

'*Tai gui le.* Too expensive.'

Suggestion of a more realistic figure from Mr Peng prompted a tirade from the aggrieved shopkeeper, no doubt a lecture on letting the side down. Mr Peng grinned sheepishly at us.

The Mutianyu section of the wall is typical of the well visited stretch of wall to the north of Beijing. Constructed mainly of large granite blocks topped with brick, it is one of the better preserved sections of the Great Wall, though subject to much new renovation. Older defensive wall used sun-dried bricks, but the bricks making up this stretch of

Ming wall were kiln-fired, hard, and much more resistant to erosion. Local kilns were set up and specific sections were built by local labour under official command. Snaking along a forested knife-edge ridge, it has an unusual number of watchtowers which also served as beacon towers. If attacking nomads were spotted, fires would be lit on top to spread the alarm and alert the defending forces. In the daytime, when the light of the fires would not be so visible, what was called 'wolf smoke' would be created. One imaginative suggestion is that this term originated because wolf dung was put on the fires to create darker smoke, but it is more likely that it was a reference to prowling steppe warriors. Old photos of the Wall to the north of Beijing show bare rocky hill slopes, but recent restriction of grazing by goats has encouraged vegetation growth.

Although Rowena and I gladly took advantage of the cable car trip up to the wall, it was an uncomfortable reminder of the increasing commercialism surrounding this iconic structure. Many of the tourist access points to the Great Wall near Beijing have attracted ancillary activities, and Mutianyu was no exception. After a short stroll along the steep ramparts, we decided to pass up the option of a toboggan ride back down to the bottom and chose to walk down through the woods.

Over the next couple of days Mr Ren had worked out a lovely route winding along quiet roads up narrow valleys and over precipitous forested hills, negotiating a couple of high passes and another dark tunnel. We rode past chestnut and apricot groves and through pretty villages with red brick courtyard houses clinging to the hillslopes, and along a river valley where a cluster of fish pond restaurants gaily adorned with large red Chinese lanterns lined a road beside a pebbly river. At Nanyecun, a very house-proud lady nearly had a heart attack when she saw our cavalcade advancing up the narrow alleyway to her little courtyard house at the foot of a rocky slope. It required further haggling and a call to her boss before the horses were allowed into a neat sandy yard with a vegetable patch and a few fruit trees.

'She say we shower before eight o'clock,' warned Guo Sheng slowly, pointing at his watch. In most countries I have been to this would have meant only cold water was available after that. But in fact, our hostess meant that the cold water supply was turned off then. Like many houses in China, the hot water was heated and stored in a solar tank on the roof. So when we did not make the deadline, instead of a cold shower, we were faced with a burst of scalding hot water. But the white-tiled bathroom with squat loo and photo tile of naked lady on the shower wall was spotless.

One chilly autumn morning when mist hung in the dark branches of the persimmon trees and cloaked the rugged hills looming above, we rode past a flaking red wall topped with roof tiles, behind which rose the dark umbrella shapes of pine trees. Weeds sprouted like hair from the tops of pillars flanking a wide gateway blocked off with railed partitions. Seemingly abandoned, the compound behind this wall marked the northern limit of the Ming tombs, and held the Tailing tomb of the monogamous Hongzhi emperor (Xiao Zong), who was singular for being the only emperor never to keep concubines.

Only three of the thirteen Ming tombs are open to the public. The other ten, including this one, still need renovation and are closed to the public. Standing behind low railings across the valley about a kilometre away, we came to a tall stone stele, or pillar-like tablet, topped by entwined dragons and supported by a stone *bixi* or dragon-headed turtle. This traditional feature of Ming and Qing tombs was at the entrance to the Kangling tomb, also off-limits, where the Hongzhi emperor's only son, the Zhengdi emperor, is buried. He reportedly died from an illness contracted after drunkenly falling overboard while fishing. Perhaps the moral that can be drawn is 'Don't drink and fish'.

After the quiet rural scenery, it was a shock to reach a horrendous road in a narrow north-south valley clogged with a sluggish river of nose-to-tail lorries crawling past in either direction. The G110 from Yanqing served as a reminder that we were now less than fifty kilometres from the centre of Beijing, and this was no doubt one of the few passable routes from the north through the otherwise impenetrable hills. I wondered if attacking nomadic forces had ever used it. It was a half-mile tramp up the narrow verge with exhaust fumes spewing over us before we found somewhere to cross, though at least the trucks were unable to get up much speed on the choked road. Mr Ren guided us along a quiet country lane on the other side, passing a sign advertising 'Tour and family plucking in the village'. It sounded rather gruesome and we did not hang about to find out what it meant.

We passed the SUV parked in a layby. Guo Sheng was in the driver's seat, head back and snoring. I turned to Mr Peng and tried out my few words of Chinese.

'*Kan. Guo Sheng shui jiao.* Look, Guo Sheng is asleep.'

Mr Peng smiled and nodded and I was tempted to try out a little more. I jokingly suggested Guo Sheng needed to wake up.

'*Ta dei qi chuang.*'

Mr Peng grinned, the edges of his eyes crinkling into laughter lines.

'*Ni shuo cuo le.* You said it wrong.'

Lifting himself up in the saddle he mimed getting out of bed.

'*Ni yinggai shuo "xing".* You should say "*xing*".' I had made the beginner's mistake of mixing up the Chinese phrase to get out of bed with the word for to wake up. It was a simple error, but it made us both chuckle companionably together, and in that small moment I felt my connection with Mr Peng grow.

That evening was our last on the road, and we had an entertaining stay at a chicken farm just off the Badaling Expressway near Nankou, only a day's ride from central Beijing. Chickens of every conceivable colour flapped and squawked in a long row of mesh divided pens which opened off a long brick shed at the back. A couple of pens contained strutting pheasants with reddish-blue plumage and tiny white collars, perhaps bound for upmarket Beijing restaurants. Unexpectedly the farm doubled up as a part-time event venue, and as well as a modest function room, there was a karaoke stage in a courtyard strung with coloured lights. A few snakes writhed through branches in a small mesh-fronted cage to the side. We may have been the only guests, but we were treated to the works. A steaming Beijing hot pot appeared, bubbling on a brazier at the centre of our round table in the courtyard, but no sooner had we picked up our chopsticks than the heavens opened. Everything was hurriedly shifted onto the stage as large drops of rain spattered down. A bottle of *baijiu* materialised, heralding a merry round of toasting and *'Ganbei!'*. Our host was keen to make a good impression on his now well lubricated guests, and it was not long before the karaoke machine was in full swing with song scripts displayed in Chinese on a television screen. So while the rain poured down and steam rose from the hotpot on the cramped stage, Mr Ren regaled us with stirring songs of Mongolian steeds galloping across the grasslands. The performance was embellished by various warblings from Mr Peng, Guo Sheng, and the host's son and daughter, evidently old stagers, but Rowena and I thankfully managed to avoid the ignominy of displaying our vocal talents. The finale was a disco complete with strobe lights. Disturbingly, I have a faint recollection of prancing around in my jodhpurs before we tottered off considerably the worse for wear to collapse on our beds.

Our final day dawned crisp and clear and we set off with a bursting sense of anticipation that our goal was near at hand. North of Nankou the Badaling Expressway enters the gorge-like Guan Gou river valley where it narrows to cut through the Jundu hills. We took the old road which runs parallel to the expressway and sometimes clings to the hillside above. It was far from being a pleasant option as there was no hard shoulder, and the many tour buses taking tourists to Juyong Pass and Badaling Great Wall swished past in both directions. There was no attempt to slow down for the horses, and whenever we gesticulated at them to reduce speed, the drivers waved back cheerily and blasted their horns.

The fears of our Chinese friends were finally borne out when we met an icy wind blowing down the valley from Mongolia, an abrupt change from the balmy weather we had been experiencing. But thanks to their warnings we were well prepared, and were wrapped up in thermal underwear, warm padded jackets and gloves. Eventually we began to overtake and mingle with crowds of people walking up the road to the Great Wall, and at last we rounded a corner to see the Badaling gateway ahead of us. I am not one to give public displays of emotion, but a mixture of excitement and relief bubbled up inside me, and I grinned at the others. We had overcome lameness, bad backs and officious police, and made it safely to Badaling. We may only have covered a tiny fraction of the distance which lay ahead, but in that moment, I felt as much satisfaction as if I had already ridden right across Eurasia. In spite of all the setbacks, we had survived the first leg unscathed and were on our way. Most importantly, useful contacts had been made and we had learnt a lot which would help to plan for the following year. I now truly felt that the whole mad scheme was feasible.

'*Quiezi!*' Guo Sheng cried out as the team lined up for photos with the Great Wall twisting up the hillside behind. A huge Olympic sign was fittingly displayed below. Then we pushed onwards through the crowds, and Mr Ren shepherded us around to pose in front of every monument or plaque he deemed remotely relevant, including the Children's Charity Monument.

But it was not quite all over. Two days later, Wutzala and Kubi, in their roles as representatives of the Chinese Equestrian Association, had organised an official launch of the Sino-British International Friendship Ride as it was now dubbed. Members gathered on hired horses outside the smart new tourist guesthouse we had stayed in the previous two nights. Mr Ren had dug out my Welsh flag from the depths of the SUV and mounted it on a stick. He spun Xiao Hei, and whirled the flag around his head like an oriental Owain Glyndwr, the heroic Welsh ruler who fought against the English.

With cries of '*Jia!, jia!*', the Chinese version of 'Giddy-up!', the cavalcade charged en masse a few hundred yards up the road to Chadao village, a reconstructed heritage town and military fortress. Up the stone ramp onto the battlements over the gatehouse everyone clattered. Then, like the grand old Duke of York's troops, down we came again. After which, with the exception of the *laowai* who kept to a more sedate pace, the assembled company galloped full tilt up the road outside the town wall to the ancient Ming gateway at the far side for photos and speeches. While Xinlian translated, I thanked everyone I could and foresaw that the ride across China would be a great success with the help of the Chinese Equestrian Association. Wutzala countered with a lengthy and rambling speech in Chinese, of which I hardly understood a word.

'I think he expected your speech to be much longer,' said Xinlian in a disappointed tone of voice. It seemed that in China the longer the speech, the more prestige it accrues. I was not surprised to read sometime later that the mayor of Guangzhou had proposed limiting official speeches to less than an hour to stop audiences falling asleep in meetings.

It was sad to leave the horses in the stables at the Jihe stud. Rowena had become quite fond of the stolid Bei Bei, and although she had a mouth and sides like iron and tried to bite me on the first day, Jing Jing and I had developed a mutual understanding. Guo Sheng put out a hand to stroke her when we arrived at the stud but jumped back as she swung her head towards him with teeth bared.

'This is how you do it, Guo Sheng,' I teased, rubbing Jing Jing's neck as she stood like a rock with drooping head. As I anticipated, she snapped at Guo Sheng the moment he tried again. Mr Zhao found homes for them within the week, and I was able to recoup most of the money they had cost. They had served us well but it would have been prohibitively expensive to pay for keep over the winter, and I had now been promised free horses from the Shandan stud.

That evening Rowena and I gave a dinner for all the people that really mattered and who had made the first leg happen. Xinlian, my Chinese teacher who had been a great support from the beginning; Mr Zhao, who had found horses for us; Mr Ji, the farrier who had shod the horses so well; Mr Peng, who came to the rescue with his little Mongolian geldings and got up at 5am to feed; Mr Ren, who had made a real effort to find *xiao lu* or back roads for us; and Guo Sheng, who had encouraged and protected us all the way. Without their help the ride would never have got off the ground. I had made some great new friends and felt really optimistic about the future of the ride. There was much toasting and '*Ganbei!*', a great sense of camaraderie, and a touch of sadness that it was over – at least for now.

Driving back to Beijing on the expressway a truck hooted at us. It was Mr Peng with Xiao Hei and Qing Qing in the back. We stopped on the hard shoulder to say a last '*Zai jian*' or 'Until I see you'. It would only be another five months to wait.

CHAPTER SIX

A FALSE START

临渴掘井
lín kě jué jǐng
Dig the well before you are thirsty.

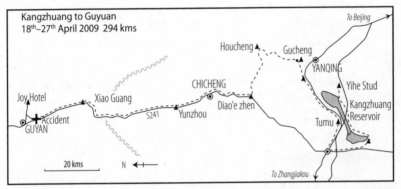

Kangzhuang to Guyuan
18th–27th April 2009 294 kms

To Beijing

Houcheng ▲ ····· Gucheng ▲
YANQING ◉
Yihe Stud ▲

CHICHENG ◉
Xiao Guang Diao'e zhen ◉ Kangzhuang ▲
Joy Hotel S241 Yunzhou Reservoir
◉ Accident Tumu ▲
GUYAN

20 kms   N ←—

To Zhangjiakou

Saturday, 18 April, 2009 – Launch of the Beijing to London Ride. 38 km.

The winter months had been a frenzy of preparation, organisation, and worry. Wutzala had sent a long and convoluted contract in Chinese, but I was loath to sign anything which might tie the ride finances into a legal deal I might later regret. My lack of legal knowledge and poor command of the language made everything a struggle. Translating needed to be paid for, and email was not an effective means of communication when so many issues needed to be thrashed out. I desperately needed a mutually acceptable compromise to guarantee the enormous support the CEA would undoubtedly be able to provide. However, help was at hand, and as always from the most unexpected quarter, in this case a young lawyer learning Chinese in Beijing who was the son of the friend of a friend of my old friend Dr Rowena Mathew.

David McNeill had the requisite legal background, communicated easily in Chinese, was on the spot and would be happy to help out. He proved utterly indispensable, meeting up with Wutzala and Kubi on several occasions to thrash matters out. As he had a good insight into how things worked in China, he was able to come up with a very short and simple agreement which kept everyone happy. He also acted as an able interpreter when I had the rather surreal experience of a press conference by Skype with journalists in Beijing.

The thorny issue of age arose again.

'Do you think you will be able to do this journey at your age?'

I now had a stock answer up my sleeve.

"Rosie Swale-Pope from Wales is in her sixties and she has just *run* around the whole world, so I think I should manage to cross Eurasia on the back of a horse!'

An astonished silence and the topic was dropped.

With a basic agreement sorted out, everything was on the move. Fretting about the costs of crossing China, I sent off another batch of appeals for financial sponsorship together with some grant applications, to no avail. I would have to rely mainly on my pension lump sum payment which was due in 2009. But I was thrilled when Frank Hodal of Vidazorb affirmed continuation of his sponsorship for a new 'Zorbee' and there was also some very much appreciated sponsorship in kind. This included a top spec riding helmet in an appropriate gold colour from Welsh-based firm Charles Owen, and a stock of wide helmet brims from Australian company Cutana. These fitted snugly over the helmet and protected me from suffering a sunburned nose or rain dripping down my neck. As they were detachable, they also came in useful for swatting horseflies.

'Is it a special kind of Chinese helmet?' people asked, barely stifling a laugh.

The combination did look rather eccentric, but so what – safety and practicality came before elegance when one was facing weeks on the hoof.

The Chinese in particular came up trumps. Besides arranging horses from the Shandan stud, in March I had the exciting news that they had secured a new sponsor in the form of the Jiazhuo Special Vehicle Company. A Special trailer was being made for the ride, and I was sent a range of designs to pore over and comment on.

One of the first matters to be seen to on arriving in Beijing at the beginning of April 2009 was buying a four-wheel drive vehicle to pull the trailer, and a little contingent set off to trawl round the second hand truck and car yards. With us was Wong Li May, a young Chinese girl from Singapore who was taking a break from university in New Zealand. Small and stocky with a round face framed by a bob of straight black hair, she had no experience with horses, but spoke Mandarin Chinese and had joined the team as a volunteer interpreter. Ex-taxi driver Mr Peng poked under bonnets and sniffed exhaust pipes until there was unanimous agreement on a reasonably priced metallic-blue Jeep Cherokee which had even starred in a commercial in its former life. Then it was off to sort out a number plate for our celebrity automobile, an unexpectedly significant task.

'It is very important not to choose unlucky numbers,' Li May informed me. 'Number four is very unlucky.' Number four was a total no-no as the Chinese word for four 'se' is identical to the word for death except for a difference in tone. The Chinese are so superstitious about this that if you find yourself wandering along a hotel corridor in China vainly looking for Room 4, it is undoubtedly because it doesn't exist. We perused the numbers displayed on a wall screen in the registration office. 'OK 836' seemed OK and included auspicious numbers six and eight.

'But isn't it a problem that eight is the sum of two deaths?' I queried. Surely that made it doubly unlucky.

'No, that doesn't matter, the Chinese word for eight sounds like the word for fortune,' giggled Li May. In fact, number eight is considered so lucky in China that the Chinese were overjoyed to be given the Olympics in 2008, and chose to start the opening ceremony at eight minutes and eight seconds past eight o'clock on the eighth day of the eighth month, August.

It was strange to own a car without being able to drive it, but there was a certain satisfaction in being chauffeured around town like a potentate by Mr Peng and it was a relief not to be reliant on public transport.

A string of meetings followed, by far the most important of which had been arranged by Harry Tse, a successful Hong Kong businessman and horseman who had decided to take the venture under his wing. Harry, Mr Peng, and myself were ushered into a small conference room in a government building near Tiananmen Square to meet up with representatives from the grandly named China International Friendship Cities Association, and Chinese People's Association for Friendship with Foreign Countries. A trio of equally grand-looking officials faced us on the other side of a long highly polished table, but after a formal welcome I was happy to find they were truly extending the hand of friendship. Printed certificates authorising the ride were organised, specifying our names and with an important-looking official stamp at the bottom. These documents proved to be of inestimable worth in dealing with the police and other occasionally suspicious officials on our way across China. My concern with regard to running the gauntlet of local bureaucracy was now completely removed, particularly as we were also provided with emergency telephone numbers in case of problems. But with the certificates at the ready, these were never needed. Without this official support it is most unlikely that our journey through more sensitive areas of China would have gone so smoothly, and it might even have ground to a halt. I was to remain ever grateful to Harry and his official contacts.

The next major excitement was the arrival of the horses from Shandan on April 10. They were being delivered to the hotel and riding centre south of Beijing where the CEA were putting us up to attend a press conference following a forty-mile endurance race. I still found it strange to see all the endurance horses arriving in open trucks. Mr Ma, who had driven his two horses 4,000 kilometres from Yining on the Kazakhstan border, had erected a protective canvas cover on his vehicle. Our horses were not so lucky and six lean and hairy beasts turned up having travelled the two days and two nights from Gansu province loose in the back of an open lorry enclosed with metal railings. Four of them were ours, but which four? The truck was reversed up to a bank and one by one the horses were haltered and jumped off the back. I was glad to see two poorer specimens were bound for another destination, and we led the remaining four geldings to an outside pen.

They did not look an inspiring bunch. Although Shandan horses are always called horses, these ones could more accurately be described as ponies[1]. They had obviously wintered out on meagre grazing as their backbones protruded and their coats were dull. Of the three bays, one looked too small and another too scrawny for the rigours of the journey ahead. However, there was a larger, deep-bodied gelding with a patchy coat and plain head, and a lean, rangy black gelding that I liked the look of. We gave them feed, hay, and water and left them to recuperate after their long haul. From now on they would be given grain three or four times a day and would hopefully quickly improve in condition. The next morning, we attempted to handle them a little. The big gelding was head-shy but easy to catch, and Mr Peng soon had halters on the scrawny bay and the more nervous small bay, but the black horse was as wild as a fiend, whipping round and lashing out with his heels, catching poor Mr Peng on the thigh and leaving an impressive bruise. I re-assessed my plans to ride it.

The evening after the endurance race, Wutzala had organised a big press conference in the hotel dining room. A rather dour lady representative from the Shandan stud, Wutzala, Mr Peng and myself, together with Xinlian as interpreter, sat in front of a large banner promoting the ride. Facing us was a roomful of reporters

---

[1] In the West a horse is officially any equine 15 hands or over to the top of the wither or shoulder, a hand being four inches. Anything below this is a pony. However this does not apply in all cases, for example with a cob, which is a sturdy type of horse or pony. Certain breeds such as Arabian, Mongolian and Shandan are always called horses even if they are pony height.

and TV cameras. This would have been quite daunting a few weeks previously, but I was quickly becoming accustomed to all the media attention and happily made a short speech and answered questions. The conference was followed by an awards ceremony for the endurance race and then it was an evening of jollity with a Chinese banquet and lashings of *maotai*, joined by David McNeill who had turned up for the day.

On Tuesday, April 14, we loaded up the horses once again and set off to spend a couple of days at Harry Tse's stables in the north-eastern suburbs of Beijing. Harry was instrumental in setting up the growing sport of horseball in China. Developed in Argentina three hundred years ago and revived in France in the 1930s, it is sometimes described as a cross between rugby and basketball played on horseback. Mercifully, the live duck it seems was originally used has now been replaced with a six-handled ball. Very perceptively, Harry realised that it was a sport that did not require the importation of expensive foreign bred performance horses. As long as they were of medium height and athletic, almost any ordinary Chinese horse had the potential to become a useful horseball mount. He trained in natural horsemanship techniques and qualified as a horseball coach in Britain. He had then set up a horseball centre in Beijing, buying in local horses cheaply, and selecting a team of enthusiastic young Chinese for training in the methods he had studied. Some of them were graduates and for many it was their first experience of working with horses. Harry had managed to cram all the necessary facilities onto the small property he had secured, with a central sand school/ horseball court, accommodation for the students at one end, and two round pens and a long outhouse containing loose boxes, tack room, and offices at the other. Everything was neat and well kept, and an atmosphere of calm content pervaded.

Our horses were worked in the round pen and ridden in the sand school, soon responding positively to the gentle handling they were receiving. The bigger head-shy gelding had seemed very indifferent on arrival, giving every sign of having been roughly handled in the past. He now stopped jerking his head away every time we put a hand out towards it, and appeared to enjoy the attention he was receiving. In the absence of inspiration, I called him Bajiu or eighty-nine in Chinese after the number eighty-nine branded on his backside, not to be confused with the alcoholic spirit *baijiu*. Hopefully I would not need a shot of *baijiu* to ride Bajiu and he would make a solid and dependable ride for an old age pensioner like me.

Whereas Bajiu now turned his head to look at me when I walked past, the thin bony gelding remained detached and apathetic. He was a quiet, willing ride with a short, quick stride. The real revelation was the small bay that I was unsure would be up to the job. One of the boys dashed around the sand school on his back with a broad smile on his face and I was enticed to have a try. What he lacked in size he made up for in spirit. Unschooled but active, he had a mouth like silk – a touch too harsh on the reins and his head would shoot up in the air. He could also pace, the smooth gait making one wobble from side to side rather than bounce up and down. He quickly became my preferred choice and I named him Zorbee for my sponsor Vidazorb. Unfortunately, the black gelding was still wild, and it seemed doubtful that he would be ready to ride in time for the official start.

The customised trailer provided by the Jiazhuo trailer company had been delivered to the yard. It was partitioned to provide two horse stalls at the back, and this area would mainly be used to carry feed, fodder and horse equipment. At the front there was a small kitchen compartment which included cupboards, a sink, and gas cooker, as well as a substantial water container. A big bonus were the solar panels on the roof which not only supplied electric light to the trailer but power to a plug point, so we could charge a variety of electrical equipment such as mobile phones, laptops and cameras. This was pure luxury. I had also directed that there would be ample tie rings on both sides so we would never be struggling to find somewhere safe to tie the horses up at night as we had on the first stage.

We were now joined by horseman Li Jing. An ex-librarian and

native Chinese who had taken Russian citizenship, he had just spent over a year and a half riding from Votkinsk, about 300 kilometres west of the Ural mountains in Russia, to Beijing. The intention had been to arrive in time for the Olympics, but in the event, he did not arrive until sometime after. It now meant that two Chinese on the team had experienced long distance travel by horse. With shoulder-length hair tied back in a pony tail, sporting a wispy beard and moustache, and enveloped in a huge green canvas cloak inscribed with Chinese poetry in red characters, Li Jing had swept down through Manchuria on his horse, Yura, like a character from a romantic legend. The press reports that had been forwarded to me made him seem larger than life, but he turned out to quite small in stature and with the sparrow-like delicacy of many Chinese. Fluent in Russian, he also spoke rather rusty English and, together with my halting Mandarin, we could communicate fairly effectively. This achieved an increased significance since, to my intense annoyance, Li May suddenly announced at the eleventh hour that she had decided not to come along.

The morning before the launch the horses were loaded once more onto a truck and whole shebang moved once again to the Yihe stud where we had finished riding the previous autumn. Mr Ji the farrier was not available, so the horses were ridden into a nearby village to be shod by a local blacksmith in the traditional way, strapped up to a wooden shoeing frame. Supplies of feed, hay, and water were loaded up into the trailer, and I packed and re-packed my luggage, which included one small holdall of clothes and a second holdall containing electricals such as camera and video camera, satellite phone, a variety of chargers and solar chargers, various leads, and so on. There was also a large bag containing spare equestrian equipment, and another with copious veterinary supplies for the horses – this compared with a small medical kit for the humans! I had my two Free 'n' Easy saddles, and Li Jing had brought along his own rather fearsome Mongolian saddle. Unlike my saddles with their flexible and adjustable panels, this consisted of a rigid wooden 'tree' or frame with a raised seat on fixed panels. Traditionally the ornate seats of Mongolian saddles have thin padding, and the high pommels and cantles (the front and back of the saddle) rear up to form a winged 'V' shape, difficult to fall out of, but hardly the height of comfort. Next to my padded saddles and fluffy sheepskin seat covers, Li Jing's hard saddle seat with its tattered lining looked like an instrument of torture. Wide leather saddle flaps hung down on either side to avoid friction between the horse's sides and rider's legs. Li Jing could wrap them round the frame and carry the whole thing under his arm when he was not riding. When riding he put a thick saddle pad on the horse's back under the saddle, and secured everything with two narrow straps under the horse's belly, the front girth strap tightened to keep the saddle in place, the looser back belly band to keep it stable.

Li Jing had agreed to join the team and share costs, and Li May would have been paying her own way, had she not changed her mind about coming. Harry took me aside.

'I think there is a problem. Did you understand that Mr Peng expected to receive a weekly wage for the journey?'

'But I thought he realised he was coming as a member of the team and I would pay his expenses only.'

'He doesn't have a lot of money and cannot afford to go off for two or three months without any income. He has his son to think of.' Mr Peng had a teenage son from his former marriage who he was devoted to.

'How much does he want?'

Although not unreasonable, the figure was more than my pension, which I was relying on for ongoing living expenses. It was a huge blow.

'I quite understand, but I am a pensioner on a strict budget and cannot afford this much.'

'I really think you need to have him with you. He is very dependable and can help you if you run into trouble.'

Fully aware of this, I was engulfed by a wave of despair. The loss of his services could be hugely detrimental to the success of the ride and Harry was insistent that he come along for reasons that became evident later on. I needed to re-assess the situation and my finances. It seemed possible if Mr Peng was prepared to compromise, and with the help of Harry and David, we thankfully managed to negotiate a mutually acceptable deal and I was able to breathe yet another sigh of relief. The CEA had found a volunteer driver called Mr Wan and as Li May out of the blue changed her mind yet again and decided she did want to come along after all, we would now be a party of five.

The start of the ride was planned to coincide with the Second Guangting Endurance ride held on the Kangxi grasslands outside Kangzhuang on Saturday, 18 April, 2009. The eighty kilometre endurance ride would follow the edge of the immense Guangting reservoir which provides water and hydropower for Beijing. The venue was only a couple of kilometres from the Yihe stud, and the plan was for a small group of us to hack over on the morning of the joint events. Having opted to ride Zorbee, who was still a bit of an unknown quantity, I was a little nervous as I tacked up on the yard. But he was manageable if a bit over-excited as we jogged down earth tracks through bare arable fields behind the Yihe contingent. A stable lad pranced ahead on a grey Arabian stallion, followed by Li Jing on his bay mare Yura, and Mr Peng on Bajiu leading the thin gelding. The wild black horse had been left behind at the ranch, as we had decided he was too unmanageable.

Chinese endurance riders milled around on a flat, well-trampled area in front of a clubhouse on the grassland running down to the reservoir. It was a very different scene to endurance events in Britain as cowboy gear seemed to be de rigueur and Stetsons predominated over safety helmets. We lined up in front of the clubhouse to await the opening ceremony. Thankfully it consisted of only a few short speeches from the podium before our respective national anthems were played, and Li Jing, Mr Peng and myself were presented with Olympic flags by a representative of the Chinese Equestrian Association. Then we paraded around waving our flags to the strains of some suitably stirring music over the loudspeaker followed by a cohort of the CEA members also brandishing flags. I swapped to Bajiu in case Zorbee took exception to my flag and I ended up in London earlier than expected, but in fact he was perfectly well-behaved. The Chinese media were out in force taking photos, filming and conducting interviews with the team, and I spoke by mobile to a newspaper in France. The trailer was on display being signed by anyone who was anyone, including Harry and his sons Jeremy and Jeremiah who had come along to support, as had David and Xinlian.

The endurance riders disappeared into the morning mist which hung over the plain, while we took a little time to get going as Li Jing was faffing around having taken off his bridle and lost it. I found his disorganisation somewhat irritating until I realised I had packed it away thinking it was an old one of mine. Then we discovered our girths were much too loose as I had not had a chance to buy shorter ones. But like a magician, Harry produced a hole puncher out of thin air.

'*Zou ba*! Let's go!' Peng called out, and at last we were truly on our way.

The Kangxi grasslands stretched into a murky grey haze which hid the reservoir from view. Dusty paths criss-crossed the level expanse of the plain, which was covered scantily with thin grass interspersed with ploughed areas. As we rode, great pale windmills loomed silently out of the mist like alien machines from a science fiction movie. At the base of one, a farmer tilled the earth with a couple of donkeys harnessed to a small plough, an odd juxtaposition of old and new China. We made our way down to a deserted shoreline, trotting briskly across narrow sand flats and picking our way round rocky headlands as the long day drew out. Scattering glints on the crinkled surface of the lake reflected the late afternoon sun as we passed little fishing skiffs drawn up on the beach. A final scramble up a steep slope through a small village and it was a short walk down the road and across a narrow dam to our first stop overlooking the lake. We had covered nearly thirty-eight kilometres since leaving the stud. The lodgings had basic rooms attached to a restaurant, but the only washing facility was a basin in the dining area. Chairman Mao stared down sternly from a poster on the wall above, as if to check whether we were brushing our teeth properly.

We had been concerned that the bony bay gelding was still too thin to stand up to the stresses of the ride, so it was decided to swap him for the wild black fiend who had been left behind at the Yihe stud. The following morning, we left Zorbee, Bajiu and Yura tied up at the restaurant with plenty of hay, bundled the thin horse onto the trailer, and whisked him back to the ranch.

We watched as the black fiend was subjected to a crash course in a round pen by horse trainer Mr Wang, using natural horsemanship techniques. Rearing, spinning, and kicking was to no avail, by the end of the day Mr Wang had him bridled, saddled, ridden, shod, and loaded onto the trailer. Now he was an official team member, Li Jing bestowed him with the romantic and rather fitting name of Hei Feng or Black Wind.

From now on we had to allow ten minutes every morning for whoever was riding Hei Feng to gently gain his trust before quietly mounting, but the time period grew shorter each time.

That evening we ate supper under the watchful eye of Mao Zedong, all of us no doubt harbouring our own thoughts regarding the journey ahead. For my part, I was elated to be on the brink of setting out on the journey proper. Thanks to the involvement of the CEA I now had horses, official endorsement and back-up support. All the current capital expenses had been dealt with and I knew daily living costs fell comfortably within my budget. For the time being I could sleep at night without worrying I would run out of money, be arrested by the police or end up stranded in the middle of nowhere without help. I did not expect the path to be completely smooth, but there was absolutely no reason to suppose I could not reach the other end of the Great Wall of China by the end of July, as long as I didn't fall off my horse and break something. We raised our bottles of Qingdao beer for a toast to future success.

CHAPTER SEVEN

ACCIDENT

风向转变时,有人筑墙,有人造风车
Fēng xiàng zhuàn biàn shí, yǒu rén zhú qiáng,
yǒu rén zào fēng chē
When baffled in one direction a man of energy will not despair,
but will find another way to his object.

Monday, 20 April – Monday, 27 April, 2009.
Kangzhuang reservoir to Guyuan.
256 km. Daily average 33 km.

'If you go by Zhangjiakou it is not good for horses,' urged Wutzala. 'You should not go that way. It is much better to ride north into Inner Mongolia.' Kubi nodded his head vigorously in agreement.

I stared at them in disbelief and disappointment. From Kangzhuang I had intended to head north-west towards Zhangjiakou and re-join the Ming Great Wall which then runs in a south westerly direction through Shanxi province and across the Ordos plateau. I had set my heart on this route partly as I knew that relatively intact sections of the wall continued round the edge of the Ordos desert. It would be a dream come true to ride directly alongside the wall on the flatter plateau land there.

Sadly, I had to admit Wutzala and Kubi had a point. Shanxi province, lying to the west of Zhangjiakou, is China's leading producer of coal, and this has been accompanied by the development of heavy industry. Choking pollution and industrial traffic could make navigating this stretch a deeply unpleasant experience for human and horse alike. At the end of the day, I accepted that I needed to follow the advice of my Chinese sponsors, although it was a bitter blow to miss out the middle section of the Great Wall which I had been resolute in my determination to follow.

I was even more taken aback when Wutzala declared he wanted us to ride eastwards in completely the opposite direction. Apparently, this was to enable photo opportunities in a scenic area, but it could also add several days onto a journey which had already been extended in length. To my chagrin I found myself heading away from London.

The weather was crisp and sunny, but a cold wind from Mongolia blew dust into our faces, and I was grateful for my neck scarf which I pulled up, bandit-style, over my nose and mouth. As Li Jing still had his own horse Yura with him, Peng took turns to ride Hei Feng for a couple of days. I alternated in riding and leading Bajiu and Zorbee, though in Bajiu's case it was more dragging than leading.

We stopped overnight in an ancient hotel block – grubby and tattered on the outside but with polished marble floors and dark wood on the inside – beyond Tumu, a drab town strung out along the main road. In 1449 this inconsequential location witnessed a momentous battle which could be regarded as the single most important factor behind the existence of the Ming Great Wall of China as we know it today. It was here that the Ming army suffered a catastrophic defeat at the hands of the Mongols.

It was a period when not only was China being menaced by the reunited Mongol tribes, but eunuch officials wielded considerable power and influence in the Ming Chinese court. The young emperor Zhengtong had been persuaded by his head eunuch Wang Zhen to lead an ill-fated expedition against the Mongols, a disastrous decision culminating at Tumu in a complete rout, the death of Wang Zhen, and the capture of the emperor. Seeing a profitable opportunity, the Mongol leader Esen Khan offered to return the imperial hostage in return for a large ransom, but his plans were foiled when the Chinese court installed Zhengtong's brother as emperor and basically said 'Thanks, but no thanks,' to the offer. In the end Zhengtong was returned ignominiously without ransom, though some time later he was reinstated as Emperor Tianshun. The significance of this event lay in the fact that it was deeply traumatising for the Ming to be defeated so comprehensively by people they regarded as uncivilised barbarians.

It shaped their policies for years afterwards and resulted in a period of active Great Wall building.

I found reading about Chinese emperors extraordinarily confusing until I realised they were known by several different names. To start with they have a birth name, consisting of a family and a personal name, in the same way as Windsor is the British royal family surname. The birth name of the first Ming emperor Zhu Yuanzhang contains his family name Zhu, which is in the birth names of all his male descendants, including Zhengtong who was born Zhu Qizhen. On becoming emperor, they acquired an era name which refers to a specific period of reign, and many emperors, particularly of the later Song and Ming dynasties are known by these names. Ming emperor Zhu Yuanzhang is more commonly known by his era name Hongwu, and this also explains why Zhengtong acquired a new era name of Tianshun on his reinstatement, though he is the only emperor to do so. If that was not enough, on their deaths they could also receive both a posthumous and a temple name. The posthumous names are lengthy monikers which are not usually referred to, unlike the short temple names given by the imperial family. The Tang emperors are commonly known by their temple names, for example Emperor Gaozu (Birth name Li Yuan, era name Wudi) and Emperor Taizong (Birth name Li Shimin, era name Zhenguan). One history book I read used Zhengtong's temple name of Ying Zong with no mention of Zhengtong, Tianshun or Zhu Qizhen. As a result, it can sometimes take a little time for the uninitiated to unravel who's who!

For most of the way we now followed a busy road with straggling ribbon development on both sides. Where straight lines of trees bordered the road, the whitewashed lower trunks gave a neatly ordered feel to the otherwise untidy sprawl. To the north, a grey body of hills lay outlined like a jawbone of sharp teeth.

'I think it is called Wolf Mountain,' said Hua, referring to the fact that we had just left Langshanxiang or Wolf Mountain town. I warily scanned the ominously serrated silhouette and shivered.

'... but I don't think there are wolves there any more,' Hua added comfortingly.

I looked away across the valley to the south where the Kangxi windmills slowly turned in the distance. Only the pink and white spring blossom on orchard trees brightened the dreary scene. Ahead, Li Jing had dropped his reins and was doing his morning tai chi exercises on horseback, slowly raising his arms to the side and extending them forward like a praying mantis.

We now had another setback.

'Mr Wan says he is ill,' Li May told me. 'He wants to go home to his family. He says he will join us again when he is feeling better.'

But I suspect his complaint was cold feet and it was a ploy to opt out of the venture without losing face, as he never returned. In the meantime, Li Jing had decided to ride Hei Feng and swap the thin horse for Yura, who he was giving to Kubi. This could be done at the same time as taking Mr Wan to meet his family at Kangzhuang, killing three birds with one stone. Peng would take over driving duties and the thin horse could travel by trailer until such time as his condition improved. Hopefully this would be the end of the chopping and changing or I would lose track of what horses we had.

So now we were down to two riders – Li Jing on Hei Feng and myself on Bajiu leading Zorbee – while the thin horse was transported in the trailer. I had a nasty moment on the busy road when Zorbee side-stepped the wrong side of a tree. The lead rope yanked out of my hand, and when I leant over and clutched at his head collar, it came off. Luckily all our horses were bombproof in traffic and I quickly caught him in spite of traffic speeding by. On the third day riding east, we reached Gucheng (Old Wall), a traditional village with mud brick courtyard houses closely packed together. A gaunt man on an equally gaunt chestnut horse met us and led us up a narrow alleyway and through double doors into a neat but rather cramped courtyard. The horses were untacked and packed into a brick lean-to with their heads poking out onto the yard, and were soon happily tucking into a pile of maize stalks. The main long dwelling with four simple guest rooms leading one off another was spotless, and traditionally positioned in the south-west corner of the yard was a slit-in-the-floor loo. I immediately grabbed my washing things to take advantage of a deliciously hot solar shower in a little washroom on the other corner. One never knew when the next opportunity would be.

It transpired that this was where Wutzala kept his horse, a big chestnut from the Yili valley in Xinjiang. It seemed this was the actual reason he wanted us to ride this way.

Snug in my sleeping bag, I woke the next morning to rain drumming down on the roof of the house. Wutzala's plans of a scenic ride were dashed as our small mounted party set off through mist and drizzle to follow a long gravelly track winding into the range of hills to the north. Faint wiry blurs emerged from the moist grey to grow into the black leafless branches of tormented trees. We climbed higher and higher, the mist shifting in slow grey wafts around us, blotting out any hope of views over craggy valleys. Scrubby vegetation covered the near slopes, and a loose branch became entangled in Zorbee's tail. He panicked, pulled the reins out of my hands and bolted back down the track. Li Jing galloped off with cape damply flapping to retrieve him, and pointedly suggested that he lead him from now on. After the debacle on the road I did not argue.

At the very top of the ridge the track cut through a nondescript embankment of overgrown earth and stones that rambled away into the cloud.

'Very old wall. Spring and Autumn period,' Wutzala announced, reining in his horse. I looked at it with a bit more interest. If he was correct it would make this seemingly insignificant pile of rubble well over two thousand years old.

The Spring and Autumn period lasted from 722-481BC, pre-dating the first emperor Qin Shihuangdi and his Qin wall. It was a turbulent time when China was split into many feudal states who vied for supremacy, building walls to keep out not only the northern tribes but each other. It is intriguing that this period of turmoil also produced some of the great Chinese thinkers, notably the founders of Confucianism and Daoism, Confucius (Kongzi) and Laozi, but perhaps less surprisingly,

Sunzi, the author of the Chinese classic The Art of War. *The wall we were crossing probably more accurately dated from the slightly later Warring States period (402-221BC) when only seven of the more powerful states remained. One of these, the Yan state, ruled a region roughly corresponding to modern Hebei, and this wall could well have been built to protect this state from invasion by the nomadic Donghu tribe to the north. The trouble is that most of the older walls have purely been identified by historic descriptions of their routes, and with the proliferation of ancient walls from different periods in North China it can be difficult to ascertain what is what.*

It looked ancient nonetheless, though I was far too cold and miserable to fully appreciate its antiquity at the time. If I had, I might have been less willing to follow Wutzala's exhortations to scramble on top with Bajiu for a sodden photo opportunity. There was only just time to scramble back down, when without warning Wutzala and his lady friend dashed off ahead down the track on the other side with the rest of the group in hot pursuit. Bajiu strained his mouth wide open as he pulled to catch up and, bumping downhill without a crupper, my saddle began to slip forward on his low withers. It was not comfortable or secure, and I was increasingly disgruntled. My hands were freezing and rain was seeping through my boots. This whole scenario was not what I had planned. How on earth had we been persuaded to make this detour?

Thankfully it was not too long before we found ourselves riding up a narrow street in the small one donkey town of Houcheng (Behind the Wall), and the horses were tied up in the drizzle outside a restaurant. A tremendous spread arrived and, digging my chopsticks into a variety of steaming dishes, I began to feel more cheerful.

'Zhe shi lu rou,' said Mr Peng, nodding at the meat in my bowl.

'That is donkey meat,' translated Wutzala unnecessarily as I knew exactly what it meant. He produced a bottle of hooch.

'I made it myself,' he pronounced proudly, pouring the strong spirit into a row of little cups. It was throat-blistering stuff and a warm glow raced through my veins as I sipped it warily. Perhaps life wasn't so

Jing Jing being bridled in the courtyard of Mr Xi's house near Kangzhuang.

The start of the ride from Shanhaiguan. Rowena on Bei Bei and myself with Jing Jing displaying the Welsh dragon with Old Dragon's Head behind us.

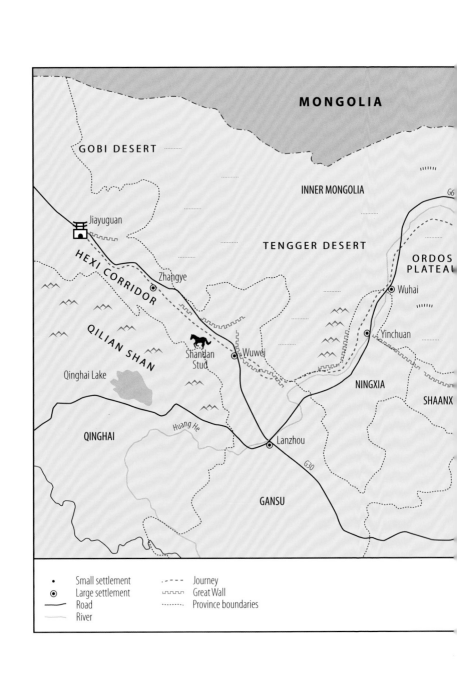

MONGOLIA

GOBI DESERT

INNER MONGOLIA

G6

Jiayuguan

TENGGER DESERT

ORDOS PLATEAU

HEXI CORRIDOR

Zhangye

Wuhai

QILIAN SHAN

Shandan Stud

Wuwei

Yinchuan

Qinghai Lake

NINGXIA

SHAANX

Huang He

QINGHAI

Lanzhou

G30

GANSU

- Small settlement
- ⊙ Large settlement
- ── Road
- ── River
- - - - Journey
- ⌇⌇⌇ Great Wall
- ·········· Province boundaries

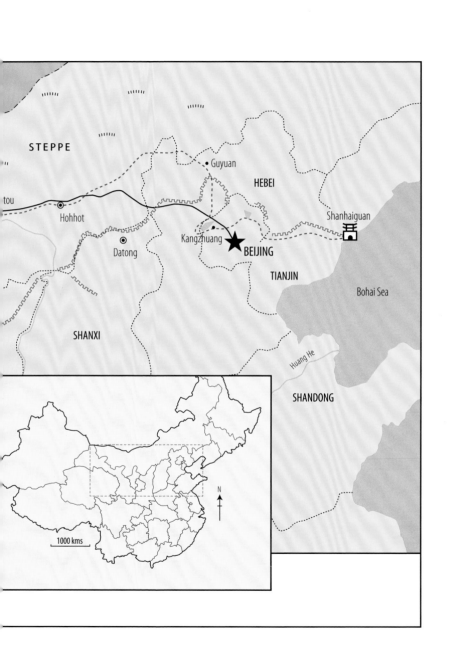

Toilets at our guest house in Shanhaiguan. These were fairly typical but certainly at the upmarket end of the spectrum.

Riding up the road to the Great Wall at Huangyaguan. Mr Ren and Rowena on Xiao Hei and Bei Bei.

Rowena and I on Bei Bei and Jing Jing near Liujiaying with Great Wall beacon towers on the skyline behind us. (Courtesy R. Gulland)

A typical sight on country roads.

Negotiating a street market on the road out of Zunhua.

Rowena and I with Bei Bei, Jing Jing and Zorbee by one of the horses on the Spirit Way to the Qing Tombs. (Courtesy R. Gulland)

By the Great Wall at Juyongguan on the last stretch to Badaling. (Courtesy R.Gulland)

With members of the Chinese Equestrian Association in front of the reconstructed town gate at Chadao ancient village near Badaling.

Celebratory dinner at the end of the trial stage with the people that made it happen. L to R Ren Hong, Liu Xinlian, Rowena Gulland, me, Peng Wenchao, Ji Yongshi, He Guosheng, Zhao Wenxing.

The horses arrive in Beijing after the two day journey from Shandan stud. The truck is backed up to a bank so they can jump off. Bajiu has his head over the side.

Li Jing on Yura, myself on Bajiu and Peng Wenchao on Zorbee at the opening ceremony near Kangzhuang.

Mr Peng on Bajiu, Li Jing on Yura, Mr Wan on Shandan and me on Zorbee. Riding through windfarm on the Kangxi grasslands.

bad after all. But the whole detour became totally worthwhile when we arrived at our surreal overnight accommodation up a secluded side valley nearby. At the foot of soaring crags under a dismal sky crouched a desolate Soviet-style complex painted almost entirely in gunmetal grey. It comprised a few bleak factory and amenity buildings, several sad-looking apartment blocks and a four-storey hotel overlooking a small leaden lake. All completely abandoned apart from a couple of caretakers.

'Factory for Kalashnikov,' Wutala explained to my amazement.

Apparently, this secretive location had been a centre for manufacture of the Russian designed AK-47 rifles, though exactly why it ceased production I did not find out. The horses' hooves echoed eerily as we led them through a hall and into an empty, dimly-lit auditorium. At one end was a stage bordered by red pillars. I wondered how many Communist functionaries had presided here, perhaps even Chairman Mao himself. Would they turn in their graves if they knew it was now stabling for a foreign devil? The horses were unperturbed by their unusual surroundings and we left them to wander loose, the clack of their shoes reverberating round their cavernous quarters.

At the empty hotel, a solitary caretaker led us up a silent stairway and along a gloomy corridor to rooms on the third floor. Li May and I were shown to a room with an en suite bathroom where an elderly boiler was suspended above the western flush loo, and I cheered up at thought of a hot shower. In Soviet fashion, the sixties-style furnishings included bedside lamps with no light bulbs and a television that didn't work. Unfortunately, the hot water boiler didn't work either and my hopes of a shower evaporated. I explored a ghostly corridor to find a room creepily set up for a non-existent board meeting. I found the horror movie atmosphere unsettling, but it freaked out Li May.

'Please wait for me. Don't leave me by myself,' she pleaded in the morning as I started to walk out. But in any case, we found we were locked into the compound and had to wait for the caretaker with the keys, though Peng managed to shin over the gate to go and feed the horses.

After stopping for breakfast of hot *youtiao,* or fried breadsticks, in Houcheng, I felt quite light-hearted as we set off in a westerly compass direction at last, stopping after thirty kilometres at the *Hong Jiang Yan Fandian* or Red River Riverside Hotel.

It sounded grand, but the river consisted mainly of pebbles and our hotel room was a cubicle in the basement opening straight to the outside. As I was rapidly discovering, the term *fandian* could refer to anything from a five star hotel to a two-room village house, as long as it offered food and lodging.

To my dismay, the next day we found ourselves heading north again. It became colder and colder as an icy wind swept down from Mongolia. I hunched down into my padded jacket as I tramped crossly along the road up a bleak valley through stark countryside, with occasional glimpses of snow-capped peaks in the distance. It seemed Wutzala was determined to freeze us to death. The wind pinched my cheeks and thighs, and it was a relief to stop at the town of Chicheng after a couple of days to stock up on thermal underwear, as usual attracting a small curious audience.

Another irritation was that Hei Feng had a smooth, fast, running walk so I had to jog incessantly to keep up with Li Jing. Although Zorbee was capable of pacing which was a little more comfortable, I did not have the expertise to keep him going at this gait for very long. His bouncy trot became immensely tiring after a couple of hours, and it also meant I had no chance to take photos. If I tried to hang back and ride at a steadier pace, he became unsettled, so it was a losing battle. Eventually, Li Jing begrudgingly agreed to slow down, but although I stressed that I was happy to occasionally intersperse walking with a faster pace, he now pointedly kept Hei Feng to a walk. I was beginning to sense that he was not a team player.

All too often we had to brave long, dark tunnels piercing high, striated rock faces. In stolid British Horse Society style I dismounted, put on my reflective gear, and led Zorbee carefully through, walking on the pedestrian walkway at the side where possible, while Li Jing sauntered up the middle of the road on Hei Feng without a care in the world. On the outskirts of an adobe village an enormous white mule broke free from its tether and galloped after us. Li Jing caught it and tied it to a tree at the side of the road where I assume it was eventually found by its owner.

As we neared Inner Mongolia we began to come out onto flatter land. Spring had yet to arrive here, and a washed out landscape of browns and greys stretched to the horizon, flanked by a low ragged line of bare hills without a hint of colour. Small clouds scudded across a bitter blue sky, throwing dark shadows which slipped fluidly over rocky slopes. In places the dry stony fields were separated by spindly grey treelines. Chinese farmers were everywhere ploughing the crumbling earth with donkeys and mules. A lean chestnut mare pulling a plough bent into her collar until her bony spine protruded, guided from behind by a farmer holding a long rope attached to her headcollar. He steadied the plough blade which scratched the dry earth to expose a growing rectangle of darker brown soil. At their side a shaggy black foal nosed fruitlessly among the naked clods. It seemed impossible that anything could flourish in this harsh environment.

We could now take advantage of *tu lu* or earth tracks through the fields, and they sometimes led us through simple brick villages where people stared or smiled, or ox carts trundled past. Compared with the more prosperous looking settlements set among trees and orchards around Beijing, these villages looked bleak.

Stopping for a rest by the side of the road we were surrounded by a gaggle of jolly women in dark trousers, work jackets, and head scarves, intrigued by a female *waiguoren* on horseback, and determined to extract my age.

'*Duo da*? How old are you?'

'*Liu shi sui*. Sixty.'

A chorus of 'aahs' signalled their surprise and approbation.

Li Jing and I stopped to take photos at the edge of a large marshy lake where a pair of lapwing curved through the air overhead.

Four days after leaving Houcheng, we crossed to the north

of the most northerly point of the Ming Great Wall at Dushikou. Somewhere across the Inner Mongolian plateau ahead of us lay the remnants of the Qin and Han walls.

After the death of Qin Shi Huangdi, in 207BC, the Han dynasty was founded by an original 'revolting peasant' Liu Bang, who rose from being a rebel leader to become the Emperor Gaodi. The Han dynasty (206BC – 220AD) lasted for over four hundred years and brought in a period when a unified China increased in power and influence. The term 'Han' came to be used to describe peoples of ethnic Chinese origin, including all ethnic Chinese groups speaking Mandarin Chinese and other Chinese dialects such as Hakka, Cantonese and Sichuanese, but not non-Chinese groups such as Uighur and Mongolian. Making up about 92% of Chinese and 19% of global population, the Han Chinese are the largest ethnic group in the world. The term 'han' also appears in the Chinese words for the official Mandarin Chinese language hanyu and Chinese characters hanzi.

The main nomadic threat from the north at this time was from the Xiongnu or Hunnu, considered by some to be the ancestors of the Huns. Gaodi renovated and reinforced the Qin wall which ran through Northern Hebei and Inner Mongolia, but was unable to extend control over the Xiongnu.

It was Monday, April 27. We had covered about twenty-five kilometres and had about four to go to our evening's destination of Guyuan. Li Jing was riding ahead of me along an emaciated treeline round a ploughed field. One minute I was relaxed and enjoying the scenery and then I suddenly found myself flying backwards through the air. I had a vision of my feet in the stirrups and worrying they would not come out and the next thing I remember was lying on the ground with the breath knocked out of my body. For some reason, Zorbee had panicked and shot forward, and I had been catapulted backwards out of the saddle onto my head and right shoulder.

Li Jing was soon at my side.

'OK?'

'I'm OK. I'm OK.'

But when I looked down and saw my collarbone sticking out at an odd angle under the skin I realised that I was not OK at all. I cursed silently. This would mean delaying the ride for at least a couple of weeks. In fifty years of riding I had never broken anything more serious than my little finger. But I consoled myself that race jockeys broke their bones all the time and were back in the saddle within days.

We carried a walkie-talkie and it was not long before I was being helped to the jeep. Luckily there was a hospital in nearby Guyuan where I joined a row of patients sitting outside a consulting room. They peered at me curiously. The X-ray showed that I had not only snapped my collarbone, but had four broken ribs. After a short discussion, we decided that as there was nothing much that could be done and as we were only about seven hours drive from Beijing where there would be better medical facilities, we should return there. The horses were settled into stables attached to a holiday complex not far away and Peng drove carefully back to Beijing. We met up with Kath Naday at the SOS International Clinic, and I had another X-ray.

'I am afraid you have broken six ribs not four,' announced the young European doctor. '... But you look amazingly well, considering your age and the amount of damage showing on the X-ray.'

By now it was dark and there was nothing further the SOS clinic could do. I was unable to contact my insurance company at this late hour to sort out medical care, so we went on to a Chinese hospital, where I had yet another X-ray. The Chinese doctors decided to encase my shoulders in plaster to keep my collarbone in place so it could heal and I was strapped up with my arms at right angles to my body. I looked like a demoniac chicken. The cast pressed into the underside of my arms, almost cutting off the blood flow. I was not in much of a state to argue, and when I complained feebly the doctors did not look too sympathetic.

But they had reckoned without the formidable Kath, who had acted as a tour guide in China and was used to dealing with all manner of situations. Ignoring their protestations, she took control.

'You must cut the plaster cast off at once. Can't you see it is hurting her?'

The doctors reluctantly removed it, but a waiver form and pen was pointedly shoved into my hands.

The result of the X-ray came back. Not only had I snapped my collarbone and broken six ribs, but I had punctured my lung. I began to think it might be better not to have any more X-rays in case they found something else. I was laid down on a hospital couch and given an injection into my side. The doctor produced a large tube resembling the kind I used at home in Wales for resuscitating poorly lambs. He tried to push it in between my broken ribs. The pain was excruciating.

'Kath, I can't do this. Can't they put me out or something?'

'They don't think anaesthetic is a good idea.'

'Seriously, I have given birth to three children and it was nothing compared to this.'

The Chinese are evidently made of sterner stuff, and it was obvious the doctors thought I was being a wimp. But Kath stuck to her guns and in the end they were prevailed upon to give a second injection. It made me feel nauseous, but at least I was just about able to endure the agony as the tube was forced through my broken ribcage into my lung, which was now half-filled with blood. The blood was to drain slowly out through the tube into a small plastic container which had to follow me everywhere for several days like a little dog on a lead. I was given the option of staying in the hospital or finding somewhere to wait until I had sorted out medical care elsewhere with my insurance company. Kath had been in contact with Ed Jocelyn. He was out of town and kindly offered me the use of his flat. It was a no-brainer.

For the next couple of days I rested at Ed's, propped up on pillows on the sofa as I could not lie flat. Huge bunches of flowers and baskets of fruit arrived from well-wishers including the CEA and Harry. Kath recommended the Beijing Family Hospital, and I moved in once my insurance company had given the go ahead. It was an excellent choice as the care there was second to none. I had a luxurious private room with en suite shower room and television, and Kath kept me supplied with DVDs. Guo Sheng, Mr Peng, Harry, Kubi, and Li May came to visit at various times.

'Wutzala and Kubi are worrying you will not want to carry on with the ride after this,' ventured Li May.

I looked at her in surprise. The thought had never even crossed my mind.

'Of course I want to continue. Tell them I will be back riding soon,' I said firmly.

On Wednesday, 6 May, ten days after my accident my collarbone was pinned up by excellent surgeon, Dr Chen Hao Hui (surgeons are not plain Mr as in Britain), who had spent two years in Southampton. The operation went well, but the bad news was that I could not expect to be back in the saddle for at least two to three months. Quite apart from the collarbone, several of my ribs had suffered complete breaks rather than fractures, and they would take time to heal. To my intense frustration, everything would have to be delayed until at least the end of July. It did not in any way dent my resolve to be back as soon as I had the all clear, and I made sure Wutzala and Kubi were in no doubt about my determination. I needed them to keep the ball rolling as much as they needed me.

A week later I was allowed out of hospital. The punctured lung had healed enough to allow removal of the drainage tube, but not enough for clearance to fly home. My insurance company proved to be very helpful and there was no quibbling about my choice to stay at the comfortable Rosedale hotel for another ten days. There was a television with a diet of English language Z movies, and a work surface with waist height plug points. My ribs were far too painful to allow me to reach plug points at floor level. There was also internet connection, though after a few days it appeared that the authorities were having a post-Olympic clampdown, as I could not access my blog. My daily exercise consisted of shuffling across the small park outside to treat myself at a little patisserie Kath had introduced me to, always being careful to wear my sling. In fact, after my collarbone had been pinned, my shoulder was relatively comfortable. My ribs were a different matter and I always kept my sling on in public to warn people that I was injured in some way, as my relatively normal exterior hid considerable interior damage. Any minute jolt to my ribcage caused an agonizing stab of pain, and I did not want people carelessly bumping into me.

At long last on Tuesday, 19 May, three weeks after my accident, I was allowed to board my flight home. It was an immense relief to recuperate in familiar surroundings at home. I was still very frail and unable to lie down horizontally, but Iestyn brought me cups of tea in bed while I rested. Gradually my ribs mended and my strength improved. From taking half an hour to make my way slowly up the hill at the back of the farm with frequent halts to catch my breath, I was able to walk all the way up without stopping. I swam regularly at the local pool, and at last came the day when my friend Dr Rowena took me out for a gentle ride on one of her horses. I was ready to join the fray once more and I could not wait to get started.

CHAPTER EIGHT

ZOU BA!

不怕慢, 就怕停
bú pà màn, jiù pà tíng
Be not afraid of going slowly, be afraid only of standing still.

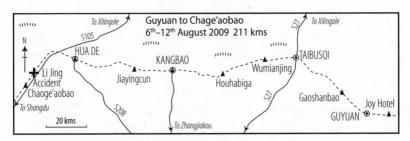

Thursday, 6 August – Friday, 7 August, 2009.
Guyuan to Wumianjing.
69 km. Daily average 35 km.

Sunday, August 2, 2009. We sped northwards up the road from Kangzhuang, and I winced as overtaking cars hurtled towards us on the wrong side of the road, often forcing us onto the dusty hard shoulder which acted as a third lane. Grey hills rose rugged and barren on either side, but the previously bare earth fields along the valley floors were now luxuriantly covered with an emerald patchwork of maturing crops outlined by dark green bands of trees. Piles of melons were stacked for sale at the side of the road. Had we really ridden up this road three months ago? It was an amazing transformation from the landscape I had left behind in April. As we neared Guyuan, I looked in vain for the marshy wetlands we had skirted then. The water had long since evaporated and only grassland remained.

In the jeep with me were Li Jing, Li May and the ever-dependable Peng, as well as a new addition to the team. A tall lanky Chinese

91

with a square jaw and metal framed glasses, Wang Jingbing, alias Hua, was a naturalised Chinese Canadian originating from Beijing. A graduate of Beijing University working in IT, he had lived in Japan as well as San Francisco, and spoke good English. Hua had chosen James as his English name, though we never used it. His nickname, Hua, referred to the fact that he enjoyed skiing (*hua* can mean to slide, skate or ski) and Hua was the name we would all continue to use. I had also gradually and naturally fallen into calling Mr Peng by the more informal 'Peng'. After all, I was an older woman talking to a younger man, and Peng was already calling me by my Christian name. Besides, given all our shared experiences, he now felt like an old friend.

Presently, we swung in through an ornate Chinese gate flanked by stone lions. The Joy Hotel complex, where we had left the horses and the trailer over three months previously, was sited by a reservoir in a grassland area just outside Guyuan. The complex consisted of hotel accommodation blocks, a couple of reception halls and a small racecourse with attached stables. Li May and I were shown to a clean room with western-style en suite and hot shower in a low barrack block. It appeared that the *lao ban* had been very sympathetic on hearing of my accident and had taken a great interest in the project. He had magnanimously undertaken to look after the horses while I recovered, and had been planning a grand send-off when I returned. Tragically, he had died unexpectedly in the interim, but the deputy boss was eager to impress upon us that it was a matter of respect that they fulfilled his wishes.

We went to inspect the horses. It was not good news. Hei Feng had slipped over on the concrete yard and suffered serious injuries to his hind legs, and as he was so wild they had been unable to treat him properly. Sadly, there was no way he could continue and tragically he would probably need to be put down. From the start I had been forced to accept that I could not become too emotionally invested in the horses we used. Hei Feng was not my horse and I had no final say in his fate. In all honesty, I preferred not to know. However, the other three geldings were in fine fettle with shiny coats, and the thin horse no longer looked like a toast rack. He could officially join the team, and Peng called him Shandan. It seemed none of us were very inspirational when it came to naming horses.

My main worry was that the stable boys had been riding Bajiu to get him ready for us. They were trying to be helpful, but had used one of their own saddles which had given him a nasty girth gall, or friction sore, caused by the girth. My heart sank as I was still feeling decidedly frail and had been relying on the steady little gelding to carry me at least initially. I immediately started treating the sore, hoping it would not cause more delay. Zorbee and Shandan had apparently not been ridden. One of the stable boys trotted off on Zorbee who immediately gave an impressive bucking bronco display, and then ran away with and decanted another lad shortly after. I felt a little gratified that I was not his only victim. Thankfully Shandan presented no problems.

The horses were shod the next day the traditional Chinese way, trussed up to a metal shoeing frame resembling goalposts. Suspended from the cross bar by two wide belts round their bellies, the horses were also restrained by ropes along their flanks. The frame even had a pulley system to lift the belts. One by one the horse's front legs were doubled up and bound with rope to immobilise the front foot for shoeing, but the relevant back leg was strapped to the end post. It was an ancient and basic method, but it got the job done with little danger of injury to the farrier. He suggested I round up the cost of shoeing the horses from 90 yuan to 100 yuan. As this came to well under £10 for all three, I readily agreed!

To the horror of the Chinese stable staff who almost cut their horses in half when tightening girths, I decided to try and sidestep the girth sore problem by riding Bajiu with a very loose girth covered in a sheepskin sleeve. The advantage of my Free 'n' Easy saddle was that it was so stable it was almost guaranteed not to slip round. Peng on Zorbee and Hua on Shandan rode with me over the grasslands and along shady tracks to the exact spot where I had fallen off three months previously. I did not want to leave any gaps in my journey. Farmers were loading cauliflowers into agricultural trucks, and a little donkey foal standing by its mother pricked its long ears to see us pass. Another day we rode along the reservoir where birds waded, and through green flax fields dotted with blue flowers, cantering up to a little Chinese pavilion at the top of a low hill, Bajiu with his choppy motion huffing and puffing his way up. The girth gall was fine after all this, and so I felt completely confident to start out the following afternoon on the allotted launch day. Thanks to my Free 'n' Easy saddle, I was able to carry on riding Bajiu and the sore healed up completely over the next few days.

I was now the proud possessor of a dongle but used the more reliable hotel office internet connection to email home and do a spot of blogging. When I arrived in Beijing in April, I had discovered I was unable to publish the blog posts with which I hoped to engage public interest in the ride and promote the charity aspect. Evidently, following a relaxation over the Olympics, the Chinese authorities had cracked down once more on social media. I could not really believe that my wittering about thermal underwear and lung drainage constituted any threat to the fabric of Chinese society, though it was mildly flattering to imagine that the powers that be thought otherwise. I was smugly relieved to be shown sneaky ways of circumventing the 'Great Firewall of China' by expat Andy McEwan, Ed Jocelyn's Long March companion. The game was cat and mouse and the connection erratic, but at least I managed to post sporadically over the next couple of months.

The standard Chinese buffet breakfast at the hotel hardly filled me with delight, consisting as it did of pickled vegetables, not to mention the inevitable *zhou* or congee, a watery Asian rice porridge tasting like wallpaper paste, though I was able to fill up on boiled eggs and *mantou* (steamed white buns). But as it was Inner Mongolia, we now had an urn of milk tea served with fried millet. As is Mongolian tradition, this had salt added, but thankfully not as heavily salted as I had previously experienced on a trip to Mongolia proper. I had found that unpalatable unless I thought of it as soup rather than tea, but I actually came to quite like the more lightly salted Inner Mongolian version.

The hotel catered for parties and conferences, and every day there seemed to be some sort of celebration banquet in progress in the main dining hall. If it was not for the deputy head of Yangqing province financial department, it was for a district policemen's convention. Huge fake trees flanked a stage at one end of the hall, and the sylvan theme was continued on the ceiling which was thickly festooned with a green mat of fake branches and leaves. The banquets were enlivened by mock Mongolian rituals and much karaoke singing; admittedly a very commercial Chinese take on Mongolian culture, but it looked a load of fun.

One breezy evening we went for a short drive out into unfenced steppe. A turbulent swell of grassland rolled endlessly away to the horizon beneath wild wisps of cloud in an all-encompassing sky. A straggle of saddled and bridled horses galloped steadily over the steppe alongside us with ears pricked forward.

'Where are the riders?' I puzzled.

'I think they were horses for hire,' said Hua. 'They just let the horses free after working, and they know how to go home by themselves.'

I felt a poignant fleeting thrill. They seemed to embody the unfettered nomadic spirit of the Mongolian steppes. It made me wonder what remained of the nomadic life which had existed for millennia on the open grasslands ahead of us. How much had survived the invasion of Chinese commercialisation?

On the day of the launch the boss would have been proud, as we had the full Mongolian banquet treatment. Wutzala and Kubi had turned up for the occasion, and both Wutzala and the deputy boss gave the inevitable marathon speeches in Chinese while Hua translated my modest offering in English. The team lined up on the stage to take part in the Mongolian ceremony. Rousing music over the loudspeaker accompanied a small procession in Mongolian dress parading up the aisle. At the front walked a staff member wearing a brightly patterned blue silk Mongolian *deel*, a traditional item of clothing somewhat like a dressing gown held together by a sash round the waist. His beige work trousers protruded incongruously from the bottom and he wielded what appeared to be an enormous floor mop topped by a gold trident. Behind him paced three very pretty young women in colourful *deels* carrying blue silk scarves and various ritual items for the ceremony to come, shadowed by a figure brandishing a yellow flounced parasol. Trundling along in the rear was a large gaily painted red and yellow barrow on which was displayed the piece de resistance, a whole roast calf, or was it a sheep, the unfortunate creature embellished with a pair of fake golden horns.

The entire procession trooped up onto the stage and the ceremony unfolded. I did not have much clue what was going on and decided to copy Li Jing on my left. Little bowls of *baijiu* were handed round. One by one we were exhorted to flick a few drops upwards to heaven, a few drops downwards to earth, and a few drops horizontally to friends, before anointing our foreheads. Then came the best bit, knocking back the rest. The young women draped the blue silk scarves or *khadag* round our necks. Small rounds of bread were offered and Li Jing took one. I watched carefully and followed suit. Mild consternation ensued. Apparently, it was customary to break off a small piece, and there was a surreptitious flurry while enough bread was produced for the rest of the participants. As guest of honour I was then asked to step forward and a large knife was placed in my hand. For a horrible moment I feared I was expected to carve up the whole carcass for the assembled company. But it was just to make ritual vertical and horizontal cuts on the forehead of the carcass before we all cut off and exchanged slices of meat.

While the team, supporters and media people tucked into the banquet, the entertainment troupe who ran the show performed Mongolian songs and dances and played the traditional horse-head fiddle. As one might expect this string instrument derives its name from the carved horse head at the top. The two strings are traditionally made of horse hair, as is the bow string, but it is played like a cello rather than a violin. The performers were very impressive, and I was quite made up when two of the handsome young men from the troupe insisted on having their photo taken with me.

We were met outside by the horses, already tacked up, and a small media scrum. A young woman journalist accosted me.

'Can you give an interview for local television, please?'

'Of course.'

A microphone was stuck in my face and a pregnant pause ensued while we stared at each other expectantly. Finally, I cracked.

'Go ahead. What do you want to ask?'

'Please talk.'

'Aren't you going to ask any questions?'

'No. Please talk about your ride.'

A mental 'Cut!' flipped through my mind. I quickly halted proceedings to compose a short resume and try again. Next time I would be ready.

The official send-off was to take place in front of the small grandstand on the racecourse, and we all lined up behind a large red ride banner. In front of us wavered a small chain of supporters including some enthusiastic young women in bright red *deels*. The start of the ride was announced over the loudspeaker, followed by a barrage of firecrackers almost under our noses which would undoubtedly have caused a stampede among horses in the west. But this was China and our horses hardly flinched.

'*Zou ba*! Let's go!' cried the commentator over the loudspeaker.

The human chain leapt to one side and we were off yet again, Li Jing, Peng and myself trotting off in front with a melee of mounted stable lads decked out in *deels* behind us. A couple of them led bay mares, both with foals at foot, and one carrying a young girl. Completing the spectacle and bringing up the rear was a white 'fairy princess' carriage decorated in fluttering pennants and pulled by a flashy skewbald horse – 'skewbald' meaning coloured with large patches of brown and white.

'Is it a Cleveland Bay?' Li May had asked out of the blue when she saw it. I imagined the despairing faces of Cleveland Bay enthusiasts all over the world. A clue to the colour of this aristocratic breed of driving horse lies in its name, and splashes of brown and white like a gypsy horse is definitely taboo. As I was to find out, Li May was prone to bewildering statements.

Round the racecourse our curious cavalcade swept, up the entrance drive and out under the archway past the stone lions. Our stable boy escorts accompanied us a for little way before they turned back, waving cheerfully.

It was a motley trio that set out to walk and jog across the steppe and through Guyuan into the countryside to the north: a wild-looking ex-librarian with unruly facial whiskers under a tangled black mane of hair, dressed entirely in khaki beneath his long khaki cloak; a homely-looking former taxi driver in a crumpled yellow hoodie and baggy trousers; and a prim pensioner in tight black jodhpurs, red jacket and gold helmet. We had many thousands of kilometres to cover in front of us, across arid deserts and high mountain ranges, but whether horses and relationships would last the course remained to be seen.

After our luxurious sojourn at the Joy Hotel, we were brought back down to earth that evening with a thump. The courtyard farm where we stayed on the edge of the small town of Gaoshanbao, twenty-five kilometres further north, had a row of spartan rooms leading straight off a muddy yard full of sheep and goats which had been brought in for the night.

'*Cesuo zai nar*? Where is the toilet?' I asked.

Li Jing and Peng pointed over the yard wall. I walked round to the other side but could see nothing remotely resembling a toilet, though there were a couple of low foot-high walls of loose stones in full view of the main road.

I went back and tried again. '*Cesuo zai nar*?' Li Jing and Peng grinned and pointed over the wall again. At least it was getting dark.

Another day's ride across flat arable land bounded by tree lines brought us past a rather battered road sign announcing our entry into *Nei Menggu* or Inner Mongolia province. Although we saw no sign of the ancient walls which cross through this area we were now well into the former lands of the nomads.

The vast swathe of grassland steppe to the north of China proper has been fought over and controlled wholly or partially by many different peoples over the centuries, almost exclusively nomadic tribal groups. Even at times when a Chinese government has controlled these areas it was generally when nomadic groups conquered China, for example during the Mongol-led Yuan dynasty created by Kublai Khan. During the Manchu-led Qing dynasty the region was divided into the northern province of Outer Mongolia (Wai Menggu) and the southern province of Inner Mongolia (Nei Menggu). The Mongols took advantage of the collapse of the Qing dynasty in 1911 to declare independence over an area largely corresponding to the Qing Outer Mongolia. It subsequently continued to be known in the West as Outer Mongolia, but in 1990 became the democracy now known simply as Mongolia.

Inner Mongolia remained within the new Republic of China, though with some alterations to the boundaries of the province. Under the Qing, it was initially mainly populated by Mongolian herdsmen. But in the latter part of the nineteenth century the Qing government encouraged large numbers of Han Chinese farmers to settle these northern borderlands, a policy which subsequent governments have continued. About four-fifths of the population of Inner Mongolia today is Han Chinese, compared with less than a fifth of Mongolians. Inner Mongolia may be the first autonomous province recognised by the Chinese communist administration, but this population imbalance leaves ethnic Mongolians with little effective autonomy.

I was relieved when we reached the market town of Taibusqi after about thirty kilometres, as I had anticipated that this would be our overnight stop. I was still feeling very frail after my accident, and my back was aching with the unaccustomed exercise. But to my chagrin Hua had decided to find us somewhere on the other side of town.

'It is only ten kilometres,' he announced. I should have learnt by now.

It was a pleasant enough tree-lined road, but I ended up leading and then dragging an increasingly tired Bajiu. Every so often I saw what would have been idyllic camping spots by belts of shady poplar trees, but I was not yet in tune with the Chinese fear of sleeping in the wild. The ten kilometres turned out to be fourteen, and it was an exhausted and vexed figure which trudged into the semi-abandoned town of Wumianjing behind the others. We had covered forty-four kilometres that day, but it felt like a hundred.

'Hua, you must realise we can't cope with distances like this when we have just set out. I have only just started riding again after a bad accident,' I grumbled. 'And it is better for the horses if we build up distances gradually.'

Wumianjing had once been a government centre but now had only a skeleton population living in a few barrack-like streets of low brick houses in a semi-abandoned village. Hua had found accommodation at a rundown cottage hospital. The local medical officer led Li May and I along a dark corridor to a room with two creaky iron hospital beds. In the centre of the room was an old unlit iron stove, and between the beds stood a drip stand. I blew up my inflatable mattress, placed it on one of the beds, and laid my aching body gratefully on its soft surface. I had felt a bit sheepish about buying this luxury item when I saw it on offer at a Beijing outdoor shop – one would hardly expect to see it in the kit of a real adventurer – but in the circumstances it turned out to be one of the best buys I ever made. Zorbee was also out of sorts: off his feed and occasionally kicking his belly. It was the first sign of colic, and probably caused due to the sudden exertion of a long day after three months rest. Li Jing walked him around until he settled and started grazing. The following morning, we were both a lot perkier, but it was a sign that we needed to take things a bit easier for a few days.

CHAPTER NINE

LAND OF THE NOMADS

我听说' 很好', 我看到' 更好'
wǒ tīng shuō 'hěn hǎo ', wǒ kàn dào 'gèng hǎo '
'I heard' is good; 'I saw' is better.

Saturday, 8 August – Tuesday, 11 August, 2009.
Wumianjing to Huade.
96 km. Daily average 24 km.

We had now turned to the west and were riding over the Inner Mongolian grasslands. For the next few days we kept the distances down, covering about twenty kilometres a day, before gradually building up to thirty to forty kilometres a day. We followed a wide gravel track stretching ahead over endless rolling hills, with only the occasional car or lorry bumping past in a cloud of dust, although when we crossed a little spur of Hebei that poked north into Inner Mongolia the surface abruptly changed to asphalt. With few trees to shelter us, the summer sun beat down relentlessly from a bowl of blue sky, and I started to be glad we had taken a more northerly route. Once teeming with wildlife and grazed by nomadic herds of sheep, goats, cattle and horses, the grasslands are now settled by Chinese agriculturalists. Areas have been fenced off, and small villages of mud and brick houses have sprung up at intervals. Donkeys and cattle grazed on the patchy grass around the settlements, and sunflowers bloomed in the courtyards. Occasionally the grassland gave way to cultivated areas where long belts of wheat, oats, potatoes and cabbages accentuated the gentle curves of the low slopes. Here, rows of trees lined the road, and it was an immense relief to slip out of the burning midday sun into their cool, dappled shadows. A shepherd in dark trousers and heavy jacket, apparently impervious to the heat, stood guard over a flock of floppy-eared sheep huddled together in the shade. In a small shop where we stopped to buy supplies, the shopkeeper pulled aside a few boards in the concrete floor and dragged up a plastic bag full of moist *baozi* (Chinese buns with a meat or vegetable filling) from the depths of the cellar beneath, a natural cool-box.

'*Kan, yi zhi lang*! Look, a wolf!' Hua cried out.

We were resting on the brow of a hill, and a wolf-like dog trotted slyly past us over the steppe. Or was it a dog-like wolf? Numerous wolves used to roam these grasslands, preying on the animal herds, and Hua was convinced.

But trans Russia traveller Li Jing had survived the lupine infested forests of Siberia and was equally convinced it was not. A lively debate in Chinese ensued along the lines of, 'Yes, it is.' 'No, it's not.' It would not be the last argument I witnessed on our way across China.

I had just read Jiang Rong's book, *Wolf Totem*, which was hitting the bookstores in Beijing at the time and which paralleled the extermination of wolves with the demise of the Mongolian way of life on the Inner Mongolian steppes. It is certain that there have been immense changes on the Inner Mongolian grasslands. In the past a sustainable number of nomads roamed the steppes with their herds, following the seasons to drive their livestock to new pastures. In the summer, when water was a priority, the herds grazed on grass near rivers and lakes. In the winter, the cold meant animals did not need so much water and could survive on snowfall, so they retreated to the hills where the trees gave shelter. As they moved, the grass had time to regenerate behind them.

This cyclical system still survives in Mongolia to this day, but Inner Mongolia's increasing population and the introduction of fixed grazing areas has been a factor in the degradation and desertification of the grasslands. Other factors have been climate change and deforestation, and the Chinese government is trying to counter desertification by tackling all these issues. In fact, although we were some way north of the Ming Great Wall of China, we had now entered the zone of the Green Great Wall of China. This is a long standing government initiative to reverse desertification through tree planting in a wide belt of land across north China to the south of the Gobi Desert. It aims to plant millions of trees along over around 4,000 kilometres of desert borderland by 2050, and we were to encounter plenty of evidence of these planting schemes as we rode through areas directly to the south of the Gobi Desert.

We were now very approximately following the line of the old Qin and Han walls, which made their way across the steppe to Hohhot, the next major city on our route.

To fully understand the reasons why the Chinese built these great defensive walls it is necessary to consider two things. Looking firstly at the relationship between the steppe nomads and settled Chinese agriculturalists, it must be appreciated that nomadism is not self-sufficient. It is true that for centuries nomadic herdsmen have survived mainly on the produce from their livestock: meat and milk, as well as leather (for clothing, saddlery etc.), and wool (for clothing and felt for their yurts). But they also needed grain, metal (for knives, cooking pots, bridle bits, etc.) medicines and luxury items such as silk – goods which a mobile lifestyle did not allow them to produce themselves. It was the establishment of the settled agrarian economies on which nomads depended for goods and survival that enabled nomadism to develop on the grassland fringes in the first place. As such, nomads have essentially been faced with two choices: to trade or raid. In other words, if they were unable to acquire the goods they needed to survive through peaceful trading, they procured them by forceful attack.

The Chinese had different options as to how to deal with this threat, all of which had their pros and cons. They could encourage peaceful trading: bartering with herdsmen for furs, leather goods and horses. Unfortunately, nomadic peoples did not always have enough goods to trade that the Chinese wanted, and in this case the Chinese authorities generally kept the peace by providing subsidies in the form of items such as silk and even princesses. This was essentially bribery and not always a popular policy, though the powerful Tang dynasty at its height employed it effectively. An offensive option was to actively attack and push back encroaching nomadic tribes, but this could be costly both financially and in manpower, and result in disastrous defeats as occurred at Tumu. And of course some Chinese governments chose to take a defensive approach and build walls, also financially costly to construct and maintain.

Secondly, it is important to appreciate the role the horse played in the building of walls. As we have seen, when agrarian Chinese refused to trade with the northern tribes, the latter were forced to raid. Initially horses were not ridden on the steppe, but used firstly as a source of food, and then as draft animals. However, as people domesticated animals and spread onto the grasslands, they realised the advantage of riding horses to herd their flocks, and it was not long before they turned to mounted warfare. Fast mobile mounted warriors could easily outflank the watchtowers, forts and foot soldiers of settled peoples before they could retaliate. It is thought that some of the first stretches of the Han long wall were constructed between existing fortification points.

In the village of Houha Biga, we stayed at a farm compound with the traditional one-storey red-roofed buildings overlooking a neatly swept courtyard. A large black and tan guard dog of a lick-you-to-death variety was chained to a brick kennel at the gateway, and to one side was a separate overnight sheep enclosure. A row of large windows with metal framed panes of glass was set into the white tiled facade of the main house above a blue tile mosaic with a maroon border, and setting off the pretty cottagey look was a small leafy kitchen garden to either side of the door. We were welcomed by a very genial Chinese family, though the baby in his bare bottomed trousers nearly burst into tears in horror at the sight of his first foreign devil. A meal was laid on, including some rather unusual steamed honeycomb-like pasta which I have never seen before or since. This family were relatively affluent and had a mini tractor in the yard and further living quarters in a sizeable low brick building to one side. Here Li May and I were shown to a small earth-brick floored room leading straight off the courtyard and furnished with a low brown vinyl topped cupboard and a couple of iron bedsteads equipped with hard mattresses and bean bag pillows. 'The boys' slept on a *kang* in the kitchen, and I found Hua snoring beneath a garish poster of a cartoon-like fantasy Chinese landscape. A bridge painted in crude red led to a temple on an island. On the striped white and blue waters floated a couple of unusual swans with white bodies and black necks, a sort of Australopean fusion.

On 9 August we entered the busy market town of Kangbao, threading our way between small motorbikes, vans and a variety of rubber-tyred carts pulled by mini-tractors, mules and donkeys. Little spotted piglets squealed from a cage on the back of a motorbike outside a sort of piglet distribution centre, and a solitary sow strode purposefully up the main street as if searching for her missing offspring. The rows of two-storey shophouses lining the main road into town displayed colourful shop signs in large Chinese characters. Mr Peng hunted down a hotel in a five-storey block at the centre, and we tied the horses to the trailer in the tiny yard at the back before tucking into a meal and taking advantage of the hot showers downstairs.

I had made the greenhorn's mistake of packing only short sleeved tops for the hot weather, and during the heat of the day my arms were catching the sun. But in vain I scoured Kang Bao high street for a long-sleeved shirt. At all the shops the response was, '*Mei you*. We don't have one.' Apparently, there was a season for long-sleeved shirts and this was not it. I had given up hope and was walking back to the hotel when the patter of feet made me turn round. It was the shop attendant from the department store we had just visited chasing down the pavement to say they had just dug one out from the back of the storeroom. It was thin, loose-fitting, and palest pink, just perfect for my needs though possibly not a fashion statement. I could set out the following morning prepared for what the sun threw at me as we tackled the treeless steppe which rolled away to the west.

Three months of inactivity after my accident had left my muscles weak, and the long day in the saddle to Wumianjing had aggravated my back. Although we had kept the distances down since then,

Hua and Li Jing liked to keep up a speedy pace of travel. I found the incessant trotting excruciatingly uncomfortable even when I stood in the stirrups. The pain had intensified to the extent that I was in tears simply trying to carry my baggage up to my room, and pathetically I even phoned home to sniffle my sob story down my mobile to Iestyn. Enter Li Jing, who fortunately (or perhaps unfortunately) for me had just invested in a set of Chinese massage cups and was keen to enlist me as a guinea pig for his first attempt at the ancient art of cupping. An alternative medical therapy which is claimed to relieve a wide variety of complaints from pneumonia to anxiety, it is also supposed to work for back pain and stiff muscles, though there is much scepticism about its efficacy.

Li Jing instructed me to lie face down on my bed, and gave me a Chinese massage before placing the specialised cups on the upper part of my back and mechanically withdrawing air to create a vacuum. After about fifteen minutes the cups were removed. There was no mirror in the room in which to see my own back, but Peng's expression of horror when he inspected the results hardly filled me with confidence. I could feel the points where the cups had been attached burning.

'Ooh, it looks like blisters all over your back,' Li May reported dramatically. Li Jing remained silent.

There was nothing for it but to wait and see, though I can vouch for the fact that it did nothing to relieve my level of anxiety. Amazingly, whether or not it was the cupping or my wonderful air bed, there were no side effects and my back felt much better in the morning.

But not for long, as when we set out once more, the demon boy racers continued to insist on tearing along again. Li Jing favoured a method of travel which involved pacing at full speed for about an hour and then stopping to rest for an hour, rather than covering the same distance in the same time by travelling more steadily and not taking such long breaks. It was torture for me to trot on Bajiu, and I decided I had had enough. They could do what they wanted, but I was going to walk. At the next rest stop I kept on plodding. Bajiu was not too happy at leaving his companions and had a minor temper tantrum, neighing and napping. When a horse is napping it does not mean it is taking forty winks, but trying to have its own way by evasive tactics such as digging in its heels and crabbing sideways. Every time Bajiu opened his mouth and tried to whip round, I kept his head facing ahead and gave him a smack with a little stick I had broken from a tree. Eventually he realised that he was not being removed from his buddies for life, and over the next couple of days he calmed down and started to walk obediently forward.

As a result, my back hurt less and, for the first time since we set out from Guyuan, I was able to fully enjoy the day's ride. This took us across rolling grassland with shady belts of trees to the hamlet of Jiayingcun, where we stayed in a school compound. It had a large grassy school yard enclosed behind a high brick wall, so the horses could roam free for a change. Along one side was a low school building with five classrooms and headmaster's study, and on the far side of the yard were Boys' and Girls' long-drop toilets. Apparently most of the local children now attended a more modern school with better facilities, and with only five pupils left, the school was semi-abandoned. Not surprisingly, the building was uncared for with empty unswept rooms and no electricity. I found a bare classroom to camp in, and slept soundly beneath a blackboard rather poignantly still inscribed in chalk with Chinese characters from the last lesson. Above it and on either side of a Chinese flag, large red Chinese characters exhorted the pupils to '*Hao hao xue xi – tian tian xiang shang*' or 'Study carefully – every day make progress'.

As we rode out of Jiayingcun the sunflowers in the courtyards of old mud brick houses angled their radiant heads to the early morning sun, and old men led their donkeys out to graze on the edge of town. White windmills turned slowly in the distance beyond vibrant yellow and green stripes of wheat and millet divided by dark slashes of tree belts. On the white gravel of the road ahead, a chestnut mare and her mule foal ambled to one side and swung round to stare at us.

Where possible we followed *tu lu*, or earth tracks, to the side.

'*Ta weishenme jiaode tu lu?* Why is it called an earth road?' asked Li May.

'*Yinwei ta shi tu zuo de.* Because it's made of earth,' Li Jing answered patiently.

As the days rolled by, the individual characters of the little team were beginning to make themselves apparent. My stolid Bajiu was an affable but conservative fellow with a healthy appetite. If he had been human, I could imagine him down the rugby club propping up the bar and buying drinks all round, but very reluctant to expend an ounce of energy on the playing field. He was not a natural leader by a long shot, and if I relaxed the reins for a second, he would veer sideways and make a beeline for the tails of the other horses as if magnets were attached to them. If I did not let him follow behind, he would plod sluggishly along, no doubt wondering where his next beer was.

'You are doing it wrong. You should ride him like this,' instructed Hua when I grumbled, closing his long legs on Shandan's sides and pushing with his seat.

'Yes, I know, but it is easier for you. Shandan is not lazy like Bajiu.'

I was finding Hua was very good at dispensing unwanted advice and criticism, particularly in retrospect.

'Well of course it's all very well to say that now, but it's a pity you didn't say it before,' I would find myself saying, as he told me yet again why I should have done something a particular way. But I gave as good as I got, and found he never held a grudge. I began to warm to him and even enjoy the squabbles which helped to pass long days on the road, though I found his propensity for passing wind at unexpected moments a trifle disconcerting.

Li Jing was a more quixotic character. He was of Hakka descent, the Hakka being a Han Chinese people from southern China with a strong overseas presence. Forceful lovers of liberty, they have a reputation for being energetic and contentious, and Li Jing certainly seemed to enjoy debating. One of the few times I saw his face light up was when he was arguing with Hua on a variety of topics such as who was the most famous Chinese person. But there was also a touchy and stubborn side to him, and I began to see why there had been reservations about his being included as a team member. I already had the feeling he only tolerated me, and he usually preferred to ride by himself. This was not a problem in itself except when it was without regard to others, as I had already discovered. It was perhaps because he was a bit of a loner that he was drawn to the more difficult characters among our horses, first the wild Hei Feng, and now the wired up Zorbee.

With consistent gentle handling by everyone, Zorbee was settling down to his job and proving he had amazing depths of endurance. His main bugbear was still things touching his legs, and though he now allowed the boys to brush them carefully, like Shandan, he was never too bothered about human company. Shandan had evidently been treated like a machine for most of his life, and behaved like a world-weary office worker doing exactly what he needed to do and no more. The only time he showed any enthusiasm was when food arrived. But he was amenable, safe and never any trouble. Out of the three horses the friendliest was Bajiu, who was also the most likely to be found with his nose in the feed bags. He became quite a favourite, particularly with Li May. Since she had decided she wanted to be part of the venture, she had settled cheerfully into the daily routine. As she was also of Hakka ancestry, she had a natural connection with Li Jing. Like Hakka men, the women also have a reputation for independence and self-reliance, but like Manchu women it is perhaps partly due to the fact that they never practised foot binding when it was common throughout the rest of China proper. This painful tradition limited mobility and in effect helped to keep women subjugated. Li May was certainly not slow to express her opinions; neither was she the most proactive member of the team, though admittedly Hua had sidelined her role as interpreter. But I trained her to carry my bags to the jeep and make me a coffee every morning while I brushed and tacked up, which made her presence worthwhile. She was also good company for Peng when he was driving, and I often caught them giggling and laughing together.

As for Peng, he continued to be a solid, reliable rock, never losing his temper and always seeing the bright side of things. In contrast to the fiery Li Jing and voluble Hua, he exuded Confucian calm and content. It was ever the placid, hardworking Peng who was up at the crack of dawn to feed the three horses, and who always found a solution to every problem without fuss or bother. He was as indispensable as Harry Tse had predicted, and I came to depend totally on him in the days and weeks to come.

CHAPTER TEN

RACING ACROSS THE STEPPE

欲速则不达
yù sù zé bù dá
More haste, less speed.

Tuesday, 11 August – Sunday, 16 August, 2009.
Huade to Chaoge'aobao. 34 km. Xilingole.

We paused overnight at Hua De, an unappealing mining settlement with industrial enterprises set in wasteland, only to find, as we rode out early the following morning, that on the other side of town a gleaming new ultra-modern sector was sprouting. Instead of the rather dated and worn-at-the-edges central business districts we had so far encountered, a wide two-way boulevard swept through the centre with huge spanking new buildings being constructed on either side. Muzak blared out from a shining secondary school beside blocks of residential flats, rows of modern shophouses and what looked like a huge swanky department store. I was to realise that this was a common feature of almost all the larger towns we passed through from now on. The Chinese authorities were pushing industrialisation and urbanisation for all it was worth, and developers were being encouraged to spend millions on urban projects all over the country. It is an astonishing fact that in the three years 2011-2013, China produced more concrete than the US did in the whole of the twentieth century. Anywhere in an outlying area with mining or industrial potential was prime fodder as the government worked to encourage people to move into and develop these less populated regions. This had sometimes led to the emergence of 'ghost cities' in places where speculative development had progressed full tilt regardless of whether there were people ready to move in. The rate of urbanisation in China is extremely rapid, and in most cases these empty developments are eventually bought up and inhabited. But many are long term investment purchases, and there are some instances where developments have remained empty white elephants.

It was a hot uninspiring ride across a treeless plain towards the next large town of Shangdu although we were following a quiet old pot-holed road. When Hua and Li Jing stopped to rest, I kept Bajiu moving on at a walk, but he continued to fuss and whinny every time the other horses went out of sight and constantly pushing him on wore me out. In the meantime, Hua and Li Jing continued with what I regarded as their nonsensical teenage boy progress – long rest stops interspersed with gallops to catch up. Of course, the inevitable happened. I was riding ahead about ten kilometres from our intended destination when Peng and Li May came driving up from behind. Bad news. It appeared the devil horse had struck again and Li Jing had been injured in an accident with Zorbee. I waited by the trailer until Li May reappeared in the car with the casualty. It transpired that Hua had dashed off at a trot (though I suspect the word gallop would be better substituted) and Zorbee had become over-excited. Galloping in pursuit with his head in the air, he had tripped in one of the many holes on the side of the road and crashed to the ground, trapping Li Jing beneath. The high pommel and cantle of his Mongolian saddle had prevented him being flung clear, and it seemed he had broken his collarbone and his ribs also hurt. Spookily his injuries were a mirror image of the ones I incurred in my accident with Zorbee. Peng and Hua arrived riding the horses, and Peng and Li May took Li Jing off to Shangdu hospital where he was told he had not broken his ribs. By the time they returned to the trailer it was almost dark. Hua had got talking to a local who arranged for us to stay at the house of his sister-in-law at the next small village of Chaoge'aobao. So Hua, Li May and I ended the day leading the horses through the pitch dark, following our new friend on his scooter to the mudbrick house of our new hostess.

Wutzala had invited us to attend an international endurance event in the Inner Mongolian province of Xilingole on the weekend of Friday, 14 August to Sunday the 16, and with my bad back and Li Jing's injury it seemed in any case a convenient time to take a couple of days off. Peng arranged with our hostess to care for the horses, who could stay with the trailer while we drove the jeep a few hours north-east to the venue at Xilinhot. Our drive took us through scrubby bush land and an enormous wind farm, and on arrival we found we had been booked into the luxurious Yuanhe Jianguo hotel. What a joy to be treated to five star facilities in an eleventh floor room overlooking the town. At lunch I was delighted to meet up with a Malaysian contingent of riders from my childhood home of Kuala Lumpur – Noraili with young protege Din, and Asrin, supported by husband Daniel. I showed Asrin a photo of my family coincidentally taken with Malaysian friends. 'But that's Rafie!' she exclaimed. We had mutual friends!

From the first time I tried endurance I was smitten, and immediately set my sights on race rides. Although the welfare of the horse is a priority in all endurance competitions, some place more emphasis on finishing condition and some on speed. Race rides fall into the latter group, and are won by the horse with the fastest time over a set distance, usually between 80 and 160 kilometres for a one-day race ride. However, the condition of the horses is also strictly monitored and must fall within set parameters. There are regular veterinary inspections at 'vet gates' during the course of the race, the horses being tested for lameness, heart recovery rate, hydration and injury. No horse is allowed to continue until its heart recovery rate is low enough, and any horse which fails to pass within a set presentation period or is judged 'unfit to continue' is immediately eliminated from the competition, even if it has crossed the finish line. I have been at many races where a slower horse has been victorious after the leading horses failed the vet inspection. On my little Arabian stallion Silver Mint, I crossed the line first on four occasions to win a twenty mile marathon and forty, fifty and eighty mile endurance races. We were selected for the British Intermediate Team, but unfortunately his endurance career ended when he injured his back in his last race before the international competition.

I also won a second placing in a fifty mile race on my Arabian mare Silver Sea Gem, and competed three times in the twenty-two mile 'Man v Horse' marathon, run locally over the Welsh hills, with one win and two second placings.

Although the Mongolians have run long races over the steppes for centuries, organised and properly vetted endurance riding was still in its infancy in China. I had not been over-impressed by the couple of rides I had already witnessed, and as an example saw at least one horse that I considered lame pass the halfway vetting. I was eager to see how they coped with this one.

The race of seventy-five kilometres was to take place the following day under rules laid down by the Fédération Equestre Internationale (FEI), the international body for equestrian sports. After lunch, the competitors were jostled into the back of a military truck to be transported round the course like cattle, while we joined the convoy in the jeep. Just as well, as the truck soon got stuck on a bank and everyone had to decant. We gave a lift back to the hotel to the Malaysians, and Singaporean Mr Ho Nai Yue, who was there in his capacity as president of the Asian Equestrian Federation, and were able to relax and watch telly while the hoi polloi were still bumping wearily round on their course inspection.

Local horses had been sourced for the 'international set' which besides the Malaysians included riders from Singapore, Hungary, Germany and Austria. I had been delighted to be invited to participate as an unofficial representative for Britain. There is nothing like trotting and cantering effortlessly for miles across country on a fit horse, feeling their muscles working like clockwork beneath you. So it was gutting to accept that with my bad back there was no way I would be able to survive three kilometres at a pace faster than a walk, let alone seventy-five kilometres. However, I volunteered to make a token start and tackle the first couple of kilometres on condition that the horse provided for me was dead quiet. Before dinner we walked down to the racecourse for the briefing and allocation of start placings and horses. To my surprise I was presented with a deck of cards and asked to make a pick to determine my horse. I suspect that the ballot was not entirely based on luck, as young Din ended up with a sprightly looking thoroughbred, while my six of spades magically gave me the placid Mongolian gelding I had hoped for. Peng helped me heave my saddle on him and I tentatively trotted around for a while before we had a short rehearsal for the following day's parade.

The race was due to start at 9am, but was preceded by a grand ceremony. We all paraded on our horses in front of the grandstand behind a vanguard brandishing international flags. There were Mongolian dances and Chinese speeches, and in case any of the crowd were in danger of missing any of it, the whole jamboree was displayed on an enormous screen above the track. Mysterious orders were given for us to dismount, but the reason became clear when an exuberant and noisy fireworks display followed. Of course, being in China, none of the horses took much notice in any case, and my bay gelding merely twitched an ear.

In my feeble condition I had been wary of a mass start, but in fact the riders had been divided into four groups and the melee I had worried about did not materialise. My group started off at a suitably sedate pace, and I was able to trot quietly all the way round the racecourse standing gingerly in the stirrups, and a little way up the hill before calling it a day. But it was dispiriting to plod back to the racecourse, repeating 'Wode bei bu hao. My back's not good,' to the queries of passing riders going in the other direction. Ah well.

I put the gelding back in his stable, and we all jumped into the jeep to follow the progress of the race, which followed a shallow grassy valley winding through the Inner Mongolian steppe. I was pleased to see that this event was considerably better organised than the first one I attended in China. We waited at the last vet gate, where there was a large water tanker standing by, and a ger crammed with veterinarians. A ger is a round portable tent used by Asian nomads for thousands of years. They consist of a felt covering over a pole and latticework frame. Traditionally skins would have provided an overall waterproof cover, but nowadays this is more likely to be canvas. Ger is the Mongolian name for these tents, but they are sometimes more commonly known in the West by the Turkic name 'yurt'. The covers round the sides of the vet *ger* had been rolled up so the diamond-shaped wooden latticework was exposed, letting steppe air blow through to cool the vets who were packed inside in the shade.

Wutzala was first in on his chestnut horse, and vetted through with no problem, though I did not see the horse being trotted up. We watched a few more horses come through and all seemed to be going well. However, Noraili was waiting to crew for Din and seemed anxious.

'Din should have been here ages ago,' she fretted. 'He was among the leaders and his horse was looking good when it left the halfway vetting.'

Eventually we drove her back along the track and found Din with the horse, which had run out of steam and had basically tied up. This has nothing to do with ropes, but meant its muscles had stiffened up in a type of cramp so it could not move. Among other things it can be caused in grain-fed horses which are aggressively exercised after a period of rest. Young Din was very upset. He had only previously ridden horses he had helped to train himself, and the danger inherent in riding borrowed horses is that it is difficult to gauge their fitness level and capabilities. It seemed there was no official provision for horses that had dropped out of the race, but eventually vets and officials turned up and we were able to leave the horse in their capable hands. We later heard that he had been trailered back and was recovering well.

Wutzala arrived first at the racecourse to win the event but we did not stay to watch everyone else trail in. The rest of the international riders went round steadily and brought their horses back in in good condition, but found it difficult to cope with the different culture surrounding horse management, particularly with regard to offering water. In modern endurance riding it is accepted good practice to offer horses water as often as possible to keep them well hydrated. Asrin had started to give her little black horse a bucket of water at the halfway vetting, only to have it snatched away by the owner.

As it was not her horse, she felt she could not really argue about it. The other riders had the same experience, but luckily a couple of miles from the vet gate they noticed a water trough behind a farm building, and let the horses drink their fill. 'They went much better after that!' commented Asrin.

The day was rounded off with a tremendous buffet dinner at the hotel for all the competitors, officials and supporters. Photos of the riders were flashed up on the screen, awards were presented, and all the competitors were squeezed into one big crowd for a camera opportunity. After my half-mile trot I felt a bit of a fake to find that I was included in the whole ceremony. The Mongolian entertainment included talented singers and a fantastic band of horse-head violinists, whose energetic fiddling exuded the spirit of the steppe and vividly brought to mind the thundering herds of horses which undoubtedly provided inspiration.

I was privileged to be invited by Mr Ho to join a ride post mortem the following day. Mr Ho was giving recommendations, and I was able to contribute some of my thoughts, for example the need to provide for horses that drop out, and the importance of offering horses plenty of water all the way round. Unfortunately, Mongolian horse management harks back to the days of Genghis Khan, and this included the practice of withholding water before and during exercise. This might be relevant before a short intensive spurt of activity such as a sprint race but not for endurance events. I was continually frustrated when I asked people why they did something a particular way to get the response, 'Because we have done it like that for thousands of years.' While experience undoubtedly counts for a lot, the suggestion that long tradition makes something right even in the face of modern research and logic seemed nonsensical to me, and I often had to stop myself responding, 'Well perhaps it's about time for a change.'

Li Jing was of this Genghis Khan school of thinking and I was to have many tussles with him in the weeks to come. He did not water his horse until an hour after stopping, and at rest stops Zorbee was tied up without water until a few minutes before we left, the complete reverse of accepted practice in endurance circles. When I walked Bajiu in and immediately offered him a bucket of water, Li Jing looked disapprovingly at me while Zorbee pawed the ground in vexation.

'Li Jing says it is dangerous to water your horse straight away after riding. Shouldn't you wait like him?' queried Hua, who was much more open to different thinking, even if he argued about it.

'No, it is always best to water whenever you can and keep them hydrated. We water our horses regularly during endurance races with no problem. And in any case we are not going fast.'

I said nothing directly to Li Jing as by then I was pretty sure he would ignore me. He continued with his watering system, but on a rare occasion when we crossed a stream while riding, he let Zorbee put his head down to drink, which seemed to contradict his whole theory. I increasingly found the radical notion that an elderly foreign woman might occasionally have valuable suggestions was sadly an alien concept to many men I encountered on the way.

The first endurance ride I attended in China had definite welfare issues, and I had heard reports of horses dying from exhaustion at Chinese endurance events due to inadequate management and vetting. They have sometimes had to learn the hard way, but have been making huge strides in the right direction, and the introduction of official FEI regulations to equestrian events can do nothing but good for overall horse welfare.

The morning was rounded off with lunch and French wine hosted by the governor of Xilingole in an incredibly bling Renaissance-style function room.

It was late by the time we arrived back at Choage'aobao, but minus one member of the team. Li Jing had gone to hospital in the night as he was still in pain, and it turned out that he had in fact fractured a couple of ribs after all. It seemed most sensible for him to go back to Beijing to recuperate. It would just be the four of us continuing over the steppes to the banks of the mighty Huang He river. Only Hua and I would be riding. I hoped I would be able to persuade him to stick to a steadier pace and keep me company.

CHAPTER ELEVEN

A MONGOLIAN WELCOME

活到老, 学到老
huó dào lǎo, xué dào lǎo
One is never too old to learn.

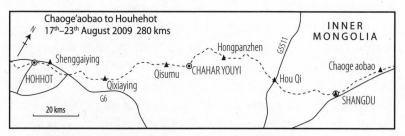

Monday, 17 August – Sunday, 23 August, 2009.
Chaoge'aobao to Hohhot.
280 km. Daily average 40 km.

I lay snug in my sleeping bag on the double bed I was sharing with Li May and looked up to the exposed poles and branches holding up the low earth and tile roof. We were in the village courtyard house where we had left the horses. The house was the ubiquitous Chinese mud brick cottage with two rooms on either side of a central brick-floored entrance hall-cum-kitchen, and we were in the room to the left which often doubles up as a storeroom. Sacks of grain were stacked waist high at the back of the room and along the end wall a plethora of personal belongings were piled up, including quilts, boxes, bins, toilet paper, a suitcase and a cheap gilt mantlepiece clock.

In the central kitchen, the tiled stove to the right of the door boasted two wok holders. Other than that, the kitchen furniture was limited to a couple of simple freestanding kitchen cupboards on legs, a low table propped against the wall, and a metal stand holding a plastic washbasin and a used piece of soap. Water was stored in a couple of white plastic buckets which had previously held some unidentified agricultural product.

The boys slept on the other side of the hall in the main bedroom on a *kang* over which hung a large poster showing a western 1960s-style living room with pale carpet, three-piece suite and potted plant. These gaily coloured posters were a common decorative feature in poorer homes and eating places, and often depicted the lifestyles people aspired to, usually a touch behind the times.

Peng had been up at the crack of dawn as usual to feed the horses, and as I came out into the bright morning sun I found them munching placidly on straw. One corner of the yard contained a leafy vegetable garden inside a low mud wall. Six brilliant white cockerels with red combs flapped and strutted, one crowing from the top of a prehistoric red tractor with a tyre-less wheel propped up on bricks, while six white rabbits scrabbled around in a cage. All of them except our horses were bound for the pot. Our hostess sat on the ground by the gate in Chinese trousers and flowery blouse, gossiping with a group of female friends. I surveyed the contented scene. I had enjoyed our luxurious break in a five star hotel, but felt glad to be back in the warm simplicity of village life. Perhaps I would feel differently in the middle of winter with no central heating or running water.

Peng opted to ride with me on the old road to Shangdu, and Zorbee nearly claimed another victim when he caught his foot in some wire and panicked. Peng fell off, but was happily none the worse. Added to this, Bajiu managed to get cast upside down on a bush while rolling at a rest stop, and the boys fluttered around, unsure what to do next.

'Get the tethering rope round his far hind leg and help me pull him over.' My words hit a wall of male scepticism again.

'Are you sure it will work?' Hua asked doubtfully as Bajiu continued his struggle to right himself.

'Of course, I have done it loads of times.'

Bajiu was pulled over in a second and scrambled to his feet.

Another aggravation was dodging the numerous foot-deep holes which pitted the sides of many roads in Inner Mongolia like mini bomb craters. It was one of these that had been Zorbee's downfall. Hua told me they were the result of unfinished tree planting campaigns. As local government was funded for the numbers of trees planted, they were understandably very enthusiastic about digging holes as evidence it was being done even if there were no trees to fill them. Between the holes and Zorbee's wire phobia, we had to keep our eyes peeled at all times.

Shangdu was a sizeable town so Hua soon managed to find a truck stop we could stay at overnight. Truck stops are common all over China and always include a large yard with space for transport vehicles of all sizes. In essence these truck stops are the modern equivalent of the former caravanserai, which were roadside inns catering for travellers on the old trade routes of Eurasia. But instead of more ancient forms of transport such as camels, donkeys, mules and horses as well as other livestock being moved such as sheep and cattle, the yards were now filled with long distance lorries. They were perfect for us as there was plenty of room to accommodate the jeep and trailer with the horses tied to the side, and as the ground was already soiled with oil leaks from the lorries, proprietors were not so fussed about any mess the horses might make, although Peng always cleaned it up as best he could. Accommodation was usually in the form of long blocks of rectangular rooms with doors opening straight onto the yard. Sometimes the accommodation offered showers or restaurant facilities, but these could not be guaranteed. Like most basic accommodation in China the rooms generally contained iron bedsteads, each with a hard mattress, cheap quilt, and bean bag pillow. A thermos of hot water was provided for washing, and this could be supplemented from the cold water tap outside. I had packed a plastic basin, and soon became proficient at taking a basin bath in my room, working downwards from face to feet, finally washing my knickers and socks in the grey water.

A dual carriageway swept across the bleak and unappealing landscape to the east of Shangdu. Hua and I padded through sticky clay wasteland and across sparse grassland where scattered sheep picked at blades of grass among tethered cows and donkeys. A weak sun filtered down through the afternoon haze as we climbed a stony hillside. Every so often we passed a small village, the washed-out landscape of beige and ochre occasionally broken by the unexpected emerald green pocket of a vegetable garden behind crumbling walls, the neat leafy rows of cabbages and lettuces interspersed with spiky onion plants, ripening tomatoes and orange pumpkins. It was forty-two kilometres to the grubby two-storey guest house we stayed at in the rundown settlement of Hou Qi. Rain from a passing thunderstorm lashed the window of our overnight lodgings, the iron staircase at the back of the building, the open-sided brick greenhouses.

It was still drizzling miserably in the morning. After his fall, Peng seemed to have resigned himself to the role of driver while Hua continued riding Zorbee. We struck out along a small road across the grasslands. Twice within the first hour Zorbee panicked at bits of wire from broken fencing, but with his long legs clamped firmly on Zorbee's sides, Hua stayed on board. Having removed his glasses because of the rain, he decided it was expedient to put them back on so he could scout out potential hazards. It may have been a dreary start to the day, but the wet gave the open steppe a wild and boundless feel. The road meandered past a small grey lake set in a clayey marsh, and over damp undulating grasslands which reached out through the drizzle to remote hills on the far horizon. We paused to chat to a shepherd, and at midday stopped for noodles at a roadside eating house. Patches of light brushed the swell of hills ahead, and the rain-heavy clouds rolled away to be replaced by fluffy cotton wool balls in a deep blue sky. As we rode into the village of Hong Pan Zhen, a farmer hauling buckets by hand from an ancient concrete well paused to watch us pass, his tethered donkey waiting patiently while her foal suckled.

Our *fandian* next to a disused PetroChina pump canopy just outside Hong Pan Zhen was owned by a skinny young bachelor immaculately dressed in black trousers and white shirt. The simple rooms in the small white-tiled guest house could have done with a coat of paint, but our host was evidently a particular sort of chap and a well-used straw broom and dustpan were leaning against the kitchen wall. Next to the single wok brick stove stood a large black Shanghai jar for storing water. It was unusually fed from an internal stand pipe, the height of luxury.

'But the water doesn't come on until seven o'clock in the morning,' Hua informed me.

Hong Pan Zhen itself was a ragged village with low mudbrick buildings lounging on either side of the main street. The evening sun struck at an angle, lighting up tiled roofs and shop facades as we strolled down to buy a few necessities. Surprisingly for such a small place there were six shops stocking a variety of goods such as cigarettes, vegetables and *mantou* (Chinese savoury buns without a filling), and we were able to buy noodles, biscuits and peanuts, as well as a new plastic washbasin. They all had bottles of liquor prominently displayed on shelves. I suppose there is nothing much else to do but drown your sorrows when you live out in the sticks. Three smiling young women in trousers and long-sleeved tops stood chatting at the entrance to the largest establishment, which seemed to double up as a social club. A few motorbikes were propped up on their kick stands outside, and grouped around a couple of small tables in the dark interior, several men were hunched solemnly over cards and mah-jong. They might just as well have been at a funeral wake for all the enthusiasm they were showing, but their poker faces turned to astonishment when I walked in.

With only two riding, we decided to trailer the spare horse, and the following morning Peng led a reluctant Zorbee at an angle onto the ramp, turning to face him when Zorbee refused to walk in.

'Tell him to try leading straight and not facing the horse,' I suggested to Li May.

I took Zorbee and briefly showed Peng my approach.

'Why don't you let him do it his own way?' Li May butted in.

I was getting a little tired of her habit of giving advice on things she knew nothing about, and snapped back testily, 'I have been loading horses for years, but Peng has not.'

But Peng was always willing to try out new suggestions, and although I occasionally offered advice, I invariably left him to it. He was infinitely more patient than I was.

Zorbee left soft dents in the sand as Hua rode ahead of me along a dry riverbed. After skirting round the sprawling industrial town of Chahar Youyi Zhongqi, we had realised this watercourse ran parallel to the quiet metalled road we had been following. A quick look at the map suggested that it led in the general direction we were headed and we scrambled down to follow it for two perfect days. Initially it sliced its way in a gully through the red alluvial deposits of a shallow wooded valley, crumbling earth cliffs curving round the outside of the bends. Terraced fields stepped gently up beyond scattered trees along the banks, and in one place the strolling white shapes of a herd of grazing goats contrasted sharply with the lush green grass growing beneath.

Beyond Qisumu the riverbed gradually widened, but the hills on either side closed in and overshadowed us, squeezing the fields to a narrow green belt where sheaves of grain were neatly stacked on the stubble left behind. River deposits filled the valley floor to form a flat flood plain from which the steep hillsides rose abruptly on either side, sometimes barren and sometimes covered with sparse vegetation clinging between slabs of rock. The riverbed meandered to and fro, its sandy and stony wasteland taking up more and more of the valley. A small stream of water appeared, growing into a small river twinkling over a pebbly bed. Eventually the valley narrowed suddenly to a gap between forested hills and we were forced to scramble over rocks beside rushing rapids and negotiate a weir before persuading the horses to jump over a small concrete water leat.

The valley spread out again into a cultivated expanse, and we now picked our way along the top of the river bank between the earth river cliff and fields of rustling maize, leafy green potato plants and sesame blooming with blue flowers. Sometimes there was a grove of trees where a fat donkey or sleek mule was tethered by one foot. The river bed itself broadened and became braided, offering open stretches of sand and gravel which tempted Hua to canter Zorbee ahead. He swung along at a comfortable lope, but it was still agony for me to bounce along behind with my bad back on bumpy Bajiu even though I stood in the stirrups. Supporting myself with one hand on the cantle, or back of the saddle, gave me another painful muscle in my shoulder, and I pleaded constantly with Hua to reduce the pace. At first it was to no avail. But when he nearly managed to get Zorbee stuck in a quicksand from which they only floundered out with difficulty, he became a little more circumspect.

The small parallel road which connected a string of little villages along the valley was not busy but carried a fairly regular traffic of coal lorries, so we were fortunate to be able to follow the watercourse for nearly sixty kilometres over the two days. I reflected on how idyllic it would be if we could always travel like this, following natural features and small tracks across unspoilt countryside in a way it would once have been possible to do. But it was not long before we were threading our way through fume-spewing traffic into the dusty wild west town of Qixiaying, where we stayed at a grimy truck-weighing yard. It had been far more peaceful at the deserted government building we had slept in the night before in Qisumu, in spite of the barking guard dog, which flung itself to the end of its long chain whenever we crossed a yard overgrown with weeds to reach the toilets.

As we came out onto a level plain and took a tree-lined road towards Hohhot, Hua continued to act like an excitable puppy the moment a blade of grass appeared on the verge. Off he dashed on Zorbee, unsettling Bajiu who jiggled around so my back twinged painfully. An incongruous mock castle constructed out of pale red and grey bricks for a Genghis Khan epic appeared across a stretch of thin feathery grass at the base of billowing hills and gave me an idea. I fished out my video camera.

'Hua, why don't you ride around in front of the castle and let me film you.'

Much to my relief, Hua fell for my diversionary tactics. As I had hoped, his film star ambitions got the better of him and he careered happily around with the battlements in the background while I stayed in one spot and emulated a movie director.

'Go about fifty metres away and gallop towards me. Now canter from right to left with the castle behind you. No, no, you went too slow, try it again.'

After twenty minutes of this he got rid of some of his boyish high spirits and calmed down. We trudged quietly along the road the rest of the forty kilometres to the outskirts of Hohhot, where we stayed at a dire roadside dive in Shenggaiying. Li May and I shared a dismal windowless inner room with dicey plug points and loose electrical wires sticking out everywhere, and the toilet was a yard at the back.

A yellow haze hung over the city of Hohhot as we made our way through the tattered outskirts along a road carrying a steady stream of trucks. We had been riding for just over a week since our trip to Xilingole, and had covered 280 kilometres; quite good going. It should not be long until we reached our next major city destination of Baotou on the Yellow River. I was getting quite good at reading simple Chinese characters by now and felt encouraged by the blue road sign stating the distance there.

'Baotou 154 km'

Ten kilometres further along the road we came to another sign.

'Baotou 154 km'

It appeared even the Chinese road signs enjoyed the *'shi gongli'* game.

However, our immediate destination was the Hohhot racecourse, where we were due to be welcomed by the Hohhot horsey set. We found the assembled company waiting by the grandstand in a *ger* where snacks and milk tea were pressed on us by girls in colourful Mongolian *deels*. Before we could say 'Genghis Khan', Peng and I were marched off and dressed up in Mongolian wedding outfits to pose for photos for the entertainment of all present. In vain did I insist that I had a perfectly adequate husband at home. Apart from a green silk *deel* and yellow cummerbund, my bridal costume involved an extraordinary ornate multi-coloured piece of headgear at least a foot high which tottered precariously on my head like the Leaning Tower of Pisa. In this appendage I was ushered in front of a television camera to give an interview for Inner Mongolian TV. Thankfully I was spared the mortification of wearing it while parading through town in a cavalcade to our next venue, though we were draped in blue votive *khadags*.

Led by two riders in silk *deels* and pointed Mongolian hats carrying banners and mounted on Mongolian '*zoulu*' or pacing horses, their tails traditionally bound halfway up, we clattered en masse through the hot streets, creating a local sensation. Every so often we stopped for swigs of bottled water. Next to me rode the pretty long-haired wife of the local beef jerky manufacturer who was sponsoring the reception. Dressed in a purple *deel*, she rode a piebald horse and told me she was a teacher. We entered a large park and stopped at an ornate pavilion by a lake where wedding couples were posing for photos. For an awful moment I thought Peng and I might be dragged off to join them. Instead everyone tied their horses to the trees and lined up for group photos in front of a large banner with a string of Chinese characters which were later translated rather mystifyingly for me as, 'A warm welcome to the Chinese and British heroes from the time travel.'

After a short rest, the time-travelling Chinese and British heroes mounted up again and were swept along by the mini Mongol horde to a large *ger* erected in a far corner of the park. Our truck was already there, so the horses were tied to the rings while a permanent marker was produced so everyone could add to the spaghetti-like tangle of signatures scrawled on the trailer. Inside the *ger* a feast was waiting. I am afraid to say I was glad the Mongolian influence was not too apparent, as the only time I have been to Mongolia proper, the cuisine seemed to consist almost entirely of boiled sheep and hard cheese. But this was a Chinese style banquet with a stunning array of succulent dishes simmering on braziers and many shots of *baijiu* washed down to calls of '*Ganbei*', accompanied by speeches and Mongolian singing. The Chinese certainly know how to hold a party. Hua, Peng and I all took our turns in the Mongolian welcome ceremony, flicking *baijiu* to earth, sky and wind before white welcoming *khadags* were placed round our necks.

A gently spoken young Mongolian by the name of Garedy led us on a track through fields to the south. Suspecting his horse was lame, he impressed me when he immediately dismounted and led it the rest of the way – the mark of a true horseman. We arrived at a long building set in a broad expanse of open land. The horses were untacked and released into a grassy paddock. Off they trotted, shaking their manes and snorting, before their heads shot down to pull at the grass. Suddenly their legs buckled beneath them and they slumped euphorically on the ground, rolling over and over to clean the sweat from their travel-stained backs. We brushed the horses' backs religiously morning and night, but it could never replace the sheer pleasure of a good roll.

'There is our hotel,' said Hua pointing across the expanse of land.

Sitting in the middle distance were what appeared to be two enormous flying saucers, decorated in traditional pale blue and white Mongolian patterns. Was the modern five star hotel designed as a nod to alien visitors such as myself who might feel more at home? No, with a lot of imagination it was supposed to look like a couple of *gers*.

But if we thought this was to be the end of the day, we were very much mistaken, as the Hohhotans were not finished with us yet. We only had time for a quick shower before we were faced with yet another cornucopian banquet, this time set out on a revolving turntable in a plushly decorated room in the hotel. There were more speeches, toasts, *baijiu* flicking and *khadag* presentations. I was beginning to accumulate quite a pile. To my dismay my TV interview was broadcast on a large screen for all to see. A Mongolian singer belted out a traditional song. But suddenly he began to produce the most extraordinary noise: deep guttural chanting interspersed with a high twanging whistle. It seemed impossible that anyone could produce such surreal sounds without external aids.

This was traditional Mongolian throat singing, produced entirely by the singer's vocal chords, but sounding more like a cross between a didgeridoo and a jew's harp. I had never heard the human voice produce anything so unearthly and was transfixed by its strange beauty.

I asked Li May to translate the sixty-four thousand dollar question for Garedy.

'Ask him why they don't give water to horses during their long distance races.'

'He says it is because they have done it this way for thousands of years.'

CHAPTER TWELVE

YELLOW RIVER

不到黄河不死心
Bù dào Huánghé bù sǐxīn
Not giving up until one reaches the Yellow River.

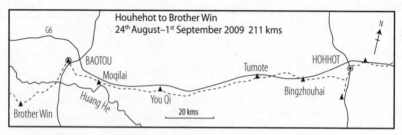

Monday, 24 August – Tuesday, 1 September, 2009.
Hohhot to Brother Win Stables.
211 km. Daily average 35 km.

After nearly three weeks in the saddle my back muscles were still excruciatingly painful at times, and showed little sign of improving. So we were glad not only to have a relaxing day off after the relentless Inner Mongolian hospitality, but also to take the opportunity to track down some sort of waist support for me. Garedy drove us round the shopping centres of Hohhot, and eventually I found a Korean-made corset like a wide elasticated cummerbund. It added to my strange appearance, but I hoped it would allow my muscles to rest and recuperate.

We learned from one of the horsey set that he was running a horse in a *nadaam* the following day, and it seemed a good opportunity to attend one. A traditional Mongolian festival involving wrestling, archery and horse racing competitions, this *nadaam* was only a couple of hours drive away. Early in the morning we followed Mr He up a misty winding road and out onto the steppe land to the north of Baotou. In the middle of the open plain vehicles were converging on a temporary scaffolding grandstand. A small bank of tiered seating had been constructed in front of a garish painted backdrop of Nadaam scenes. Teams of people in brightly coloured matching costumes were pouring out of coaches and descending on the grandstand and a small row of tents which housed, among other things, a noodle stall and a communal ladies loo. After inspecting Mr He's horse – a lanky bay thoroughbred type tied to a high line with other horses near a *ger* village – we found a place to sit at the back of the grandstand amongst the hoi polloi.

The fun and games began with a big opening ceremony accompanied by running commentary in Chinese over the loudspeaker. There were speeches by local dignitaries and a Cossack style display of trick riding. A complete orchestra of horse-head violin players in *deels* belted out Mongolian music, a young virtuoso in the front row flinging back his long mane of fine black hair as he fiddled vigorously. All of the contestants marched past in their groups – wrestlers, archers and riders followed by an interminable parade of what seemed to be representatives of every official organisation and local business in Baotou. After what seemed hours they eventually got down to the real business of the competitions, which ran consecutively. I was rather hoping to see sweaty muscle-bound Mongolian wrestlers dressed seductively in leather boots, skimpy underpants and cutaway tops, grunting and grappling with each other. Instead the wrestling appeared to be a much more casual affair, with young men tussling half-heartedly in tracksuit bottoms and even T-shirts, though they generally made some concession to traditional costume. In fact, the whole event reflected the fact that Inner Mongolia has been part of China for many years.

The first horse race was for trotters, or more accurately pacers, but it was a world away from the professional trotting and pacing races you see in the West. In America, tall leggy 'standardbreds' were developed from racing thoroughbred lines to compete in harness racing on special tracks. In these races the sleek stabled horses almost always pull a lightweight two-wheeled 'sulky' in which a driver sits. There are separate races for trotters and pacers, pacing being faster than trotting. Pacers often wear harness 'hopples', which are leather straps around their upper legs to make sure they keep to a lateral pacing gait and don't break stride. Professional harness racing is also hugely popular in other parts of the world such as Europe and Australia, though not always using standardbreds.

Here on the Inner Mongolian grasslands, the circular course was roughly marked out with flags stuck into the grassland apparently at random – no health and safety concerns here. Hairy and stocky, the little Mongolian horses were ridden not driven, and wore no extra harness hopples. Natural pacers, they skimmed round the course, scuttling past with their legs whizzing back and forth like clockwork.

Then came the race we had all come to watch. The group of around sixty waiting horses and riders in the distance on the far side away from the grandstand suddenly shot off in a melee. The leading bunch soon galloped past, riders sitting easily on the backs of their mounts, legs hanging loosely on either side. The horses ran efficiently with heads slung low, the Mongolian horses recognisable from the ribbons on their bridles and tails bandaged in the middle. The rest of the field trailed behind, but a swirling cloud of dust had now been kicked up, so it was impossible to see if Mr He's horse was among them. Around the course they thundered again, the crowd surging forward across the track as the victor galloped across the finish line. Cantering sedately in the rear and looking a tad out of place was a pair of sleek and beautifully turned out sport horses, their Chinese riders elegantly dressed in monogrammed polo shirts, pristine white jodhpurs and riding boots. One of the horses evidently decided that this sort of common free-for-all was quite beneath his dignity and had to be led off in disgrace after unseating his rider to the immense enjoyment of the crowd. But of Mr He's horse there was no sign. Apparently, it had fallen at some point, so there were no celebrations when we retired to the tent village to conduct a post mortem. The boys slurped loudly and ecstatically as they bent their heads over huge, greasy bowls of noodles, shovelling and sucking slippery strands into their mouths. In China this is regarded as respectful appreciation of the food rather than bad table manners, but I could never quite bring myself to follow suit.

We had now ridden down from the Inner Mongolia steppe land to the more populated valley of the Huang He or Yellow river. On Wednesday, 26 August we made our way through the honking streets of Hohhot and headed west along a road lined with industrial estates and small workshops. Cars and trucks rattled past and Peng and I scrambled along the side until the verge became non-existent and our attempts to avoid the traffic became futile. It was a relief when Hua found a comfortable place to stay in a row of shophouses with a Chinese Christian family whose little daughter played a mean piano. Li May and I had a clean room at the far end of a neat kitchen garden, and our hosts laid on an excellent supper and breakfast.

There is a long history of Christianity in China. Legend has it that it was Nestorian monks who originally smuggled the much prized silkworm out of China in the sixth century. They had certainly reached China by the following century, as the ancient Nestorian stele in Xian records their arrival in 635 during the Tang dynasty. Christians were expelled in the fourteenth century under the early Ming dynasty, but the Catholic Jesuits sent missionaries during the second half of the sixteenth century and they achieved influence in the later Ming court. It was not until the nineteenth century that Protestant missionaries began to work extensively in China, particularly after the First Opium War of 1842. Both Roman Catholics and Protestants played an important part in increasing western influence through establishments such as hospitals and schools; the largest missionary agency being the protestant China Inland Mission, founded in 1865 by Yorkshireman Hudson Taylor. It was through this organisation that many missionaries came to China, though they turned down Gladys Aylward, made famous by Ingrid Bergman's portrayal in the film, The Inn of the Sixth Happiness, *apparently due to her slow progress in learning Chinese.*

Although many Christians were massacred in the anti-western

Boxer rebellion at the turn of the century, it did little to dent the spread of Christianity. Several prominent pre-communist era figures such as nationalists Sun Yat Seng and Chiang Kai Shek were Christian, as was the notable warlord and nationalist Feng Yuxiang, known as the 'Christian general'. I was fascinated when one of our hosts in Hebei told Guo Sheng that his father had been the Christian general's groom! Christians have been persecuted under communism, but the Chinese government has relaxed to a certain extent in recent years. It is difficult to put an exact figure to the numbers of Christians in China today, but estimates have been as high as a hundred million.

After the previous day's horrendous experience on the road to Baotou, we tried to avoid the beaten track as far as possible, and on Thursday found a pretty little earth track along the foot of the jagged plateau edge through plum orchards and maize fields and past crumbling stone walls hiding old houses. Rustling poplar leaves cast dancing shadows across our path in the crisp bright air with a hint of autumn to come, but the peace was shattered when we passed through a military airfield where jets were taking off and roaring overhead. On the edge of Tumote, Hua and I found the jeep and trailer parked on a wide paved area in front of a line of solid buildings, in the middle of which was an extraordinary place painted brick red with white trimmings. On the facade life-size figures of voluptuous naked Grecian-style women were embossed on large white plaques decorated with gold fig-leaf wreaths. I was slightly surprised to find that this was where we were staying.

'It is a bath house,' explained Li May. 'It is for women as well as men if you want to try.'

The décor made me suspicious that there might be more than hot baths on offer, but the boys disappeared with large white towels to take advantage of the bath experience with not a slinky female in sight. I decided to give it a miss as our airy rooms overlooking the road had spotless en suite bathrooms, though the seats were missing from the flush loos.

An unsuccessful foray through the maze of maize fields beyond

Tumote left us teetering precariously along the top of a dyke between two deep trenches, before I realised from the map that there was a railway line running parallel to the main road. This almost always signals the presence of a service track running alongside and so I persuaded Hua to take a small earth road running down to the line. Bingo, there was the track, and we were able to enjoy a relaxed couple of days walking and chatting beside the line to Baotou with the occasional train rumbling past.

Hua told me a little about his five years working in Japan, where he had lived with his wife before they divorced.

'Did you enjoy living there?' I queried, interested in his answer, as historically there has been considerable enmity between the Chinese and Japanese. Large parts of China were overrun by the Japanese army during the Second Sino-Japanese War, which merged into World War Two, and the Chinese were subjected to appalling atrocities. The terrible 1937 'Rape of Nanking', where thousands of ordinary Chinese were brutalised, raped and massacred by Japanese troops, has never been forgotten.

'Yes, I enjoyed it very much. The Japanese people are very friendly and the food is very good.'

'I am afraid I have never been impressed by Japanese food, although I have never really sampled it properly,' I commented. 'It just seems to consist of tiny portions of raw fish and vegetables. I much prefer Chinese food and it seems to involve more cooking skill.'

'Oh no, you are wrong. Japanese food is very good, and very difficult to cook properly. You must go to a good restaurant. I will show you when we are back in Beijing.'

Our chats also revealed to my surprise that Hua had read quite a few English language classics, though perhaps unsurprisingly *Animal Farm* was not on the list.

Where we reached the occasional small station we led the horses along the platform to the astonished gaze of the odd local, and at You Qi we negotiated a tangle of rails and sleepers at an enormous coal depot and marshalling yard. A group of curious railway workers called out to us, '*Ni laizi nali? Ni yao qu nali?* Where have you come from? Where are you going?'

We were rapidly becoming accustomed to these questions. Hua's responses generally elicited disbelief at the answer to the first question, let alone the second. In fact, I found the Chinese were usually far more impressed by the hundreds of miles we had ridden from Beijing than the thousands of miles I still had to ride to London.

As we neared Baotou we were forced back onto the road, but I had a frisson of excitement when I saw a faraway glint of water reflecting the blue August sky. It was off to the south and had to be the great Huang He itself.

'But I thought it was yellow,' complained an aggrieved Hua.

The Huang He or Yellow River is also known both as 'the Mother of China' and 'China's Sorrow', and all its names are the result of one thing: loess. When the winds blow from the north, fine dust from the northern deserts is carried south over China. This is the dust that coats Beijing and made us pull up our scarves over our faces in the spring. Over many centuries it has been deposited in parts of northern China to form a thick, fertile layer of earth known as loess, many feet deep in places.

The Huang He flows through these loess areas, picking up the highly erodible soil which is washed down the slopes by rainwater. By the time it reaches the North China Plain, the great river is carrying more sediment than any other river in the world, and sixty times that of the Mississippi. It is this heavy burden of yellow silt that has given the river its name. As the river enters the flat land of the plain, it slows down and the load of silt clogs the channel, building up the riverbed until it is higher than the surrounding land. When meltwater from the high mountains swells the river flow in early summer, this may eventually be enough for the river to burst through its banks and cause widespread flooding. In the past the Huang He has re-routed its path to the sea many times, the cycle starting again each time. Over the centuries this has been both a blessing and a curse. On the one hand the river is regarded as the mother of China due to the fertile silt deposited over the plain during flooding. The rich soil enabled the agriculture and settlement which was the basis for the emergence of Chinese civilisation and culture. But on the other hand, the Huang He floods have drowned millions of people and caused untold sorrow.

It had been arranged for us to take a day off at a resort on the edge of Baotou, courtesy of local businessman and racehorse owner Mr Zhang. It was the usual Chinese holiday camp take on Mongolian culture with concrete *gers* scattered in woodland round a central communal centre with canteen and function room. We were given more substantial lodgings in a small office building with bedrooms overlooking a mini racetrack with stabling. Peng was waiting by a shoeing frame with a local farrier who had already re-shod Shandan, and Zorbee and Bajiu were soon taken care of. A smartly dressed woman in purple high heels appeared. It was Mrs Zhang with teenage daughter in tow. She invited us into a carpeted *ger* where we sat around a low table bearing plates of mutton chunks, omelette, potato stew, dishes of beansprouts and aubergines, sweet syrupy apples, and yoghurt. Milky tea and the inevitable *baijiu* were served. Mrs Zhang was learning English and was keen to try out her limited knowledge, as Mr Zhang was deputy director of a thoroughbred stud farm and was planning a buying trip to England.

Our day off was a chance for me to wash my hair and clothes, and sort out my technical equipment, though the internet connection was virtually non-existent. The horses rested in the shade of the trees with the occasional flick of a tail or shake of a mane. The boys all had a go on an old *zouma* or pacing horse at the stables, pounding round the track looking very pleased with themselves. Mr Zhang arrived back in the evening to take us to an amazing seafood restaurant where we were plied with shark's fin soup, steamed crabs, clams and sweet and sour giant prawns, not to mention a whole Huang He fish which looked rather like some sort of pike.

'They say it is endangered,' said Hua. '... But this one is farmed,' he added quickly as a look of horror spread across my face.

The next day was the first of September, and after an interview for Baotou TV, we set off to cross the Huang He and ride the forty kilometres to the stud farm, which was situated on the edge of the desert to the south of the river. Mr Zhang guided us, and we were accompanied for a short way by Mrs Zhang, nattily dressed for riding in blue and white check trousers, blue soldier style jacket and large riding helmet, and mounted on a little grey Arabian.

A stream of vehicles of all shapes and sizes jostled their way noisily across the bridge and round a car from which a TV camera protruded, filming our progress. Beneath us the muddy swirling waters of the Huang He moved relentlessly to the sea and Hua pivoted round on Zorbee's back to shout triumphantly above the traffic din, 'It looks yellow!'

Peng and Li May were waiting on the other side with the jeep and trailer, and a familiar face. Li Jing had returned after his two weeks recuperation in Beijing, now wearing a back and shoulder brace. Shandan was unloaded and saddled up, and they joined the group. We turned west along a sandy track on the top of the earth bund which had been built to hold back the floodwaters of the Huang He.

For millennia successive Chinese governments have struggled to control the murky waters of this remorseless giant with varying degrees of success. Flood prevention measures were first introduced over two thousand years ago, and over the years have included flood levees, storage reservoirs, canals to carry excess water away and also provide irrigation, and dams to hold back floodwater and create hydroelectricity. Recent measures have been fairly successful and the last major floods were in 1945, but the river can still be troublesome. Silt has choked dams and damaged turbines, and this has been exacerbated by increased erosion caused by deforestation, overgrazing and over cultivation, another motivation for the 'Green Great Wall of China' campaign. Although the Huang He has been tamed to a certain extent, the threat is always there and it may only be a matter of time before the next catastrophic flood happens.

The flood plain stretched away as far as the eye could see, green and yellow with sunflowers and maize, and disturbed by our cavalcade, a fat, glossy mule galloped round on its tether. As we neared a couple of canvas tents below the track Mr Zhang and Hua suddenly shot to the opposite side.

'Make way for the honeybees, quick!' Hua called back.

About sixty wooden hives were arranged in three circles between the tents, and a cloud of loudly humming bees swarmed above them, tended by a beekeeper in loose black clothing and straw hat. We hurried past, avoiding the odd flying straggler, but one managed to score a hit on Mr Zhang's stable manager. Clusters of beehives were to prove a common sight on the crop covered floodplain.

We reached the town of Zhaojun to find the mayor and a gaggle of reporters waiting. After a round of interviews we went inside for lunch, and once again were ushered to a laden table. Pride of place was taken by another whole fish from the Huang He, laid on in honour of the mayor and his guests. Hua interpreted for the mayor.

'He says the fish is very rare.' My face fell again at the vision of endangered stocks of rare Huang He fish being decimated by our passage up the river. The mayor looked anxious and consulted with Hua, who translated.

'Don't worry. He says they are not all that rare.'

After a short ride along sandy tree-lined lanes and through maize fields we were met by a posse of young mounted jockeys in baseball caps who had come to escort us to the stud. But first we had to do the Mongolian welcoming ceremony again and add another *khadag* to our collections, before jigging across sandy scrubland and a huge field of vivid green alfalfa watered by a pivoting irrigation system. The stud was a magnificent brand new set-up which had been created out of desert. It seemed no expense had been spared, and there were round pens, outdoor arenas (one with a brand new set of jumps) and brick floored stable blocks set among flower beds. White railed sand paddocks and newly planted trees lined a long paved central walkway. We looked around the alfalfa-munching horses, and after Bajiu, Zorbee and Shandan had been installed in a paddock of their own, Mr Zhang took us to see his dogs. Whippets, greyhounds and Rottweilers were confined in large pens in a separate compound. But what caught my eye was an unusual brindled Taiwan dog looking rather like a cross between a mongrel and a Tasmanian devil, and two types of Tibetan mastiff, huge big-boned herd guard dogs with thick woolly coats designed to protect them from the Himalayan winter. Some are red or gold-coloured, but Mr Zhang also showed us a gigantic black and tan Hound of the Baskervilles glaring out of a shelter. Tibetan mastiffs were extremely popular among the Chinese nouveau riche at this time and were commanding astronomical prices of well over £100,000, but due to over-breeding and a slowing economy the market has since crashed. Abandonment of unwanted dogs has created a substantial problem with packs of dogs roaming loose in parts of Tibet.

Our luxurious guest accommodation was styled after a Shanxi merchant house, with living blocks and courtyard gardens inside an outer wall, pierced at the far end by a circular doorway. The curving ribbed roofs were traditionally tiled and even had ornamental figures on the gables. Li May and I shared a plush bedroom with soft beds, en suite bathroom and television, overlooking a leafy courtyard. The silence was only disturbed by the sound of bushes rustling in the wind. I lay awake in bed for a while thinking about the route ahead. The main transport links and large towns lay to the north of this northern loop of the Huang He, but we had now crossed to the south. The maps indicated few roads and no major settlements in the narrow strip of cultivated land lying along the floodplain on the southern bank. Speculating on what we might encounter on this little known stretch, I fell into a deep sleep.

CHAPTER THIRTEEN

SWALLOWS AND SUNFLOWERS

入乡随俗

rù xiāng suí sú

When in Rome, do as the Romans do.

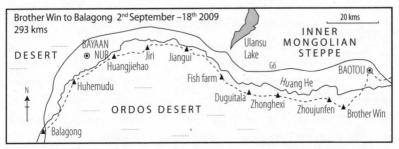

Wednesday, 2 September – Thursday, 10 September, 2009.
Brother Win Stables to Balagong.
293 km. Daily average 33 km.

I was startled awake by the sound of Russian music. Where was I? But then I remembered Li Jing was back and in the next bedroom. We had gone to bed with yet another huge meal under our belts the evening before, but it seemed Mr Zhang was not satisfied unless he was completely assured we were fortified for the whole week ahead, and lunch awaited. To our surprise, Beef Jerky Man from Hohhot turned up to join us at the table, after which we made a grand exit from the stud in the company of Mr Zhang, Beef Jerky Man and several jockeys on racehorses. The mounted procession made its way sedately down to a shallow river crossing where we were to take our leave, while Hua galloped around on Zorbee. I noticed a couple of the jockeys grinning.

Although still in Inner Mongolia, we were now at the northern edge of the Ordos plateau, an area of desert and semi-desert lying within the great northern loop of the Huang He. A couple of hundred miles to the south the remains of the Ming Great Wall mark the boundary between this sparsely populated area and the settled agriculture of the loess belt.

Nomadic tribes have grazed the Ordos since the beginning of recorded history, the name 'Ordos' probably deriving from the Turkic/Mongolic word ordu *meaning a royal camp or tent. The word has also slipped into the English language in the form of the word 'horde', no doubt through its association with invading nomadic hordes such as the Mongols.*

The location of the Ordos, where China proper borders the pastoral lands to the northwest, has meant that over the centuries it has been wrestled over by the settled Chinese and nomadic tribes. For the mounted nomads, control of the Ordos provided a base from which to strike at the heart of China. For the settled Chinese it provided a buffer zone against their barbarian enemies.

During the Qin dynasty the Xiongnu were ousted from the Ordos, partly as the Qin army adopted cavalry techniques. However the Xiongnu reclaimed it during the turmoil which followed the demise of the Qin. After a bruising defeat by the Xiongnu at Pingcheng, the Han dynasty initially used trade and subsidies to appease them, but as the prosperity and power of the dynasty grew, they took more offensive action. In the first century AD the 'Martial Emperor' Wudi drove the Xiongnu out of the Ordos again, building forts along the natural defence line of the Huang He, and extending the Han Great Wall of China to the south-east of the Ordos. The line of this wall was subsequently followed to a certain extent by the Ming dynasty wall.

Leaving the village of Zhouzhuncun the next morning we rode through sandy scrubland along the edge of the bluff marking the line where the desert dunes of the Ordos ended. A sharp distinction divides the sand-dunes, salt pans and scrub of the desert plateau to the south from the narrow belt of irrigated flood plain along the

Huang He, and far away beneath us the gleaming sheet of the great river swung across green farmland.

Dropping down the steep scarp to the cultivated land below, we found our way along rutted tracks over rough pasture and between belts of crops, occasionally scrambling across the cracked mud of dry irrigation ditches. With the help of a network of these ditches, fed by canals and channels, the floodplain supports a variety of agricultural produce. Maize rustled and waved its insect-like tendrils in the breeze, sunflowers blazed, and round green bowling balls of ripening melons littered open fields. Spaced every few miles were little hamlets with cart tracks winding between mudbrick farmhouses and tall poplars. Pigs grunted inquisitively from sties, and silky-haired flocks of pure-white Cashmere goats lazed behind makeshift fences.

We stopped to rest under trees by a mud-brick house with chickens clucking behind wire fencing and a pig lying on its side in a shelter, motionless in the midday heat. A piece of white cloth fluttered from a pole.

"It is a sign that it is a Mongolian house," explained Hua.

Outside the yard a group of people had dug a deep pit about twenty foot long by ten foot wide and lined it with a blue plastic sheet, weighted down at the sides with an assortment of items including the engine cover from a tractor. At one end maize stalks from a large pile were being fed into a chopping machine powered by the tractor. The resulting mash emptied into the pit, where a bevy of women in headscarves were treading it down. I realised it had to be a home-made silage pit to store fodder for the animals in the winter.

We relaxed in the shade while the horses grazed, swatting away the occasional insect with a swish of their tails. One of the women came over and presented us with a melon variegated in wavy green stripes. She squatted down and slashed it open to expose the succulent red innards. Sticky juice dribbled down our faces as we ate.

At longer intervals were small towns, the wide dusty verges of the main streets lined with one-storey shophouses. We could always find a simple '*binguan*' or guesthouse with basic rooms and a yard where we could leave the horses tied to the trailer overnight, and wherever there was a settlement there was always an eating house of some description. Almost every town in China contains a mobile phone tower, so internet access via my dongle was almost always possible, if slow and erratic. I could generally email even if blogging was difficult. Protruding from the landscape as church spires do in Europe, the towers marked the position of towns so we never got completely lost, and they continued to act as target landmarks all the way across China.

It had been a good decision to cross to the southern bank of the Huang He here as the northern bank is far more industrialised, and we sometimes caught distant glimpses of high-rise buildings and smokestacks to the north.

The next significant stopover was Duguitala, located at a bridge crossing over the Huang He. As we left town the usual local traffic of bicycles, mopeds, and three wheeled trucks was swelled by lorries and transporters on their way south. We picked our way up a wide degraded street between potholes and white tiled shop fronts. Telephone wires criss-crossed a leaden sky, and it was not long before rain began to pelt down. I made an attempt to jolly the troops.

'This is nothing to worry about. I ride in weather like this all the time in Wales.'

This may have been true, but Hua and Li Jing looked distinctly unimpressed.

We squelched over a waterlogged heath where a sodden wind was blowing from the north. My Cutana hat brim was protecting my glasses from trickles of rain and preventing water from creeping down my neck, but my right side was gradually becoming soaked. A long building by the road appeared through the rain-drenched mist and the boys made a beeline for it, tying the horses to a rickety fence by a rundown shed. I followed suit and we put the saddles in the shed out of the wet before dashing up to the main building through a pair of rusty gates and across a cluttered yard. The mudbrick house was not very prepossessing, but the occupants welcomed us into a couple of shabby rooms. Three men in drab clothing lounged on a *kang* watching a small television. The *kang* was heated by a wood fire in the stove, and I hung my gloves to dry on a primitive pipework central heating system on the wall which also ran off the stove. A weary young woman in a camouflage jacket offered us hot water in plastic mugs, and generously produced some *you tiao*, long sugary fried dough sticks eaten for breakfast. On a large garish poster on the wall a surprisingly youthful Mao Zedong charged headlong towards us on a fiery steed. To either side of him galloped his ministers, displaying an equestrian skill I was unaware they possessed. I recognised Zhou Enlai among them, but whether it included some of those who fell in and out of favour I cannot remember. It may be surprising to learn that Mao is still regarded as an iconic figure by much of the Chinese populace in spite of the tribulations millions of ordinary Chinese suffered as a result of the Great Leap Forward and the Cultural Revolution (of which more later). Years of propaganda will have had their effect, and the Chinese government has refrained from specific criticism as it depended to an extent on the cult of Mao for legitimacy. I was reminded of the photo of a children's choir in a Chinese magazine I had seen years before, below which the caption stated that they were singing 'Parents are kind, but not as kind as Chairman Mao'.

Li Jing disappeared while Hua and I were drying out, and when we braved the weather again it was obvious he had gone ahead on Shandan. The two remaining horses slouched side by side, dark and wet in the rain. We saddled them and set off through the mud. Hua started to complain about Zorbee.

'He feels very slow.'

'Perhaps it is the mud slowing him down.'

'No, no, I don't think so. He feels tired.'

'He can't be tired. We have only been going for an hour.'

We rode up onto the road.

'He still feels very slow,' Hua bemoaned again.

'Are you absolutely sure it is Zorbee? It looks like Shandan to me.'

To be fair it was difficult to tell in the rain. Zorbee and Shandan were both plain bays and although Shandan was distinguishable by a white pastern (the part just above his hoof) on his back foot, it was impossible to see in the mud. But the light eventually dawned. It seemed Li Jing had commandeered Zorbee again by the simple expedient of slapping on his own saddle and riding off without asking anyone.

The weather set in with a vengeance, and when Peng found a desolate restaurant overlooking a grey fish pond spattered with rain, no one contradicted the decision to stop. When the proprietress offered the use of some clean bedrooms, we decided to stay put even though the weather had started to clear.

The next morning dawned cold and overcast, but we overruled Li Jing, who wanted to stay put. Trotting across soggy grassland at the side of the road, the horses left soft hoofprints in the loam, and I was suddenly aware of being assailed by tiny chunky bodies on knife-sharp wings slicing through the air. Swallows! It was a magical experience to jog along with these little birds slinging round us on invisible wires, twittering as they went. They flicked over our heads and darted beneath the horses' noses and almost under their hooves. Cresting an embankment, we found the width of the Huang He directly in front of us, its great muddy mass agitated by watery swirls as it slid past. Surrounded by swallows, Li Jing paced ahead on Zorbee up a slippery track along the top of the dyke while Hua and I plodded behind.

Around twenty-five kilometres and several hours later, it was time to water and rest the horses, and we came back down to the road to rendezvous with the jeep. But Li Jing had taken a short cut across the grassland and the jeep was parked about a kilometre back. Hua consulted with Peng over the walkie-talkie, and relayed the outcome to me.

'We will carry on. They will come soon.'

We rode on through a belt of rolling sand dunes where the desert bulged north to the Huang He. Half an hour passed.

'Where are they, Hua?'

More consultation on the walkie-talkie.

'They say they are coming.'

Heading into the hills between Gucheng and Houcheng. Wutzala and friend lead the way, with Li Jing on Hei Feng behind.

Li Jing with Hei Feng, Shandan and Zorbee on the grasslands near Guyuan, on the day I had my accident.

Riders line up for the opening ceremony at the Xilingole endurance race. I can be recognised by my gold helmet. (Courtesy L.M.Wong)

Peng and I in Mongolian wedding outfits at Hohhot racecourse. (Courtesy L.M.Wong)

With some of our hosts in Hohhot. Hua in blue *khadag*, Beef Jerky man (with beard) and wife, Peng on far right. (Courtesy L.M.Wong)

The start of the watercourse we followed from Chahar Youyi which developed into a river valley.

The main race at the Nadaam festival.

Hua discussing directions on the way into Baotou.

With a traffic policeman in Baotou. Note the Korean corset which sorted out my back ache.

Li Jing on Shandan and Hua on Zorbee riding across the Huang He floodplain to Duguitala.

Farmer collecting willow branches near Zhoujunzhen.

Hua and I riding along the flood dyke beside the Huang He.
(Courtesy L.M.Wong)

Winnowing sunflower seeds at Houhai. Our overnight lodgings and a water tower are behind.

Braving heavy traffic was particularly horrendous where road construction was taking place, in this instance negotiating Wuda in Inner Mongolia.

Donkeys beside the No 3 canal near Shizuishan on the Ningxia floodplain.

Hua in front of the Qing fort at Zhenbeibu which now forms part of the Western China Film Studios.

At the Xixia tombs near Yinchuan with No 3 mausoleum, the tomb of Li Yuanhao, the Tangut chieftan who founded the dynasty, in the background. The Ming Great Wall runs along the foot of the Helan Shan (Helan Mts) in the distance.

A group of Hui villagers making rush matting for greenhouse covers near Guangwuxinag.

Li Jing and Hua riding along the Great Leap Forward Canal.

Li Jing and the horses take a rest by the Great Leap Forward canal.

These travelling Uighur tradesmen from Xinjiang stopped to sell us dried fruit near Hong Shui.

Herding sheep on the grasslands near Shandan stud.

Shandan mares lined up for pregnancy testing.
The ones with snipped tails are in foal.

Shandan stud. Bajiu's feet being prepared for shoeing with a planer.

A yard of pure Shandan youngsters who have recently been branded. The year of birth is branded at the top of their front leg, and an individual number on their rump.

Hua by the Great Wall between Changchengkou
and Shandan.

Shepherd and flock on the pass beneath Yanzhi mountain.

The courtyard of our lodgings at Yuanshanzi as a dust storm approaches.

Hua by a pagoda near Nanhua with the snow-capped Qilian Shan in the background.

The end of the Great Wall stage. Peng and I on Zorbee and Shandan in front of the Western Gate of Jiayuguan Fort with its reconstructed tower. (Courtesy L.M.Wong)

All photos taken by Megan Knoyle Lewis unless otherwise indicated.

An hour passed, and Hua contacted them again.

'They are cooking and then they will come.'

I frowned. Our horses had not drunk for hours and we were now in the middle of a sea of sand.

It was not until yet another hour or so had passed that they eventually caught up with us at the small village of Chengui Geliang, forty kilometres from the fish farm. For some reason Zorbee was trotting along behind the trailer on a lead rope. I was not best pleased that Shandan and Bajiu had gone without water all day when I was sharing the expenses of a support vehicle, and a row ensued, during which Li Jing rather ironically pontificated about us riding off ahead. It was not until months later that Hua told me the whole story. Li Jing had fallen off again when Zorbee became anxious at being left behind. Macho pride evidently prevented him from admitting it, and presumably Peng and Li May had been sworn to secrecy. Hua and I had carried on with our thirsty horses, none the wiser to the drama unfolding behind.

Before the rain set in again Peng negotiated rooms at a farmhouse by the road. It was a miserable damp evening, not helped by our disagreements. Water poured off the roof, slopped on the pavement, and lay in pools around the house. Beyond stretched a bleak drenched grassland plain. Wet clayey soil stuck to our boots in clumps so it was impossible not to carry mud inside. The electric plug in our room didn't work so to use the internet I had to dash through the wet to use the plug in the cold muddy trailer. Even the Chinese farmer slipped and fell on the slimy yard, and glared at me sourly when I asked if he was OK. It was easier to stay huddled up in a sleeping bag on the unheated *kang* in the clammy air of our room, although it was early evening.

The following morning Li Jing paced off far ahead of us on the gravel track running along the Huang He embankment taking a little flock of swallows with him. It seemed that it was alright for him to leave us behind, but not the other way round. Not that I minded. Hua and I ambled along together, chatting and arguing amicably. The main stream of the Huang He swung south along the bank here, the strong turbid current relentlessly gliding past, the surface ruffled by underwater turmoil and the edges fraying in little ripples against the banks.

'No alligators here,' commented Hua enigmatically.

The sandy plain stretched away from the river, covered with thin grassland interspersed with patches of sunflowers struggling to survive in the wet soil.

'Why do they always face east?' I asked Hua. 'You would expect them to face south.' But Hua was already creating a trail of hoofprints in the sludge on the track as he cantered ahead on Shandan, and I trotted Bajiu to catch up. The Korean corset was having an effect, and my back was improving all the time.

The rain continued to hold off and over the next few days we followed the earth tracks which ran alongside the canals. These were mostly wide waterways lined with concrete blocks, sometimes full of shimmering water, sometimes drained and exposing their sandy floor. Every so often it was possible to cross from one side to another by a bridge or occasional sluice gate. The canals kept us off road and provided straight easy routes through the tranquil maize fields and grasslands of the floodplain. Li Jing continued to disappear sporadically on Zorbee while Hua and I sauntered along talking to passing locals and stopping to graze the horses wherever there was a good patch of grass. Peng was concerned that our hay supplies might run out before we could stock up again at Yinchuan, although we had plenty of maize feed and could always get hold of maize stalks.

Not far from Jirigalangtu a herdsman in camouflage jacket and red baseball cap watched his herd of white goats pick their way along the slumped banks of an unlined canal. A single black goat wandered among them.

'Why is there a black goat, Hua?'

'Anti devil.'

'Ah – protection against the devil.'

'Yes, protection against the devil.'

The herdsman leant on his stick and called out across the water.

'*Nimen she zuo sha de?* What are you doing?'

'*Women shi luyou de.* We are travelling,' answered Hua. '*Qu Lundun.* Going to London.'

'*Qu Lundun luyou qi zhe ma?* Riding to London by horse?'

An element of surprise had crept into his voice.

'*Dui.* Yes.'

The herdsmen pondered.

'*Zhou you shijie?* Around the world?'

Hua laughed but answered in the affirmative.

Where the floodplain was squeezed between the river and the Ordos desert, a low line of sand dunes was clearly visible on the horizon to the south. Once we saw distant camels standing motionless by isolated buildings across a sandy waste. Another time we passed wetlands where black and grey cranes lifted off rush fringed lakes and white egrets poised around fish ponds. We followed the same canal for nearly three days, sometimes with a retinue of swallows jinking and diving and flinging parabolas around us. Grey clouds inched across the sky and the air smelt of rain though it never arrived. Far away across the bleak floodplain to our right and on the other side of the unseen river a distant pale alien city of high-rise buildings could just be made out through the haze.

'Bayaan Nuur,' said Hua.

After riding along the canal all day, we stopped for lunch near the little town of Mata Erwan. A tall figure with a splendid mane of dark curly hair tied back in a long pony tail suddenly appeared out of nowhere with a slim, blonde female companion, both on bicycles. The first westerners I had seen for weeks, they turned out to be Juan and Marta, a couple of Spanish travellers cycling around China and Mongolia. Juan's glorious locks put Li Jing's to shame, and certainly wowed the crowd of Chinese who queued to have their photos taken with him. Even Li Jing suddenly burst into life and spoke more English than I had heard from him since we left Beijing. They signed the trailer and we exchanged addresses with little expectation of seeing each other again. But the next day they cycled up at our midday rest stop and joined us for noodles at the side of the road.

We stayed in a variety of places: a simple guest house in Jirigalangtu, with a welcoming family in a Chinese home by the canal at Huangjie hao, and at Huhemudu, a small hotel where the manageress let Li May and I use her spacious room with tiled floor and desk and served us milk-free 'Mongolian tea'. We made steady progress, covering around thirty-five kilometres a day, and on 10 September, ten days after we had left Baotou, we reached the town of Balagong at the north-west corner of the Ordos loop. At this point the major transport lines from Beijing crossed from the north of the Huang He to run southwards along the east bank of the river. This included the railway and new G6 Jingzang Expressway from Beijing, which would ultimately run to Lhasa in Tibet. It also marked the end of the quieter rural area we had been riding through. We had meant to take a day off here, but the only accommodation we could find was at dismal hotel in a block of lorry workshops. There was not a blade of grass in the grubby yard full of coal dust at the back and it did not take us long to decide to move on the next day. Li Jing fell back on his cooking skills to produce supper in the little trailer kitchen, but I was unsurprised to find it was tofu, which he knew I was not keen on. I hoped this was not a prescient warning of things to come.

CHAPTER FOURTEEN

COAL COUNTRY

守得云开见月明
shǒu dé yún kāi jiàn yuè míng
Every cloud has a silver lining.

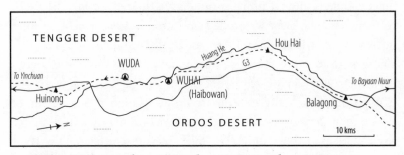

Friday, 11 September – Monday, 14 September, 2009.
Balagong to Huinong (Ningxia).
133 km. Daily average 33 km.

A bare, windswept wasteland faced us as we picked our way through stony desert to the side of the old road out of Balagong. Apart from a few cars, agricultural vehicles and the odd lorry, it was relatively quiet. The occasional train rumbled past on the parallel railway track, and Juan and Marta flashed past on their bikes, whistling and waving.

Forty kilometres further on, we found Peng parked in front of a low garage workshop in the small village of Houhai, within sight of the Huang He. A sparkler of flame spat from a welding gun held by a mechanic crouching down by the jeep, which was jacked up at the back. The weight of the water tank at the front of the trailer was beginning to cause problems with the suspension and it needed repairs. At the rear of the building was a redbrick block of three rooms fronted by metal doors and window frames, and it seemed a

151

good place to halt for the night. Li May and I were shown to a tidy room with neatly folded quilts on a *kang*. A herd of cashmere goats contemplated us from behind a ragged palisade of sticks outside, and a thick, grey layer of crushed sunflower heads was spread out on an open space about thirty foot across. A woman in a red headscarf flung shovelfuls against a large square framed sieve propped up on a stick to sift out the seeds, and Peng and I were drafted in to help. Our hostess made fresh noodles for the occasion, kneading and rolling out the dough into a thin layer on a large floured wooden board in the kitchen. The layer was rolled up into a sausage and sliced into narrow strips with a sharp knife, magically producing flat noodles. These were added to soup steaming in a wok over the wood stove.

I was rather bemused at one point in the evening when the women burst excitedly into our room and dumped a large bag of *xigua*, or watermelons, on the floor. I was on my own and unable to understand their quickfire talk. Was I cluttering up their storeroom? They returned with notebooks. It seemed I was expected to autograph them, but when I complied it was made clear they also wanted it in hanzi, or Chinese characters. This was a bit more of a problem. Luckily Hua turned up to help out, and also explained that the mysterious melons were a gift!

In rural areas the toilets were mostly outdoor slit-in-the-floor affairs tucked behind low brick walls, either in the yard or along the street, though public toilets might be in a small brick shed and contain two or more communal slits. In comparison, the twenty-slitter public convenience in Houhai village was an impressive edifice. Chinese characters for men and women, *nan* and *nu*, were painted in blue at separate entrances to a solid square white building set on a patch of wasteland. The grey concrete in the women's room was blotched and stained, but there was a line of ten cubicles created by waist-height dividing walls which provided a measure of privacy not always available in public loos. The whole building hung over a voluminous almost empty cesspit which disconcertingly puffed draughty air up one's nether regions. I wondered how long the huge pit would take to fill. Judging by the meagre contents and the rate of urbanisation in China, the local residents would have moved to modern city apartments with flush toilets long before that happened.

Although existence in rural areas was austere and facilities very basic, the simple, uncomplicated lifestyle it presented increasingly appealed to me. It was an immense privilege to be accepted so warmly into the humdrum bustle of people's daily lives and feel the enveloping sense of close community in the villages. One felt one could reach out and touch people's lives in a very real and intimate way, even if you were only a visitor. It brought home the fact that people are not so different all over the world. There are the same doting mothers with their chubby babies, the same naughty boys and shy giggling girls, the same families struggling to better their lives. Luxurious hotels in sophisticated city centres may have had all the comforts one would wish for, but their artificial environments lacked one thing: soul.

The modern world, however, was creeping in everywhere, and mobile phones were ubiquitous. It was also noticeable that even the most spartan of households contained that staple of state control, a subsidised television with a diet of carefully approved and censored programmes.

I was travelling China in a way only a handful of westerners have had the chance to do, and every day's riding was a joy. Wandering deep into parts of the country where few foreigners ventured, exploring secluded tracks through remote settlements, and connecting with ordinary rural Chinese was the immersive experience I had hoped for, and it fully lived up to my expectations. People often asked me how I felt about travelling in a strange land such as China, and of course I replied that it did not feel strange, and I loved it.

One father shared his son's gap year experience.

'Yes, he loved China too, but he felt more at home when he went to South America, because it was more European.'

I let the comment sink in, suddenly realising that although I had not been to South America, it would not have been at all the same for me. My Far Eastern childhood had seeped irrevocably into my bones, and a small part of me would always belong to Asia. From the moment I arrived in Beijing, I felt at home. The sights, sounds and smells were completely familiar, from the Chinese faces to the sing-song speech and spicy smell of street noodles. The only thing that was missing was the hot, steamy Malaysian air.

It was a pity then, that partly due to the friction with Li Jing, I was feeling increasingly excluded and miserable in the evenings. The rest of the group chattered in Chinese at a rate I could not keep up with. Peng could not speak any English, and Li Jing chose not to speak to me at all. The only reason Li May had been included in the party was to interpret for me, but irritatingly she rarely did so unless I specifically asked. Rather than sit like a lemon while everyone else laughed and joked, I began to resort to retreating to my room as soon as we had eaten, and having an early night after writing my diary.

Hua and I went for a twilight walk in an unsuccessful attempt to reach the river. We stood in a dark field of sunflowers drooping their heavy ripened heads like a weary army, a fiery streak of fading sunlight lighting the horizon, and I vented my feelings.

'I find Li Jing so difficult. He just ignores me even when I try to be friendly.'

'Don't worry about him. It is just his way.'

'And I want to improve my Chinese but you talk too fast. Can't you sometimes speak more slowly or let me know what you are talking about so I can join in.'

'We are talking about nothing.'

'What do you mean, nothing?'

'It is nothing interesting.'

'But it is interesting to me.'

'It is not interesting.'

But talking with Hua eased some of my frustrations and I returned feeling a bit more positive and resolved to 'go with the flow'. As part of the philosophy of the quintessentially Chinese Daoist religion, it seemed a good time to embrace this approach.

The area became more industrialised and although we managed to keep off the road for much of the way and ride through fields lined with poplars, and little villages where donkeys pulled rubber-wheeled carts piled with shaky loads of green maize stalks, in the distance loomed the steel and concrete towers of heavy industry. Down a sandy track we came to where the Huang He swung closer. Splashing across a flooded, mowed hay field we came to the abrupt edge of a low, crumbling river bank fringed with eyelashes of uncut grass. I leant down to dip my hand in the muddy soup of eddying water, and Hua encouraged Shandan to drink.

'You be careful he doesn't fall in, Hua.'

The current looked strong and deep, and I had nightmare visions of the bank collapsing, plunging Shandan into the water to be swept away.

We scrambled back up the flood embankment to follow the gravel track running along the top. Ahead, beneath a mackerel sky and across a wide gleaming arc of river bend, a city began to appear from a pale layer of haze. Dark silhouettes of high-rise buildings emerged in a gap-toothed row, and a necklace of pearls grew into shining white apartment blocks. Behind lay the faint outline of the Ordos plateau and the sharp pyramid of Gande'er mountain. Located on the outside bank of a meander on the Huang He, Wuhai grew up around local coal mining and is now a centre for power, steel and chemicals. Like many other Chinese towns and cities, it had been caught up in the national frenzy of construction. As we rode from the old rambling outskirts into modern redeveloped section along the top of the river cliff, we passed block upon block of brand new apartments, many still topped with cranes and almost all apparently empty.

Shandan's loose shoes clinked as we led the horses along a narrow marble path winding through a strip of park which hung above terraces overlooking the river bend.

'Shandan needs shoeing, Hua,' I pointed out. But Bajiu's shoes were also in a bad state, partly due to his tendency to drag his hind feet and wear away the front.

Peng had found a hotel in an ugly three-storey building just to the south of the town centre. Tiny rooms were crammed in along narrow corridors. Li May and I found ourselves in an inner windowless room. The light was activated by a sort of toggle switch at the end of an electric wire hanging out of the wall.

'I can't say I feel very safe here,' I said gloomily. 'It is a real fire trap.'

'But at least the electrics are good,' said Li May brightly.

For the next two days we rode deeper into an industrial zone of cement works, power stations and chemical works. The hills to the east were faint in the smog of drifting polluted air, and stretching to the south of Wuhai was a confusion of roads. Land was being grubbed up for modern development and new transport systems, shouldering aside the green rows of broccoli and cucumbers in surrounding market gardens. We led the horses over a narrow bridge in the fumes of a river of traffic steadily rumbling past, and detoured past roadworks along rubble-strewn tracks through choking dust thrown up by trucks. Occasionally a new sweep of road had been gouged out of the landscape and we were able to follow the tamped earth surface, picking our way between heavy construction machinery but away from the madness of the traffic.

On one busy road we passed a masonry work yard with rows of decorative stone lions lined up at the front. Designed to stand as a guardian pair on either side of entrances, they included a female with her paw on a cub, and a male with his paw on a ball. They reminded me of the Chinese tongue twister:

'Sì shì sì, shí shì shí, shísì shì shísì, sìshí shì sìshí, sìshísì zhī shí shīzi shì sǐ de.'

'Four is four, ten is ten, fourteen is fourteen, forty is forty.

Forty-four stone lions are dead.'

Meaningless without the right tone inflections, it is good practice for Chinese learners!

We crossed back to the western bank of the Huang He via a long narrow bridge crowded with clamorous vehicles, and entered Wuda, an industrial district officially part of Wuhai city.

The horses desperately needed shoeing. Peng had managed to put rubber tyre shoes on Shandan the day before by securing him to the side of the trailer with ropes, but this was not ideal. A row of young trees by a line of shops presented an opportunity, and Peng wedged a pole between two of them at head height to make a primitive shoeing frame. Zorbee and Bajiu were also going to be shod with rubber tyre. The remains of the metal shoes were prised off and the hooves cut back. Peng had already cut out square pieces from a suitable tyre, and these were nailed carefully onto the foot, before trimming off the excess with a sharp paring knife. Gone was the clatter of horse shoes down the metalled road. From now on the horses plopped softly along in their new sneakers.

We stayed overnight at a depressing truck stop, with a yard chock a block full of lorries. Our dingy room had a filthy stained sheet for a curtain, and I abstained from using an uninviting shower room behind the boiler. Equally dispiriting was the following day's ride through Wuda, dodging a turmoil of traffic. The horses intermingled perilously with trucks, coaches, cars, bicycles and mopeds at junctions, and squeezed through tiny gaps at traffic jams, while a pall of yellow dust rose over the roar. I was so busy marvelling how Hua inserted Shandan into narrow spaces between vehicles that it was only when I later studied a photo I had taken of him in action that I saw that one of the vehicles he was squeezing past was a police car. Hua rode like a bandit with a red bandana pulled up over the lower part of his face, all the while keeping me entertained with snippets of amusing information. He pointed across a busy road lined with low grimy buildings.

'The double linguistic Free School.'

'What?'

'Bilingual Free School – how do you say – ugly duckling?'

'Ugly duckling? Ah – the ugly duckling becomes a beautiful swan!'

'Yes – the Ugly Duckling Bilingual Free School.'

Another time he chuckled as we passed a sign for a bus stop.

'It is for, how do you say – stinky well.'

I wondered if anyone got off at a location with such an unfortunate name.

As we neared the Ningxia border, I became a little concerned that Bajiu was a touch lame in one of his hind feet. An insignificant unlevel gait could quickly develop into a lameness which might delay our progress for days, though with my endurance riding background I could be a bit paranoid and over-cautious. It could mean everything or nothing. Perhaps it was just a minor knock, or a little soreness from foot trimming before the rubber shoe was nailed on. More worryingly it could also be a misplaced nail, bruised sole, or something even more serious. One of the nails did look a little high, and possibly it had pricked the sensitive interior of his foot inside the hoof. The pity is that horses cannot talk, so we often had to resort to guessing where the problem lay, or even if a problem existed at all. I decided to play safe and walk Bajiu so as not to aggravate any potential issue.

Li Jing had gone ahead on Zorbee as usual. When Hua started to trot off after him, Bajiu yanked at the bit, tossed his head and jiggled around, completely defeating the purpose of walking.

'Can you walk with me, Hua?'

'Why can't you trot?'

'Because I am worried Bajiu may be a little lame. Please walk with me.'

'Why? It doesn't make any difference if you walk or trot when a horse is lame.'

He trotted off after Li Jing. After a day of being deafened by snarling traffic and breathing in a brew of exhaust fumes and dust, this ridiculous lack of cooperation was the last straw and I dissolved into tears.

All at once a tollgate appeared ahead, topped with three domes patterned in blue and white Mongolian swirls. It heralded our exit from Inner Mongolia and entry into Ningxia province. We stopped to take photos, a bit sniffly in my case, but I soon cheered up as we crossed the border into our next province. After spending six weeks in Inner Mongolia it was a real excitement to reach Ningxia, and get another chunk of the journey under my belt.

Although we had been riding through an area where industrial sprawl was rapidly consuming desert and farmland, and cement works, chemical factories and power stations lined the dust-choked roads, even this unappealing region was filled with unique interest. The landscape might be dreary and frustrations constant, but it all added to the rich experience of travelling through China.

'Look, we are 1,111 kilometres from Beijing,' said Hua as we passed a stone distance marker on the old 110 National road we were following. Of course, our detours meant we must have covered an even greater distance, but it still felt like a landmark achievement. A little further on Peng found a truck stop with pleasant rooms overlooking a yard shaded by trees, though coal dust drifted in from the railroad coal terminal nearby. It had a large dingy communal shower room with floor to ceiling white tiles, eight taps in place of shower heads, and a curtain for a door. I posted Li May to guard the entrance in case I gave any truckers a nasty shock while I enjoyed a 'shower'.

Lying in my sleeping bag on our first night in Ningxia, I was happy that I had persuaded Peng to let Bajiu take a break and ride in the trailer until we were sure he was sound, and Li Jing had agreed to join them. For the moment it would be just Hua and I on Zorbee and Shandan as we tackled the new province.

CHAPTER FIFTEEN

TOMBS AND MOSQUES

师傅领进门，修行在个人
Shī fu lǐng jìn mén, xiū xíng zài gè rén
Teachers open the door. You enter by yourself.

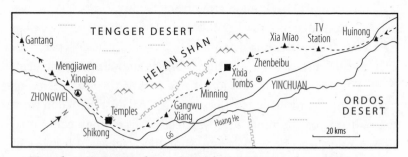

Tuesday, 15 September – Saturday, 26 September, 2009.
Huinong to Gantang.
363 km. Daily average 36 km.

It was both an excitement and an anticlimax to suddenly come across a northern outlier of the Ming Great Wall of China where it intersected the road near Hongguozi about twenty-five kilometres south of the Ningxia border. A thrill to be back after so many months, but a disappointment to find that instead of the immense stone and brick structure which switchbacks over the hills to the north of Beijing, there was now a Not So Great Wall. A degraded earth bank about five foot high ran off through a gap between tatty shophouses towards the Helan mountains. At intervals short crumbling segments of the wall about ten foot high jutted upwards like rotting teeth, the edges worn and rounded by years of weathering. Here in the west, the wall was built of layers of tamped earth, often incorporating sand, stones and binding layers of reeds. It might then be faced with wood, or locally-fired mud bricks sometimes mortared with sticky glutinous rice. In places the wall was just a mud embankment. This wall was obviously not so resistant to weathering as the wall further east, and its deterioration was accelerated by locals helping themselves to the brick facings. We rode the horses up onto the low bank to have our photos taken by the remaining wall segments, on which faint lines about a foot in depth indicated the original tamped layers.

Although Ningxia is one of the smallest provinces in China, like the Ordos directly to the east it has historically been an area of great strategic importance. By the eleventh century the Xi Xia or Western Xia had established themselves here, but they were defeated by Genghis Khan. The Mongol-led Yuan dynasty, founded by Genghis's grandson Kublai, was overthrown in 1368 by ethnic Han Chinese to bring in the Ming dynasty. The Ming dynasty Great Wall of China was built over the next couple of centuries to keep out the Mongols, though this wall follows the line of the old Han wall to some extent. Through Ningxia the wall loops north keeping out the dry Ordos plateau to the east and enclosing the fertile Yinchuan plain where the Huang He valley broadens out below the Qingtong gorge. The wall turns south again along the bare Helan Shan, or Helan mountains, to flank the plain on the west.

The irrigated Yinchuan plain forms a huge oasis in an area of barren desert and semi-desert, and explains why successive Chinese emperors were so intent on keeping it within the bounds of China Proper. Watered by the Huang He, it is well served by canals, some of them up to two thousand years old. I had hoped to use the quiet tracks running alongside them, as did Robin and Louella Hanbury-Tenison during their journey along the Great Wall in 1985. But without decent maps it was difficult to identify a route, and we continued for over thirty kilometres along the old 110 National Highway. This was still quite busy even though most of the traffic was siphoned off by the new G6 Jingzang Expressway, the same road which runs past Kangzhuang from Beijing. Up until now we had partly relied on the Chinese members of the team quizzing locals for directions, and word of mouth came to our aid again. A passing motorcyclist told us of a stables near Shizuishan, and a crab breeder who came to talk to us gave directions for a short cut down a side road to a gravel track running along the quiet tree-lined No 3 canal. We accepted an invitation to drink tea with him and admire the narrow tanks of live long-armed crabs and huge gulping carp stacked up inside his shop.

The stables were located by the canal and attached to a resort run by a local television station. They housed about twenty horses used for filming, and Zorbee, Shandan and Bajiu joined the film stars in a large bare paddock while we were given a guided tour of the premises. Centred round a tall television mast, the complex included various stage sets and an extraordinary orchard of real trees growing under a huge steel frame building with a glass roof. It was apparently used for 'alfresco' functions, not I assume of the bacchanalian variety. At the back of the plot was a mosquito-ridden lake fringed with rushes. The manageress took us for a Ningxia version of fondue in the restaurant where woks were set into the tiled tops of brick tables. We added ingredients of our choice (lamb, leafy vegetables and noodles) to a boiling stew in our table-centre wok, picking them out with our chopsticks when they were cooked. This was accompanied by a hot fruit tea, a local speciality made with the red *goji* or wolfberries for which Ningxia is famous.

It seemed a good place to take a day off, in particular as the television studio wanted to interview us. The next morning the horses were dragged out of the paddock for filming. I declined the opportunity to ride a large black Yili horse, a breed from the Yili valley in Xinjiang. Was I glad I had done so when the horse suffered a complete brake and steering failure and carted the stable girl riding him ignominiously back to the stables. A few minutes later I realised to my horror that she had saddled Bajiu and was wrenching his head round and kicking her heels hard into his sides to gallop off, or at least as fast as the poor animal could manage. So much for his day off.

'*Qing bu qi, ta shi bo jiao*. Please don't ride him. He is lame,' I pleaded. My Chinese vocabulary was pretty limited, but it did stretch to a range of words and phrases relating to horses.

I succeeded in saving Bajiu from further abuse, but then had to endure the sight of her meting out the same treatment to sensitive little Zorbee.

On Thursday, 17 September, Hua and I continued with Zorbee and Shandan for around thirty-five kilometres along No 3 canal. We dodged the water sprinklers in an enormous landscaped water park of huge lakes to the southeast of Shizuishan, and rode out into peaceful countryside where a work force of villagers was building the earth wall of a house. Eventually we cut across to the noisy main road, coming out a couple of kilometres beyond the lodgings at Xia Miao that Peng had found. It was possibly the worst place I stayed at the whole time I was in China. The horses were tied to the trailer in a grimy rubble-strewn coal and sand yard at the back, while Li May and I glumly surveyed the stained bedding on four bunk beds crammed into a filthy room with ceiling panels hanging down around a bare light bulb. Loops of electric wires were festooned between the smudged walls and when I ran my finger along the top bar of my bunk it came away black with coal dust. Getting to the toilets across the road in the rapidly falling dark meant running the gauntlet of blinding headlights from a constant stream of vehicles kicking coal dust into our faces. The meal at the restaurant next door would have been fine if we had not all been coughing so much. If nothing else it made me realise what an excellent decision it had been to follow the advice given by our Chinese backers to avoid the coal mining area of Shanxi, and how wrong I had been to grumble about our detour to the north.

To add insult to injury, when we set off the next morning, I realised I had left my mobile phone behind. By the time Peng had driven back to search, it had disappeared and the proprietor denied any knowledge of its whereabouts.

In contrast, our hotel at Zhenbeibu near Yinchuan was expensive, but the basic bedrooms, bedding and shower rooms were spotless, and an added plus was the view from the window across a dry field to the bulwarks of an old Qing fort and movie studios whose proximity was no doubt a reason for the inflated prices. Hua and I wandered up past the forty-foot high walls where colourful pennants fluttered above the cracked and pockmarked sides. Replica siege ladders and wooden chariots were lined up outside a reconstructed archway to the interior. It was all rather commercialised and we decided not to pay the fee to go inside as it was late and we were tired.

The complex, which also contained the ruins of an old Ming fort partially destroyed in an earthquake, was developed by the Western China Film Studios after writer Zhang Xianlang encouraged its use as a film location in the early 1980s. He had become aware of the old forts when he was sent to a work camp nearby during the Cultural Revolution. I was later intrigued to find out that scenes from Zhang Yimou's famous film *Red Sorghum* and other well-known movies were shot here, and regretted not making more effort to look around on our day off. Instead, this was spent sorting out new supplies of hay for the horses, and day tripping to Yinchuan where local horseman Mr He treated us to another Ningxia fondue with all the trimmings. A planned visit to the Western Xia tombs was foiled when we found them closed, but fortuitously our route the next day took us right past the entrance.

In the 1930s a young German aviation pioneer by the rambling name of Wulf-Diether Graf zu Castell-Rüdenhausen took aerial photos of what he described as 'strange earthen mounds' on the gravel alluvial plain at the base of the Helan Shan to the west of Yinchuan. On publishing a photo in his 1938 book Chinaflug *he described it as depicting the 'Hsia[2] royal tombs'. This was surprising, since amazingly it seemed that all the experts studying the ruined Western Xia city of Khara-Khoto further north were totally ignorant*

---

[2] Wade-Giles version of 'Xia'

of these archaeological remains. To all intents and purposes these curious conical structures had stayed forgotten and unacknowledged for nearly seven hundred and fifty years. And incredibly, although Castell-Rüdenhausen's aerial 'find' suggested that some people were aware of these tombs, it was not until 1972 that they were officially re-discovered by a Chinese army unit who accidentally dug up pieces of clay pots and inscribed bricks while constructing an airfield in the area. Archaeologists were sent to the site and within ten days had dug up an ancient tomb chamber which was formally identified as a Western Xia imperial mausoleum. To top it all, over the next twenty years or so, nine imperial tombs and over two hundred and fifty lesser tombs were rediscovered scattered over an area ten kilometres long by five kilometres wide. Who were the people who built this immense abandoned necropolis?

The Western Xia or Xi Xia dynasty was founded in the first half of the eleventh century by the Dangxiang or Tangut people who originated from the Tibet-Qinghai region to the west. The Xi Xia dynasty co-existed uneasily with the Song empire during the eleventh and twelfth centuries. Tantric Buddhists who developed an economically and culturally advanced regime centred on their first capital Qingjing (present day Yinchuan) on the fertile Yinchuan plain, the Western Xia held sway for almost two hundred years over an area which also encompassed the Ordos loop of the Huang He, and the grasslands of the Hexi Corridor to the west. They were agriculturalists and breeders of Dangxiang horses on the Gansu grasslands to the west, devoting an entire government department to livestock breeding. Heavily influenced by the neighbouring Han Chinese, they developed their own legal code and more particularly their own unique script (resembling but not copying hanzi) which was used in a myriad of printed documents. Then, quite abruptly, they disappeared from history leaving hardly a trace of their civilisation. What cataclysmic event caused this to happen?

Quite simply, they fell foul of Genghis Khan, the ambitious and ruthless Mongol leader who was aggressively expanding his domain in the thirteenth century. And woe betide anyone who stood in his way.

The Western Xia emperors made the fatal mistake of failing to fully cooperate with Genghis Khan and more seriously failing to surrender immediately to his attacking forces in 1227. When the last emperor Mozhu finally capitulated, the Western Xia civilisation was wiped from the face of the earth.

Genghis Khan in fact met his death on this campaign although even the details of this event are shrouded in mystery. One legend relates that he was poisoned to death by a captured Western Xia princess, but many scholars now believe he may have died belatedly from injuries incurred in falls from his horse. There is also a school of thought contending that the obliteration of the Western Xia dynasty may have been carried out posthumously on orders from his deathbed. Whatever the truth, it is almost certain that he died somewhere in the region, although controversy also rages as to whether he was interred locally or his body was carried back to Mongolia.

Peng had re-shod Bajiu, he appeared sound, and it seemed probable that it had been a misplaced nail. Li Jing, Hua and I all set out on the forty-three kilometres to Minningzhen, of course making an obligatory stop at the *Xi Xia Ling* or Western Xia tombs.

I felt the 60 yuan (£5) entrance fee to the tombs was a trifle steep considering it only included access to one mausoleum, but I suppose the tombs were too widely spaced to conveniently allow more comprehensive access. At the entrance to the gift shop a sign mysteriously proclaimed 'Forbids to Climb' over a stick depiction of a man climbing a ladder. Where were the ladders and why couldn't we climb them? The general aura of mystery continued, as the tourist shop frustratingly contained not a single detailed English guide book. The site signs were all in hanzi and none of the team were with me to translate, so I wandered round the mausoleum in a complete haze of ignorance.

A line of grotesque squat stone figures crouched at the top of a low stone ramp. Perhaps these were representatives of the fearful 'kneeling statues unearthed with sticking teeth, glower and plump breasts with unknown significance and functions' I subsequently saw described in an online Chinese guide. The description certainly seemed to fit. Beyond them within a wide courtyard surrounded by a pitted earth wall clad with the remnants of brick facings, one of the curious pyramid-like features Castell-Rüdenhausen had seen from his aeroplane towered twenty-five metres above me. The bulky earth structure was ridged with earth layers and honeycombed with holes so it seemed like an enormous beehive, but there did not appear to be an entrance. What did it all mean?

It was only when I got home and did a bit of research that I discovered this was No. 3 mausoleum, the tomb of the great Li Yuanhao, the able and ambitious Tangut chieftain who founded the dynasty in 1038. Li Yuanhao was apparently also a sneaky military strategist, as one story tells how he tricked the Song commander Ren Fu's army by placing a hundred pigeons in clay boxes at an ambush site on their route. A few Tangut soldiers feigned retreat to draw the Song army to the ambush point, where the curious Song soldiers opened the boxes. A flock of released birds swirled up, acting both as an attack alert and a location marker for the Tangut forces who swooped down, killing Ren Fu and routing his army.

According to one scholar, whereas the tomb itself lies in an underground chamber reached by a hidden passage accessed from a different part of the courtyard, the 'beehive' may be a form of Buddhist stupa or shrine. The honeycomb holes in the structure of the 'beehives' and the existence of pieces of coloured tile around them suggest that they once supported brilliant pagoda-like roofs.

'Allahu akhbar.' It seemed strange to hear the haunting wail of the imam at the local mosque calling the faithful to prayer. The sound spread through the rosy morning air as we rode out of our truck stop lodgings at Minningzhen, an evocative reminder of the mosque's Middle Eastern origins. The Western Xia were devout Buddhists, but a more recent feature of Ningxia is its large population of Hui people, an ethnic Chinese group who practice Islam. Making up about a third of the population of the province, as well as having a strong presence in other parts of China, they are a constant reminder that Ningxia lies at the western end of the Silk Road, along which first Buddhism and then Islam was carried from the west. Apart from the white skull caps worn by the men, the Muslim Hui population is not particularly distinguishable from other Chinese. The women wear headscarves, but so do many non-Muslim Chinese women. However, it meant that we could expect some restaurants not to serve pork dishes, and lamb was an integral part of the Ningxia cuisine, as we had already experienced. The signs outside the low lines of shops and restaurants on either side of the roads occasionally displayed snippets of Arabic writing, and I noticed that many of the posters decorating interior walls now showed domed and towered mosques in Middle Eastern landscapes surrounded by borders of Arabic script, rather than the usual stirring depictions of Mao, idyllic landscapes with waterfalls or idealised western lifestyles. One fact which caught my interest was that the Chinese word for horse (*ma*) is also used as a shortened form of Mohammed to create the common Hui surname Ma. I was surprised to read that Zheng He, the famous Ming admiral and eunuch who sailed as far as East Africa, was born a Hui named Ma He.

After a tedious day trudging forty-seven kilometres along the main road to stay at a truck stop near Guangwuxiang, we attempted to scramble across country to a canal we had noticed running parallel on our map. Climbing over a small hillock we came across a small group of Hui making rush mats. Four women in jackets, trousers, head scarves, protective gloves and gauze face-nets fed bundles of stiff dry stalks into a primitive wooden loom. Twelve large bobbins on the top supplied twine to the contraption, and a thick wad of matting gradually emerged in a strip about six foot wide on the other side. The mats were almost certainly being made for use on traditional Chinese greenhouses, long rows of which are commonly found near major towns. The rectangular three-sided brick sheds can be hundreds of yards in length. A curved frame on the open side supports plastic sheeting which lets the light and warmth in. Rolled up strips of rush matting are then fixed to the apex of the greenhouses, and can be rolled up or down over the plastic sheeting to control the temperature and light. An elderly man in white skull cap and goatee supervised the mat production and looked at us suspiciously. But he willingly gave directions down to the canal and we struggled over a deep ditch and through a maize field to where a rough track – sometimes rutted earth, sometimes gravel – ran along the bank.

'It is called the Leap Forward Canal,' said Hua, consulting the map. 'In 1958 probably, there was a movement or campaign called …'

'… the Great Leap Forward,' I interjected.

The so-called Great Leap Forward was Chairman Mao's disastrous attempt in 1958-62 to thrust China into the modern world by means of rapid industrialisation and collectivisation. In fact, it turned out to be more of a great leap back. Rushed planning and lack of adequate expertise resulted in poor decision-making and badly executed campaigns. One of his more lunatic ideas was the promotion of 'backyard furnaces' in which ordinary people were coerced into creating steel by melting down scrap metal, including their own agricultural implements and utensils. Of course, the steel was substandard and virtually useless, added to which villagers were so busy smelting their cooking pots that they had no time to farm. The negative impact of the Great Leap Forward is held to be responsible for the Great Chinese Famine in which countless millions of Chinese died. The marginalisation of Mao after this fiasco led him to initiate the Cultural Revolution to regain power.

'Yes, I was wondering if it was built then.'

Hua checked the map again and commented smugly, 'We will follow this canal and "leap forward" probably all the way to just after Zhongwei.'

In fact, we were forced off the canal path several kilometres before Zhongwei, but for two days it provided a quiet, rural route. In one place it ran along an embankment lined with towering old trees, in another it sliced through deep red-earth cuttings. Sometimes we caught a far glimpse of a long train on the parallel railway line to the north, or the glint of the Huang He to the south. Once or twice we came across a narrow concrete channel constructed to carry canal water over a water course: then I got off and led Bajiu carefully across the three-foot-wide concrete slabs covering part of the channel while Hua rode ahead, impervious to any danger. As we passed settlements, chained guard dogs barked at us, or lap dogs running free yapped frantically. On a dusty track through maize fields on the first afternoon, a little flock of grey birds with black caps and long tails shadowed us, flitting through the bushes on the other side of the canal. Later on, small flocks of another sort flew past: chattering schoolchildren on bicycles wobbling along the path and turning to look at us curiously. A scarecrow stood sentinel in a yellowing field of rice, two plastic shopping bags hanging from his stick arms.

Just beyond Shikong where we stayed overnight, we rode into a village along a concrete path through rice fields and a grove of slender trees.

'Date trees,' pronounced Hua.

I was a little confused. I thought dates grew on palms, but what did I know? Perhaps it was different in China. Or perhaps he meant olives.

At the end of the village street we came to a bridge over the canal. And what an unexpected treat lay on the other side. Desert sand trickled over the brow of a low south-facing rocky bluff, and nestled against it were the tiers and curved ribbed roofs of a small temple complex. A carpet of red goji berries drying on a brick pavement in front made a bright splash of colour.

'Hey, our car's here,' called out Hua. I glanced over to see the unhitched jeep parked at the side.

'Of course, it must be a Buddhist temple, and that's why Peng's stopped to see it.'

We tied up the horses and went for a wander. Heavy carved wooden doors bright with ornate paintings of birds and flowers opened onto inner courtyards. Painted panels displayed black and white cranes, symbols of longevity, twisting their elegant necks under feathery green pine branches, and scaly fish swam through eddies of blue water beneath pink-tipped lotus. An ancient retainer reverently unlocked doors to a temple chamber set into the rock face. The fierce bearded faces of temple guardians, enveloped in swirling robes, stared menacingly from the decorated facade.

'He says the cave temple at the back is from the Tang dynasty,' said Hua, and I caught my breath. This meant it was at least eleven hundred years old, and probably much older.

Buddhism has come to form part of the traditional Three Doctrines of China. But unlike the home-grown Confucian philosophy and Daoist religion, it is an imported school of thought. Originating in India, Buddhism originally reached China during the Han dynasty in AD67, infiltrating via the Silk Road. It received a large boost in the early Tang dynasty after the monk Xuanzang travelled to India between 629-649. He spent several years studying at Buddhist centres and returned to China loaded with Buddhist texts. The Tang emperor Taizong, who had initially disapproved of Buddhism, now supported Xuangzang's efforts to translate the texts, helping to popularise and spread Buddhism in China. Although Buddhism differs from Daoism, there are many similarities which draw them together, probably the most significant being that neither believe in the existence of a single omnificent god. Chinese Buddhism has adapted to local traditions, and Zen Buddhism is in fact a combination of Buddhism and Daoism.

It is difficult to gauge exactly how many Buddhists there are in China now, though with the introduction of communism, numbers of practising Buddhists have certainly fallen. Some surveys have put the percentage of the population who are Buddhist as between 10 to 20%. Most religions have recently been tolerated, though not encouraged by the communist government. Of our team, it was only Peng who identified himself with any particular religion. However, although the majority of Chinese are officially non-religious, folk and religious traditions remain interwoven inextricably with Chinese life.

China is hardly short of Buddhist temples, and this was by no means the most impressive I had seen. But it was not only the unforeseen delight of accidentally coming across this tiny hidden gem tucked away off the tourist map which made it an intensely personal experience, but also the fact that we had arrived by horse in the same way people would have done for hundreds of years in the past. And to add to this, a few crumbling remnants on top of the bluff were pointed out to us.

'*Chang Cheng*,' announced the ancient retainer.

We had not noticed that the Great Wall had come back to join us at the southern end of the Helan Shan. I had been a little sad that we had not been able to follow it for at least some way along the mountain range south of Yinchuan.

Australians Brendan Fletcher and Emma Nicholas walked the wall in 2006-2007.

'This was by far the most impressive section we've seen in the roughly 1200 km we've walked since leaving Jiayuguan,' stated Brendan in their blog, which included superb shots of ten metre high stretches of wall. The wall was not so impressive here, and upstream of Zhongwei the swirling waters of the Huang He and the spectacular Qingtong gorge form a natural barrier which rendered a defensive wall unnecessary for some distance. We would not expect to see it again for several days.

Hua and I rode into Zhongwei along a wide new road stretching for kilometres along the bank of the Huang He, pausing to talk to a lone road sweeper in regulation orange optimistically brushing sand off the endless surface with a besom. It was a scene reminiscent of the Walrus and the Carpenter.

'If seven maids with seven mops
Swept it for half a year,
Do you suppose,' the Walrus said,
'That they could get it clear?'
'I doubt it,' said the Carpenter,
And shed a bitter tear.'

I didn't shed a bitter tear, but it looked a hopeless task.

After a night at a cramped Zhongwei truck stop squeezed between four-storey buildings on a busy street, and where a distracting feature was the large glass window set in the door of the truckers' toilet, we set off to cross the town centre. At least we would have, had it not been for the officious policeman who collared us and made us divert round the outskirts. Shandan had somehow managed to tear a flap of skin in his stifle (the top front of his hind leg) on the trailer overnight, so Peng had ferried him ahead in the trailer to our lodgings seventeen kilometres away at Xin Qiao. Li May and I were allocated Room 101 and to my considerable relief it was not a Big Brother interrogation chamber but a cheerful dormitory decked out with red checked bedspreads. The local vet had been called, and in no time at all Shandan was roped up and pulled down onto his side in the yard. After injecting a local anaesthetic, the vet made a neat job of cleaning and stitching the wound, and I was left with a short course of further injections to administer over the next few days. A reward for everyone's efforts seemed called for, and as karaoke is extremely popular in China, we repaired to a private room at the local karaoke bar to tuck into *jiaozi* and listen to the warblings of Peng and Hua, which I might best describe as individual.

We were now travelling to the south of the Tengger desert, the fourth largest desert in China. The winds blow sand to the south, and at Shapatou sand dunes reach right up to the outside bank of the Huang He where it swings in a great meander, creating a spectacular sandy river cliff much admired by tourists. We made our way along the road which clung round the top of the cliff between the desert sands and the steep drop to the river. A freight train rumbled past on the railway running close beside the road, and on the Huang He far below the tiny figures of sightseers in bright orange life-vests drifted downriver on rafts. The desert sandhill on the other side of the railway line looked as if a woolly green fishing net entangled with weeds had been flung over it. In fact, this was an intricate network of grasses and straw matting laid down as part of a scheme to stabilise the dunes and prevent sand encroaching further south.

This was also our last sight of the great muddy river we had followed for so long, as we branched west and away from the Huang He valley. Because of Shandan's wound we kept the day's ride short and stopped down the road at the little hamlet of Mengjiawen. An articulated lorry drew up, its load secured under a couple of long tarpaulins, and the driver engaged in conversation with the boys. Hua pointed out the hanzi and arabic lettering on the side of the cab showing where it had come from.

'He is bringing *hami gua,* melons from Hami,' Hua told me. 'Hami is very famous for its sweet melons.'

Hami was an oasis town on my route through Xinjiang province, but well over a thousand kilometres away even by crow. The driver walked round to the back of the lorry and fumbled under the tarpaulin before bringing me my first *hami gua,* a type of muskmelon or cantaloupe. Pale veins patterned the green skin on the rugby ball-shaped fruit, or was it a vegetable? Thankfully it did not resurrect The Great Watermelon Debate that had been raging for weeks among the team. What was the sweetest melon? What botanical family did it belong to? These were apparently all topics which could raise high emotions. Hua defended a lone corner by insisting it was a vegetable.

'But it is definitely a fruit. My auntie has a melon farm in Johore and she should know,' insisted Li May. But whether fruit or vegetable, it was as sweet and juicy as I had been promised.

We set out across the sandy scrub desert the next day, following a line of rumpled hills to the south. The verge was occasionally brightened by the reddish-pink blooms of trumpet like flowers, and random clumps of alfalfa which the horses snacked on. Had it fallen off a lorry? The new G6 which was still under construction here, swung in from the south to run parallel to our road. Where possible we crossed over to walk and jog along the bare levelled earth surface, avoiding the stream of trucks and cars on the National road. They stirred up a line of dust which could be seen extending across the plain for miles.

Li Jing spent much of the time by himself pacing Zorbee far ahead, stiff as a poker in the saddle with one arm tucked behind his back, and looking fixedly ahead of him. I failed to understand what pleasure one could garner from travelling like this without seemingly taking any interest in one's surroundings.

'He says he likes to concentrate on his horse,' explained Hua.

But at the next rest stop Li Jing appeared leading Zorbee who was markedly lame in front. It was probably a shoulder injury from which he would take some time to recover, and at our truck stop lodgings in Gantang, Li Jing announced he was going home. Ironically, with the prospect of seeing the back of me in front of him, as it were, he suddenly became quite animated and friendly. I can't say I wasn't a touch relieved, though, when Peng gave him a lift to the train station in town. I was not relishing the thought of trailing after a monolith all the way to London.

CHAPTER SIXTEEN

THE SILK ROAD

但愿人长久，千里共婵娟
dàn yuàn rén cháng jiǔ, qiān lǐ gòng chán juān
Wishing us a long life to share the beauty of the
moon though we are far apart.
(Saying for the Mid-Autumn festival)

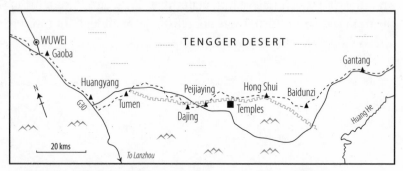

Sunday, 27 September – Saturday, 3 October, 2009.
Gantang to Gaoba (Gansu).
211 km. Daily average 30 km.

Bajiu padded across a desert wasteland littered with small rocks and straggly scrub. Ahead of me, Hua's legs waggled back and forth as he urged Shandan on. Now Li Jing had gone back to Beijing and our pacesetter Zorbee was travelling in the trailer, the other two horses needed constant encouragement. The balmy weather meant I could ride in a short-sleeved blouse, but Hua resolutely continued wearing his blue jacket and gloves. However, he had ditched his riding helmet in favour of a battered canvas hat with a floppy brim which shaded him from the sun but made him look curiously like a fisherman. A low backbone of naked crumpled hills gradually emerged from the dust haze, and we entered a valley with a few bare terraces stepping down to a narrow, irrigated floodplain brushed with green. The day before we had crossed into Gansu province, staying overnight at the small junction settlement of Baidunzi, where we left the road to Lanzhou to take a quieter short cut to the west. But not so quiet as to prevent huge transporters occasionally roaring past with long gleaming windmill blades for some far off windmill farm.

Peng had found somewhere to stay at the home of an elderly couple living next to a petrol station near the hamlet of Hong Shui. From the outside the rectangular tiled block embellished with red Chinese characters was decidedly uninviting, but once we pushed past a tired hessian curtain covering the metal door, we entered a comfortable living room with a well-polished black stove at the centre of a beige tiled floor. A fleece rug bizarrely decorated with koalas and the word 'Australia' was flung over a patterned sofa by a coffee table with a pink plastic cover, and two white stick back chairs stood at a three-legged table. Low stools were stored neatly beneath a bench under the metal framed window. In a tidy bedroom leading off to the side were a couple of sixties style wardrobes, a *kang* and a bed with folded quilts – quite enough room for the four of us though I slept on my airbed on the floor.

Across the road a square pockmarked earth bastion about forty foot high looked down on us from a hillock. It was a Ming dynasty beacon tower, signalling that we were once again back on the line of the Great Wall. If we had followed the line of the wall in an easterly direction for around eighty kilometres or so we would have found ourselves on the edge of the Huang He gorge, which formed a barrier in itself. But we were heading west, and for the next few days the wall weaved to and fro across our path, sometimes an almost indistinguishable spine along the hill ridges, sometimes a substantial slab-like barrier crossing the lowland. For several miles on the first day, Hua and I rode over a low, dry pass beside a broken two metre high earth bank which was all that remained of the wall. It was so degraded that it looked more like earthworks thrown up by road development than an ancient construction, and it was low enough for us to ride along the top.

'Two thousand and eighty metres above sea level according to my watch,' said Hua proudly, twisting his wrist round for me to look at his new toy.

There was evidence of tree planting attempts in the dry soil.

'According to local people there hasn't been rain here for years,' said Hua. 'This year there has been no rain, but the government has actually set up this irrigation systems, kind of uploading drainwater from the Yellow River to the East ...' I assumed he meant water which had been drained from the river rather than water from the drains. '... So people have no problem of growing crops for themselves,' he explained.

As we passed through villages further on, this was borne out by regular signs to *jia shui* or 'add water' painted in hanzi on squares of blue plastic above coils of hosepipe. With a true Chinese nose for commerce, the villagers were developing a sideline by selling the water on to passing traffic.

While we were resting by the side of the road, a couple of three-wheeled motorbikes drew up. Under tarpaulins at the back, stalls were laid out with a colourful array of dried fruit. The piece de resistance was a delectable sticky slab of mixed fruit, nuts and seeds about a foot square and nine inches deep, like a gigantic trail bar, decorated on the top with patterns of crystallized fruit. We bought raisins, apricots and a few slices of the slab from the dark-skinned Turkic-looking vendors. One wore a natty embroidered pill box hat.

'They have come all the way from Xinjiang,' Hua announced, stuffing some fruit slab into his pocket.

These travelling vendors were in fact among the first representatives of the Uighur people that I had come across. A Turkic ethnic group I was to become well acquainted with on the ride, they inhabit the Xinjiang Autonomous Region of western China, in particular the oases surrounding the Tarim Basin. Like the Hui, they are Muslim, but unlike the Hui they are ethnically and culturally Central Asian rather than Chinese. As a result, there has been considerable friction between the Chinese Uighur population and the Chinese authorities and this has sometimes erupted into violence.

'They want to know if we are a travelling circus,' Hua added nonchalantly.

I nearly choked on my piece of Uighur trail bar. Were we really that much of a spectacle? But I suppose so, as it was not the last time we were asked the question.

A couple of nights later we stayed at a small *binguan* in Dajing directly opposite a relatively intact section of the Great Wall. The heavily eroded slab of earth, nearly twenty foot high in places, pushed up from the ground as if it had always been an integral part of the landscape, and marched solemnly away over the brow of the next rise. When evening came, one side glowed like fire in the setting sun, while the other side was plunged into cold inky shadow. The hotel had a washroom with a hot trickle posing as a shower (welcome nonetheless), and also an international clientele as the proprietor boasted proudly, since only a year previously a couple of Norwegians walking the wall had stayed there.

We took the afternoon off and returned to the hill pass where Peng had heard there was a Daoist temple complex. Just beyond the small village of Laocheng we turned south off the road onto a gravel road cutting through a gap in the wall, and drove about two kilometres up a deep valley into the forested hills. Parking the jeep at the foot of a precipitous hillside, we climbed a steep cart track zigzagging its way up into the trees. It was a stiff haul, but what a view at the top. Between spindly pines a panorama over the lowlands far below revealed itself, spreading out into the distant haze. And once again we found we were the sole visitors to a hidden delight off the beaten track. Several small temples were perched on the top and strung along a high ridge line. Under curved tiled roofs, painted doors opened onto rooms decorated with vibrant murals and populated by gaudy painted statues of Daoist deities. Daoism is a very ancient religious and philosophical Chinese set of beliefs based on *dao* or 'the way'. It encourages people to live harmoniously with nature, which is why most Daoist temples are sited on mountains. Although in some ways Daoism is more a philosophy than a religion, it has many gods, some borrowed from other cultures. In China it is interwoven with Confucianism and Buddhism to the extent that they are sometimes almost indistinguishable to the uninformed such as myself.

A huge patterned bronze bell hung outside the first and largest temple. Inside, three vividly painted figures draped in real red silk robes were seated on a platform in front of a bright blue back wall. No doubt they represented the *Sanqing* or 'Three Pure Ones' who are the highest gods in Daoism. To either side were top-knotted figures holding books. One was feeling decidedly queasy judging by his turquoise face. And not surprisingly, as he stood in front of a mural illustrating the Daoist Ten Halls of Hell. Ten judges presided over ten courts for designated bad behaviour. But no being rapped over the knuckles or sent to the corner here. Grisly scenes of dismemberment, disembowelling, boiling alive in cauldrons and drowning in pools of blood depicted the various gory punishments awaiting the unfortunate criminals. In the Fifth 'Wailing Hall of Hell', naked miscreants were being thrown onto protruding swords. With some justification this was the punishment meted out for cruelty to animals and being a litterbug, I read later. But also rather worryingly the penalty for opening and reading other people's letters; perhaps a smidgeon over the top, even without permission.

We climbed a winding path up the ridge to further temples, one of which was vaguely unsettling. Two goddesses bundled up in red and yellow silk robes sat in front of a stuccoed wall of crudely painted tortured branches on which were perched strange little voodoo-like dolls. Were they fertility symbols or for sticking pins into, or both? Another plain brick temple was a kaleidoscope of colour inside, with intricately carved red and gold dragons twisted round red pillars. A couple of ornate pink and yellow lanterns in plastic covers, and the homely addition of a tiny teapot among tassels, hung in front of a sumptuously decorated goddess. Other female figures in vibrantly hued costumes lurked shyly around the room, wearing enigmatic half-smiles on their faces as if they were sharing a joke at my expense. But perhaps it was at my surprise when a particular one caught my eye. This was evidently a figure of some importance, as she was seated and richly dressed, but she was exposing her red-nippled breasts. Who was she and why was she flashing her boobs?

It seemed the isolated hill top position of this temple complex had saved it from the worst excesses of the Cultural Revolution launched in 1966. On the face of it, the Cultural Revolution was a drive by communist leaders to shake up and break down the remnants of a capitalist class-ridden Chinese feudal society of rich landlords and poverty stricken peasants. But it has been widely acknowledged that Mao Zedong used it as a ploy to develop a personality cult and regain power after he had been marginalised following his disastrous 'Great Leap Forward'. Initially harnessing the revolutionary zeal of students, 'Red Guard' units were mobilised to criticise teachers, colleagues, officials or anyone deemed to show 'counter-revolutionary' attitudes opposed to Maoist thought. Exaggerated or fabricated accusations were directed at innocent victims. Being from a 'bad' family, listening to western music or wearing make-up could identify one as a 'capitalist roader'. Supposed counter-revolutionaries were forced to 'confess', paraded, humiliated, and often violently attacked during public 'struggle sessions'. Victims were made to wear dunces' caps, painted with ink, beaten, or forced for long periods to kneel or assume the infamous 'jet-plane' position with body pushed forward and arms and head wrenched back. Many lost their lives or committed suicide rather than face the stress of struggle.

The movement spread to involve urban workers, the military and party members, and was widely used to settle personal grudges as people split into violently opposed factions, all claiming revolutionary ideals. Mao manipulated the chaos to purge anyone he saw as a threat to his personal power, and this included Vice Chairman Liu Shaoqi, originally Mao's chosen successor, who was targeted after antagonising Mao. He was denounced and beaten at public meetings, and died in 1969 having been refused medical attention for diabetes and pneumonia. Disgraced Chief of Joint Staff General Liu Ruiqing was permanently crippled after breaking both legs jumping from a third floor window in a failed suicide attempt to avoid criticism sessions.

The Cultural Revolution officially ended in 1969, but in practice rumbled on until Mao's death in 1976, causing a whole generation of young Chinese to miss out on their education.

Initially one of the foremost drives of the movement was the destruction of the 'Four Olds', namely old customs, culture, habits and ideas, and during the course of the movement many antiques, ancient texts and old temples were destroyed or damaged by the Red Guards before the madness was brought to an end. The temple complexes we had recently visited appeared to be unscathed, but as we were shortly to find out, not all temples escaped ransacking and destruction.

On the first day of October, Hua and I plodded into the bustling town of Tumen. Mischievous little boys ran alongside, shouting *'Jia, jia,'* at the horses. Many Chinese seemed to think the sole purpose of a horse was for galloping.

'Weixian, ta ti. Be careful, he kicks,' I warned, though more as a means of keeping them from hassling Bajiu than out of concern that the tolerant little gelding would actually boot anyone.

We turned into the neat courtyard of a two-storey hotel, untacked and started to settle in. But suddenly a small, wiry gentleman with greying hair and glasses appeared from nowhere, over-excited and jabbering unintelligibly. I asked Hua to explain what was going on. It transpired a nearby Daoist temple that had been destroyed during the Cultural Revolution was being rebuilt. It was dedicated to Guan Yu, a significant Han general from the Three Kingdoms period who subsequently become widely revered as a Daoist deity. However, there was also some sort of 'horse temple' at the side.

'It is for the horse and sister,' said Hua. I was mystified. What had the horse's sister got to do with anything? Was it some sort of anthropomorphic horse?

But the excited gentleman was beside himself with delight as it was most auspicious that horse travellers from afar had turned up at this juncture, and even more so that it included a *laowai*. We must all take the horses to the horse and sister temple to bring good luck, and who were we to disappoint him?

We obediently tacked up the horses again. The excited gentleman had left suddenly, but now reappeared accompanied by other enthusiastic temple patrons and an armful of red silk scarves. We tied some around the horses' foreheads and the others over our shoulders. A small crowd had gathered by the time we reached the temple, and a salvo of fire crackers announced our arrival as we paused on the threshold before leading the horses through the gateway into what was still a building site. Piles of rocks, sand and lime cluttered the courtyard, and the front of the temple was obscured by scaffolding. To the accompaniment of drilling, we tentatively squeezed the horses under the network of low rails and into the muddy site at the side of the main temple where the horse and sister temple was to be built. The excited gentleman bustled around, dragging us into position for photos, and more fire crackers were abruptly let off. The horses looked bored. Then it was back to the hotel in the falling dusk, followed by a small retinue of people, including an old man in a straw hat, a mother with a child, a couple of youths on bikes and a sprinkling of little boys. The whole event merited a celebration, and we were treated to a slap-up meal at the hotel with the temple worthies. A bottle of *baijiu* and a tray with two tiny cups materialised and much toasting commenced, although there was more *baijiu* on the tray than in the cups as the excited gentlemen kept knocking them over.

I determined to get to the bottom of this horse and sister story.

'I still don't understand, Hua. Why is the temple dedicated to a horse and sister?'

'It is for the horse and sister; the horse and sister from long ago.'

'What do you mean, the horse and sister from long ago?'

'You know, like the parent from long ago.'

I puzzled over this but eventually the penny dropped.

'Ohhh, you mean a horse *ancestor*.'

'Yes, horse and sister. That is what I said.'

I can't say I was fully enlightened, but at least it made more sense.

When the party was finished, we all wended our way through deserted moonlit backstreets to visit the house of one of the worthies who was a professional calligrapher. In the middle of a back room stood a work table, and all around the walls hung beautiful examples of Chinese calligraphy, the elegant handwritten Chinese characters delicately cascading down the scrolls. I felt very privileged to experience these works of art in the process of creation, and sad that they were out of my budget. But at a noodle breakfast the next morning courtesy of our Tumen friends I was lucky enough to be presented with a memento – a calligraphic painting by one of the temple patrons.

I had been dreading joining the 312 National road to Wuwei, but in fact we reached it to find the brand new G30 Expressway was in operation. This expressway, much of which was then still under construction, runs over 4,000 kilometres from the Chinese coast all the way to the Kazakhstan border at Khorgas. It is the longest road with the same designated letter and number in China, and I would follow it on and off the rest of my way across the country. Here it had channelled away most of the heavy traffic from the old 312 National road, or 'Mother Road', whose role it replaced, so we only had local traffic to cope with and there was a sandy verge to ride on. But more excitingly both these roads followed the main trunk of the fabled silk route from the ancient city of Xian before it branched off into a network of routes further west. Camel caravans and donkey trains once plodded where traffic now roars. This was the Hexi or Gansu Corridor, which has held huge significance in Chinese history. A narrow belt of fertile land hemmed in by the high snow-capped Qilian mountains to the south and the arid Gobi desert to the north, it runs approximately from Lanzhou in Gansu to Yumenguan in Xinjiang. Fed by snow melt, the belt of grassland and scrub at the foot of the Qilian mountains supports a string of oases, and from time immemorial it has acted as a natural funnel for travel and trade between China and lands further west. It was this corridor that the eastern extensions of the Great Walls of the Han and Ming dynasties were built to protect.

As the horses padded along the National road, it was sobering to think of the countless people who had travelled this route over the centuries, carrying goods, ideas and religions between east and west.

It was the ancient importance of silk trading between China and the West which led to the term Silk Road for this vital overland network of trade routes crossing mountains and deserts, although many other goods besides silk travelled along it. Rhubarb, paper, and tea were transported from China, and carpets, ivory, cucumbers and horses in the other direction. But as silk was a much sought after and valuable luxury item, it was not surprising that the Chinese, who discovered the secret of silk production in around the fourth century BC, jealously guarded this skill and held an almost total monopoly for over 5,000 years. Trading along the silk route was hit after silk eggs were smuggled out of China and silk started to be produced in the West. One story relates that in the fifth century AD a Han princess carried silk cocoons along this route out of China hidden in her head-dress. Another story points the finger at a couple of Nestorian monks in the sixth century AD. But whatever the truth, it is certain that not only silk products but the secret of silk-making itself made its way west along the Silk Road through the Hexi Corridor.

We were following in the hoofsteps of many celebrated and infinitely more pioneering travellers than ourselves. Zhang Qian, the Han envoy who reported on the existence of 'heavenly horses' to Emperor Wudi after his trade and diplomacy mission to the west, journeyed this way, as did some of the 'heavenly horses' themselves. The 'Flying Horse of Gansu' bronze was in fact found near Wuwei, and appears repeatedly in the form of statues and on signs in Gansu. This was the route that the Buddhist monk Xuanzhang followed, as did three Muslim missionaries sent by the Prophet Muhammad during the Tang dynasty. Two died en route, but the third reportedly reached South China. Marco Polo recorded that he passed this way, though some contest that he ever set foot in China.

The old road led straight to the north-west through farmland watered by rivers and streams running down from the Qilian Shan. Once or twice we caught tempting glimpses of snow-capped mountains in the distance to the south, behind the naked slopes of foothills which ran parallel to the road like a line of rumpled napkins. Unseen beyond the farmland to the north lay the desert expanses which bordered the corridor on the other side. Tall poplars with peeling silvery trunks and shocked up-reaching branches lined the straight road in races of muddy water, and the finely harrowed soil of bare ploughed fields warmed in the autumn sun. We posed for photos by a whitewashed milestone etched in red with the number 2446.

'I think it is the distance from Shanghai in kilometres,' Hua ventured. The old 312 'Mother Road' started from Shanghai.

Traffic was virtually non-existent apart from the occasional bicycle, throbbing three-wheeler truck or rattling lorry. One was stopped at the side of the road, its enveloping load of rush matting perilously tipped to one side.

'Overloaded,' commented Hua.

Another carried a load of resigned pigs crammed into mesh cages. We came to a huge transporter parked in a lay-by.

'Look,' said Hua. 'Donkeys.' And indeed looking down from the top of the high carrier poked the heads and long flicking ears of a whole load of donkeys, probably headed for an abattoir.

Numerous little settlements lined the road, so it was usually easy to find a truck stop or *binguan* to stay, and the first night we stopped at Huangyangzhen, or Yellow Sheep town.

Nearing Wuwei, Bajiu seemed a bit lame on his off fore, and the rubber pad on that foot looked very worn. I got off and led him, but he was still not right when we reached our overnight stop at Gaoba just outside Wuwei. Something needed to be done, and inspecting his foot and fixing on a new hoof pad seemed to be the first step. Peng looked glum when I discussed replacing the rubber pad.

'*Bu neng.* I can't.'

'*Weishenme?* Why?'

'*Mei you xiangjiao luntai.* I don't have any rubber tyre.'

My heart sank. Peng consulted with the hotel manager, the description 'hotel' being in a very loose sense of the word. The crumbling three-storey building had shabby rooms leading off a corridor lined with broken windows, and the toilet block was a tramp across a huge yard. Hua relayed the answer to me.

'He says there is a tyre yard about thirty kilometres away.'

It meant wasting most of the day and my shoulders drooped, but needs must and Peng and I set off in the jeep. Two hundred yards down the road, he suddenly jammed on the brakes and reversed a little way back. Propped up on a brick wall to either side of a wide entrance were two rows of knobbly truck tyres. Peng grinned.

'*Wo juede tamen mai luntai.* I think they sell tyres.'

Incredibly the hotel manager seemed totally unaware that there was a substantial tyre yard within a stone's throw of his premises. Peng clambered over heaps of car tyres piled up in an apple orchard in search of the perfect *luntai*. It had to be worn down, not too thick, and containing fibre rather than metal thread. Then small squares of rubber were cut from the tyre sides to use as shoes. Back at the trailer, Peng had just started taking off the worn pad when a little stone dropped out. So that was why Bajiu was unhappy! Anyone who has had gravel trapped in their shoe will know how it feels, and this was the downside of using pads rather than open metal shoes. But no sooner had this problem been solved than we realised a pad on one of Bajiu's back feet had dropped off completely. Peng had only a few nails left, so he concentrated on replacing the back pad, and we crossed fingers that the worn front pad would last another hundred kilometres. We were now nearing the Shandan stud where our horses had come from, and which I had visited two years previously. We had been invited to take a break there, and the stud farrier would have all the right equipment, including proper metal horseshoes.

I flinched as a volley of bangs shattered the evening air in a shower of sharp cracks.

'What is going on, Hua?'

'It is a full moon tonight. They are fire crackers to celebrate the Mid-Autumn Festival.'

I groaned in frustration.

'Oh no, I can't believe it. I haven't bought any moon cakes!'

Much to my chagrin I realised that in the whirl of daily life on the road, the Chinese Mid-Autumn or Moon Festival had crept up on me without my noticing. If there was one thing I used to look forward to as a child in Malaya when the Moon Festival came round, it was eating moon cakes. I loved the round pastry cakes which commonly contain a sweet red bean or lotus seed paste filling, but was less taken with the ones containing a salty egg yolk. Popular legend has it that when the Han Chinese rose up against the Mongols during the Yuan dynasty, they hid messages in moon cakes to incite the populace to rebel. Brightly lit lanterns are also a tradition, and I remember the magic of the red cellophane lanterns in the shape of a red dragon and red fish my mother bought for my sister Rhiannon and I one Moon Festival. Swinging from the end of bamboo sticks, they cast an eery flickering glow over the hibiscus bushes as we carried them round the moonlit garden. No moon cakes or lanterns this time round, but I treated the gang to supper at the greasy spoon café next door and remembered to follow the custom of gazing at the moon and thinking of my absent family. Whether my family would be doing the same thing five thousand miles away was another matter.

CHAPTER SEVENTEEN

A VISIT TO SHANDAN
MILITARY HORSE STUD

路遥知马力, 日久见人心

lù yáo zhī mǎ lì, rì jiǔ jiàn rén xīn

*As distance tests a horse's strength, so does time
reveal a person's real character.*

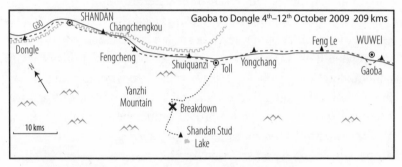

Sunday, 4 October – Monday, 12 October, 2009.
Gao Ba to Dong Le.
209 km. Daily average 30 km.

It was another three days ride to the Shandan stud, and first we
had to negotiate our way round the southern outskirts of Wuwei.
Beyond the city the road was quiet, sometimes running parallel with
the G30 and sometimes swinging away through farmland. Straight
concrete irrigation channels, water-filled ditches and lines of trees
delineated the roads and fields. The grain crops had already been
harvested and the autumn ploughland was bare apart from occasional
late stands of papery brown maize, neat green rows of soya bean plants
and untidy leafy mops of tobacco. We passed the unusual sight of a
factory sign in English, announcing the 'Gansu Best Plant Oil Develop
Co Ltd'. A few times we crossed long bridges over watercourses, the

wide moonscape of pebbly riverbed threaded with a few small braided water channels. These wastelands would become temporary raging torrents when snow melt swelled the rivers in spring, and would have presented a formidable obstacle to travellers before the bridges were built. In 1908 William Geil wrote that on the first day of travel from Wuwei (then called Liangchow) 'we had occasion to record "a day of fords"; eighty times the animals waded through snow water fresh from the lofty mountains on our left.' The rivers and streams running down from the Qilian mountains brought life-giving water and enabled settlement in the Hexi Corridor, but sank into the sands and disappeared once they reached the desert beyond.

As we were now following a well-travelled route, there was more choice of accommodation, and Peng generally managed to find a good value hotel or truck stop. In Feng Le we found ourselves in cool quiet rooms leading off a shady tree-filled yard. In a huge shed-like function building at the back was a chilly central dining area filled with large plants, which lurked round the tables like triffids. We retreated to the warm sanctuary of a cosy private dining room at the side, lounging on soft sofa seating round a low central table. Steaming bowls of white rice were served up, together with a crispy fish dish, succulent beans in ginger, and a thin soup-like lamb and vegetable stew. Bliss. The larger town of Yongchang had wide streets and rows of newly built offices and apartments. Our tidy truck stop with a neat white-tiled row of rooms round a large yard was approached through a narrow entrance between shop fronts.

The stud was located about fifty kilometres off our route along the highway, and as time was getting short, we decided to trailer the horses there and back from the nearest turnoff. On the day of arrival, Peng drove ahead to drop off Zorbee, promising to return and wait for us back at the highway. But when Hua and I reached the turn off, we found ourselves hanging around at a toll gate with no sign of Peng. We let the horses graze on an overgrown field while Hua stretched out to snooze. To the south where we were headed, the misty mountain ranges rose mysterious and foreboding.

Peng eventually turned up after a couple of hours.

'*Lu bu hao*. The road is not good,' he complained, and as we set off across the grasslands it soon became evident that he was not exaggerating. The awful potholed asphalt road turned into an even worse rutted gravel road, and the inevitable happened. While negotiating a flock of sheep in the middle of nowhere there came a loud bang, followed by hissing and steam. The strain of hauling the loaded trailer over an abysmal road had caused the jeep radiator to burst forty kilometres from the main road and twenty from the stud. A hurried phone call and the stud secretary said they would come and fetch us. We settled down to wait, and to my amazement I found I was able to access the internet with my dongle. So while skeins of honking geese flew overhead towards a lake in the ranges of blue mountains that swept up from the surrounding grasslands, I sat on the trailer tow bar and posted on my blog. 'Breakdown' I titled my post, continuing, 'No, not me with the stress of constant arguing with Hua, but our jeep.'

Evening shadows lengthened on the mountain slopes and a herdsman on a bay pacing pony scuttled round a flock of bleating sheep, driving them across the road in front of us and into pens for the night. The secretary arrived and declared that we would need to be towed in, so we had another two-hour wait until a huge tractor appeared as dusk fell. By the time we were being hauled slowly back to the stud it was pitch black, and all the headlights picked out was a bouncing circle of grass. We arrived late and tired, and were whisked off for a quick supper at the town restaurant before being taken straight down to the hotel. After my previous trip it was almost like coming home.

Although the Shandan stud was only founded in 1934, the well-watered grasslands on the northern flanks of the Qilian Shan in a strategic position between nomads and agriculturalists mean that it has long been a breeding ground for military horses. On my previous visit I had been shown ruins of old stable buildings which it was claimed dated from the Ming period, and it is certain that horses were bred here many centuries if not millennia before. The horses of the

Yuezhi and Xiongnu nomads were followed by the 'heavenly horses' imported from the Ferghana valley during the Han dynasty two thousand years ago. The Western Xia bred their Dangxiang horses here, and horse breeding by successive governments has continued right up to the present day.

The aim of the modern stud was to breed a robust riding and pack horse that would be suitable for patrolling remote and inhospitable border areas. Chiang Kai Shek, President of the Republic of China before the communist takeover, had a hand in promoting its establishment, and even Chairman Mao himself had visited. The local ponies on which the Shandan horse was based were tough but very small, so in the early 1950s Russian Don stallions were introduced to try and improve the breed. These are larger more quality riding horses, often chestnut in colour, which were developed on the Russian steppes near the Don river, and used by the Cossacks. However, this reduced adaptability so in 1963 selected local stallions were used to back cross, and this was successful in producing a larger but still tough breed of horse. After further line breeding the breed was stabilised and officially recognised in 1980. Pure Shandan horses are generally a solid bay colour, fairly plain-headed with stocky build, and around 14 hands high. Our horses were fairly typical, though perhaps not top quality examples. Quite a few of them, like Zorbee, are pacers. Thousands of mares were kept in large paddocks at the stud, which was divided into four sectors, and geldings were sold on to the Chinese army at about four years of age. Nowadays some mares are outcrossed with stallions such as Don and Arabian to produce larger more quality part-breds for the riding market.

In more recent years the demand for military horses has plummeted and at the time I was there, there were only about 300 breeding mares at the stud. These were confined to No. 1 sector, or Yi Chang, where we were staying, the other sectors having diversified into activities such as dairy farming and rapeseed oil. I got the impression that the breeding policy had originally been run along fairly scientific principles, but that the interest in bloodlines has more recently waned with the declining market for Shandan horses. In spite of Zorbee's less attractive points, one could not deny that he had a tough constitution and showed inexhaustible endurance. To my mind, these were qualities worth promoting, and I asked about his sire and dam.

'*Bu zhidao.* Don't know,' came the surprising answer, and no one seemed to have the slightest clue about his parentage. Apparently, they flung out mares and stallions together and hoped for the best, and no one kept records for individual offspring. Not the best policy for improving a breed.

Trumpet sounds startled me awake in the morning and I was momentarily disorientated. Was I arriving at the Pearly Gates? No, it was the loudspeaker blaring out the morning wake up call, followed by Chinese pop music and daily news. It was also the fanfare for a busy two days, starting with a veterinary inspection.

The little military settlement of Yi Chang was on a gentle slope in a wide secluded valley well off the beaten track. Simple brick barrack blocks of residential housing, now semi-abandoned, flanked alleyways running off a T-frame of two asphalt roads, the stem forming the main street. In the distance beyond the undulating grassy swells of the valley floor, and framed by the low buildings on either side of the street, the icing sugar peaks of the Qilian mountains shone ethereally in the clear mountain air to the south. The lack of traffic lent an almost unearthly atmosphere to the place, the only noise being the footfalls and muted chatter of a handful of people in drab clothing going about their business. To the western side of the settlement were administration buildings, and where the street ran down to a small stony river, a couple of apartment blocks painted green and yellow dominated the scene. On the other side a bleak two-storey office building sheltered by a few trees had been converted into the hotel. This had been done with the intention of promoting the stud as a tourist centre for horse trekking, but we were the only guests in the otherwise empty building. A few rooms had been done up to provide three star accommodation with flush toilets and showers, though the hot water was not what one might describe as instant.

Up at the yard we found an impressive figure in what looked like nuclear fallout gear wielding a spray gun and disinfecting the trailer. It was a member of the veterinary squad. Not so impressed were Shandan and Bajiu when they were also disinfected and had thermometers stuck up their backsides.

'What do they think of the horses?' I asked Hua smugly, waiting for a complimentary comment about the obvious improvement in their condition.

'They say their health is fair.'

To say I was a little miffed was an understatement. Thanks to Peng's care, they had been given a hard feed three to four times a day over the last two months, and compared to the skinny beasts we were presented with in the spring, they were positively blooming. But I kept my mouth shut and saddled up to be filmed with Hua as if we were just arriving. The stud had their own farrier, so after lunch the horses' rubber shoes were swapped for metal shoes to tackle the last leg to Jiajuguan. One by one they were roped up like trussed chickens to the usual Chinese shoeing frame, but I was rather taken aback when the farrier produced an electric planer to trim back their hooves.

Some of the stud's horses had been brought into the lower yards to be handled and we went down to look at them. About fifty bays, blacks, chestnuts and greys with unkempt manes and tails milled around on the dark churned earth of a walled compound. The larger chestnuts and greys were no doubt the result of outcrossing to Don and Arabian stallions. Another compound held recently branded youngsters, their rough coats showing that winter was on its way. Twenty mares were jammed sideways into a long chute between metal railings so they could not move. A veterinary surgeon in a white coat, oil cloth apron and plastic sleeve glove was at work, helped by a small team of soldiers in regulation camouflage gear. He made his way down the back of the line, pregnancy testing by the age old technique of shoving his arm up the mares' backsides to feel their uteruses, while a soldier pulled their tails to one side to prevent them being clamped down. Not very dignified but a pretty fail safe method. Another couple of soldiers followed behind, one wielding an outsize pair of scissors. The first soldier held the mare's tail steady while the 'barber' cut out a slice across the hairs at the top of the tail.

'This is to show the horses that are pregnant,' explained Hua.

Only a couple of mares did not receive the little 'short back and sides', so the stallions had obviously done their job. At the front of the line another soldier was giving vaccination jabs with an enormous syringe. It was a real production line. I thought incredulously of the industrial scale of the breeding programme that must have existed here when there were thousands rather than a few hundred mares supplying horses to the Chinese army. Although the veterinary technology may be more advanced now, it made me reflect once again on the vital strategic significance of these foothill grassland studs as an age-old production factory for military horses. And apparently not only for the Chinese.

'They say they sent many horses to the Taliban in Afghanistan when they were fighting the Russians,' said Hua.

We woke the next day to icy sleet, so it was an opportune occasion to visit the new Shandan stud museum, an imposing building at the centre of the complex reached via a paved drive under a splendid archway. It seemed they did not get many visitors as it was unlocked especially for us and half the museum was in darkness until they sorted out the lights. Much of the display concentrated on the development and diversification of the stud, but in one corner various equestrian and military artefacts, such as wooden pack saddles and battered army canteens, were on display. There was a medical kit in a leather case, and a huge sheepskin winter overcoat. The highlight was a crudely stuffed dark bay horse.

'He was the foundation stallion,' explained Hua. 'His identification number was 00.'

I stroked 00 on the nose. At his feet was a notice in hanzi. I was unfamiliar with the characters.

'What does it say, Hua?'

'Don't touch. Poisonous.'

Apparently, the preservative contained poison, but thankfully I didn't keel over foaming at the mouth. Perhaps it would have been better if I had, as I would not then have had to sign the visitors' book. On the wall hung a poster of a suitably solemn Chairman Mao writing an approving message to the stud in flowing Chinese script. Looking at the table below laid out with a calligraphy brush, ink and a large book containing blank pages, I realised to my horror that we were expected to do the same. With a flourish, Hua skilfully dashed off an artistic message in hanzi to approving smiles. In contrast, the stud secretary looked glumly at my bedraggled nursery school attempt at a signature in Roman script which looked like something the cat had dragged in. If nothing else it made me appreciate the skill of the Tumen calligraphers.

The afternoon was reserved for a film shoot with a team from Zhangye television. Escorted by four young soldiers clad in army camouflage uniform on Shandan geldings, and joined by Peng on Zorbee who seemed much improved, Hua and I rode in military formation up to a reservoir which features prominently in all the publicity shots at the stud. Not without reason as normally it would have had a stunning backdrop of the Qilian mountains, their peaks resplendent with snow. Today, however, they were shrouded in mist and rain. We were filmed artistically in silhouette traipsing down a ridge to the lake, and then a very long red banner was produced emblazoned in hanzi with '*Zhu Shandan Ma Lianjie Beijing – Lundun Aoyun Zhilu Yuan Man Chenggong.* Wishing great success to the Shandan horse Beijing to London Olympic Trip.' We all lined up behind it and paraded back and forth along the grassy slope by the lake front. In our interviews we extolled the virtues of our incomparable Shandan steeds, and in the final scene we all stood behind the banner again and in concert shouted out the epithet displayed on it, presumably in case no one had noticed it before.

'*Zhe ge hao, zhege zhen hao.* This is good, this is really good,' the director called out.

It was a wrap. We all trooped back to the stud restaurant for a slap-up meal which featured yak's tendon and pigeon stomach. The television crew, which included a couple of very pretty girls, were obviously on a mission to make a night of it, and the inevitable Chinese drinking games ensued. In quick unison, two players shot out a number of fingers from their closed fist, at the same time shouting out a number from one to ten.

'Wu! Ba!'

When one of them correctly guessed the total number of extended fingers, the loser had to drink a shot of *baijiu* as a penalty.

'Qi! San!'

They played fast and adeptly with a lot of noise, and I felt quite drunk just watching them. This popular finger guessing game is very common and can be played in several ways, for example by using both hands and guessing a number between two and twenty. But the crew had shortened the odds by playing the one-to-ten finger version, and the party became fairly lively after a few rounds. And in case anyone is wondering, the animal innards tasted exactly as you might imagine, even after several shots of *baijiu*.

As Zorbee seemed considerably better, Hua and I made the decision to leave Shandan behind and ride the other two horses on the last leg to the end of the wall at Jiayuguan. We would keep Zorbee strictly to a walk, and hope we had no further problems with lameness. It would save on the truck fee back to the Shandan stud where they were going to spend the winter, and with Zorbee as pace-setter we knew it would be easier riding. But I was surprised on the morning of Sunday, 9 October to find all three horses being loaded onto the truck to be taken back to the main road. To my intense annoyance, it transpired that Li Jing had somehow got wind of our decision and was rejoining us. I had not been consulted and made Hua phone Beijing to stress that Li Jing needed to understand that Zorbee would need to keep to a walk.

That evening we stayed at a well-kept farmhouse in the little village of Shuizhuanzi. The water supply came from a small tanker in the yard. Li May and I paid a little extra for a room with a plug point, and our hosts provided a simple supper in the kitchen.

The Great Wall had looped north, but it now reappeared alongside the G30 Expressway and the National road where they climbed over a shallow pass between two mountains. A cold mist and drizzle had descended over a bleak heathland and I huddled down into my padded jacket and raincoat, glad I had put on my thermal underwear that morning before leaving the farmhouse. Water trickled down the deserted road and damp curled the fleeces of sheep wandering alongside. They nibbled rapidly at the sparse grass, moving in short determined bursts from tuft to tuft. A disconsolate shepherd stood to one side, enveloped in rubber boots, peaked cap and a huge sheepskin cloak with the fleece to the inside. This garb seemed to be all the rage among the local shepherding fraternity, as we passed several more shepherds standing stoically by their flocks dressed in the same outfit. Along the base of the mountain to the north ran the crumbling remnants of the Great Wall, the core protruding like the dorsal fin of a lizard through the bank built up from eroded earth, while on the other side articulated lorries swished between the fences and steel barriers protecting the G30. Every so often there was a little canvas hut, and strings of orange bags strung up on lines just outside the barriers, with signs in hanzi.

'It says they are selling wild mushrooms.'

Without Hua I would have ridden in a fog of ignorance for much of the journey. I wondered about the safety issues of mushroom shopping on the verge of a major expressway, but then this was China.

We were now at 2,500 metres above sea level by Hua's watch, the highest point we would reach along the Great Wall. Paltry by Himalayan standards, but any higher and we would have to start worrying about altitude sickness. As we came down the other side of the pass the base of the clouds lifted to show a generous sprinkling of snow on the great mountain to the south.

'It has a funny name,' Hua commented quizzically, looking at his map. 'Yanzhi Mountain'. He puckered his brow reflectively. 'I don't understand why, but in English it means, how do you say, cosmetic? Cosmetic Mountain.'

I later found that *yanzhi* means rouge, and the name refers to small red flowers which grow on its slopes and are used to make rouge. According to one source I read, when the Xiongnu were driven out of the Hexi Corridor by the Han, they plaintively sang, 'Losing my Qilian mountains made my cattle unthrifty, losing my Yanzhi mountain made my women colourless'. As we came down to the small town of Fengcheng, three big mules wandered over to stare at us. They seemed remarkably fat considering the sparse grazing, but that is a reason the mule was such a popular beast of burden on the trade routes of Asia. An audience gathered to watch our travelling circus water and feed the horses outside the white-tiled house where we were staying. But when we asked our hosts for hot water to make tea, we discovered a new meaning for the phrase 'put the kettle on'. In the yard was a solar reflector, a shallow silver bowl tilted towards the sun which concentrated the reflected rays on a metal post at the centre, on top of which perched a kettle.

'You are three minutes late,' scolded Hua, as I finished drinking my solar-heated coffee the next morning. 'We agreed to leave at eight o'clock.'

I sighed. When we started out it was mainly Hua who procrastinated in the morning and we always seemed to set off an hour later than I had planned. As a result, we had decided to fix a time every day and stick to it, but the poacher-turned-gamekeeper was now becoming ridiculously pernickety.

'Three minutes here or there really doesn't matter, Hua.'

'If we say that we leave at eight, we must leave exactly at eight. That is what we agreed.' He pointedly tapped his watch.

'I just didn't want to leave an hour late, Hua. A few minutes doesn't matter. You are not always exactly on time yourself.'

'If we say we are doing something, we must do it.'

I gave up and got on Bajiu. It would no doubt provide material for a debate later on in the day.

A lean bespectacled man had stopped his car to talk to us at Hong Shui the week before. Mr Chen Huai was a local expert on the Great Wall, and he had invited us to stay at his house at our next stop of Chang Cheng Kou or 'Great Wall Gap', so called because of the gap where the National road and G30 Expressway now blast their way through the wall. Mr Chen's courtyard house was tucked away behind a row of shophouses overlooked by the wall. This had followed us all the way from Fengcheng, becoming more substantial all the way, and was now a great earth rampart about twenty foot high. We led the horses into a large enclosed grassy yard. It was a real treat for them as they were able to roam loose for the first time in a while, and Bajiu immediately had a good roll, flinging his legs ecstatically in the air. Mr Chen led us into a pretty creeper-covered courtyard surrounded by a low block of rooms. I had the use of a bed in his centrally heated study, and warm as toast, was able to dispense with my sleeping bag for a change. Over a supper of pigeons' eggs, Mr Chen told us he was friendly with British Great Wall enthusiast William Lindesay, who ran the length of the wall at a time when areas it passed through were off-limits to foreigners. I had read his book, *Alone on the Great Wall*, and had been greatly impressed and encouraged by his dogged determination to achieve his aim in spite of being jailed and deported on more than one occasion. My minor frustrations seemed completely petty by comparison, and whenever I was being pathetic about some relatively inconsequential setback I would pull myself together and think of him. He had subsequently become an authority on the Great Wall and had also stayed at Mr Chen's so I felt I was in good company. Mr Chen produced Lindesay's most recent book, *The Great Wall Revisited*, but unlike my copy, his was personally signed.

The sun broke through the chilly morning air, lighting the tops of the trees around Mr Chen's compound in a fiery glow behind us, and striking a bright dagger of light through a narrow gap in the wall and across our path ahead. The immense virtually unbroken barrier stretched away through ploughed fields to the north-west. Hua scurried ahead on Zorbee, leading the way along a well-trodden track in the gradually narrowing band of shadow at its foot. I leant over from Bajiu's back to place my hand on the cold friable surface, sensing a magical link back over 500 years to the many hands who had toiled to build this great structure. In my mind's eye I saw lines of workers tamping the earth down between wooden casings with ramming poles, adding water to dampen and compact the layers as they pounded and built them up one by one. Would they have been singing in time with the beats as workmen still do when constructing earth walls to this day? How many soldiers and forced labourers suffered and died to create this iconic fortification on the north-west frontier? Conditions on this remote front were brutal, with harsh weather, poor food and oppressive discipline, and mutinies were not unknown.

The wall became obsolete when the Ming were defeated by the nomadic Manchu Qing who extended their control over the lands beyond. So much human struggle had gone into its creation, but as we continued along its length it was sad to see the damage caused so casually by human neglect in the years after. Here and there people had dug out simple shelters in the fabric of the wall itself. We came across a crude cell with door and window openings, and further along a more ambitious double chamber with benches hewn out of the interior walls. As we progressed, the line of the wall was interrupted where tracks and irrigation channels broke through, and in places it was undercut where hungry sheep had nibbled away grass roots at the base. Every so often a great watchtower reared up against the hazy blue sky, the tamped earth core exposed to the weather. Once, guards would have scanned the horizon from these watchtowers, searching for signs of hostile nomads. Now the brick facings had long gone, no doubt taken by villagers for their own use. The scale of natural and man-made erosion had left nothing in places but bulky pinnacles marching across the landscape like a line of druidic standing stones. At one point we could see a much lower spine-like bank off to the right, almost certainly remnants of the more ancient Han dynasty wall which was built to protect the Gansu corridor around 1,500 years previously.

We rode for two or three hours to where a wide, dry river course scattered with lumps of wiry grass breached the wall. Scrambling up the bank on the other side we were confronted with a deeply ploughed field lapping the wall base. It seemed a tricky option to attempt stumbling through the clods, so we turned south and followed a track along the riverbed. This brought us out on a country road running parallel for another ten kilometres, though we were later told the wall ran all the way to Shandan.

Shandan was much like any small Chinese town, but as we stopped for noodles at an eating house on a dusty street, I had no idea that we were only a stone's throw from the memorial tombs of two extraordinary *waiguoren*. In fact, two years previously, when Wu Shuli had picked me up from Shandan station, he had mentioned something about a *yinggouren* or British person who was buried here, but at the time I was more concerned with finding horses for my journey.

On a cold evening as dusk was falling in December 1943, an old Soviet truck with a broken windshield could be seen jolting down the unmade road to Shandan. In the back, thirty-three Chinese students in padded clothes, sheepskin coats and caps with ear flaps, huddled against the biting wind, small hand towels tied over their noses to keep out the dust. Crammed in with them were bedding and supplies including four large earthenware jars of bean and pepper pickle. In the front sat a middle-aged New Zealander called Rewi Alley. Alley took his Christian name from a rebellious Maori chieftain, and perhaps it was this name that also imbued him with the stubborn spirit which characterised his life.

After gaining a military medal in World War I and scratching a living on a remote hill sheep farm in New Zealand, he found himself drawn by the lure of China, where he was inspired to improve the lot of poverty-stricken Chinese. His work took place against the background of the Japanese invasion and the struggle between Kuomintang (now the main party in Taiwan) and Communist forces. Alley was the driving force behind the formation in 1938 of Chinese Industrial

Cooperatives, a movement he called 'Gung Ho' or 'Work Together',
and as an offshoot of this he also set up 'Bailie' schools[3] to train young
Chinese in industrial skills. In 1941, he appointed a young British
reporter to run the school at Shuangshipu in Shaanxi. George Hogg
was an Oxford graduate who took to his new role with unbridled
enthusiasm and the school thrived.

However, by 1943 the Japanese advance was threatening, and
this is how it was that Alley arrived in Shandan with a vanguard of
students to start the school up again at a safer location further west.
Another thirty students arrived soon after, and with George Hogg as
headmaster they set to work creating living quarters and workshops
in old temple buildings they had managed to rent. Tragically within
eighteen months Hogg had died of tetanus from a stubbed toe while
playing basketball with the boys. He was buried outside the South Gate
in Shandan. The 2008 film The Children of Huang Shi *is based on his*
story. Alley took over running of the school, and within a few years the
students, who now included some girls, had created workshops for a
range of products from machine tools and textiles to soap and leather
goods, not to mention irrigating land for a farm and developing a
coal mine and power plant. The students were expected to work hard,
keep fit and maintain high hygiene standards. They were well fed and
learnt skills designed to stand them and their country in good stead
in the years to come.

After the communist takeover the school was moved to Lanzhou
to form part of the new technical institute, but thanks to the efforts of
Alley and other Gung Ho veterans, a new school was re-opened in 1987.
Only eight months later, Rewi Alley died. Today memorial tombs to
Rewi Alley and George Hogg lie side by side in a memorial garden by
Nanhu Park to the south of Shandan town centre. In the words of the
Oxford Dictionary, the term 'Gung Ho' came to mean 'unthinkingly
eager and enthusiastic', but I wonder how many people realise it is a
Chinese phrase first coined by this tenacious New Zealander.

---

[3] Named after American missionary to China, Joseph Bailie, who had
progressive ideas about education.

As we rode out of Shandan I felt quite appropriately 'gung ho'. I could now genuinely say I had ridden quite literally in the shadow of the Great Wall. The glossy coated horses felt strong and well, and with Zorbee as company Bajiu clipped along briskly. Day by day we were covering ground and the distance to Jiayuguan was shrinking. It was now less than 300 kilometres, and barring setbacks I should have no problem arriving at the end of the wall within a couple of weeks, well before my flight to Heathrow at the beginning of November. I felt a tinge of excitement at the thought of seeing home and family again. Our team was gelling well, and I enjoyed my lively debates with Hua as we rode together, stopping at intervals to take photos of each other posing by different landmarks. Peng and Li May were by now big buddies, and had even bought a cheap set of rackets to knock a ball around together in the evenings. The absence of Li Jing, who had still not arrived back from Beijing, had tipped the dynamics of the group in my favour so I felt much more included in conversation.

On the edge of town, a concrete sign with 'Long Wall' in hanzi was sitting on a dejected remnant of wall. Further along it reappeared in all its twenty-foot glory, striking resolutely across a flat plain and paralleling the road most of the way to our next destination of Dong Le: the village name denotes Eastern Happiness in hanzi, but written as one word in pinyin it has a less romantic connotation. It was dusk as we turned into a cluttered yard after a day's tramp of over forty-eight kilometres. A line of chained dogs barked furiously at the horses as we saw to their needs. In the simple *fandian* Li May and I found ourselves shown through the boys' sleeping quarters to reach our room, which we shared with two other occupants. A young girl smiled shyly at us and a tiny kitten mewed pathetically under Li May's bed before plucking up the courage to sleep on top. We were on the last leg to Jiayuguan.

CHAPTER EIGHTEEN

THE DRAGON'S TAIL

人心齐, 泰山移

rén xīn qí, tài shān yí

When people work with one mind,
they can even move Mount Taishan.

Tuesday, 13 October – Thursday, 22 October, 2009.
Dong Le to Jiayuguan (Di Yi Dun).
298 km. Daily average 27 km.

The thirteenth of the month is not an auspicious date, so I was not overly surprised when Li Jing turned up at a rest stop as we were nearing Zhangye, the next city after Wuwei. He immediately appropriated Zorbee and in spite of requests to walk, was soon pacing off ahead, never looking back. In the meantime, much to my disappointment, I had been forced to change my route plan yet again. The Great Wall had swung to the north once more and away from the main thoroughfares. I had planned to follow it more closely along the small roads I could see on our map, but another problem had arisen with the jeep. The tow bar was now badly bent to a dangerous extent, again the fault of the water tank at the front of the trailer. Peng was already crawling along at a snail's pace, and felt it was too risky to take the jeep and trailer over rough unmade roads too far away from larger settlements along the main road. He crept slowly down the National road into Zhangye, and called out a mechanic who quoted 600 yuan (about £40, very reasonable by British standards) and took the jeep off for repairs.

Originally called Ganzhou (Kanchow), Zhangye has been an important centre on the Silk Road for centuries, It probably dates from before the Han dynasty over 2,000 years ago and has been dominated by the Uighur and Western Xia at different times. Marco Polo reported that he stayed there for a whole year when it was controlled by the Mongol Yuan dynasty and known by the Mongolian name of Campichu. Local legend claims that Genghis Khan's emperor grandson Kubilai Khan was born here in the Buddhist Dafo temple, but William Geil who passed through in 1908 commented, 'the city is known far and wide for its lies', so who knows. The Dafo temple is also notable for housing the largest reclining Buddha in China, thirty-four metres of clay statue built during the Western Xia dynasty.

The city was strategically sited on the Heihe or Black River where it flows out from the foothills of the Qilian Shan. This is one of the main rivers watering the Hexi corridor, and it runs far out into the Gobi Desert, bringing water for irrigation along its valley. As it shrinks in its middle course and finally peters out in the sand it fittingly becomes known as the Ruo Shui or 'weak water'. It is thought it once extended much further north and brought water to the ancient Tangut or Xixia city of Khara-Khoto. This city continued to flourish after the Mongol invasion, taking the Mongol name of Etsina, and the river was known as the Etsin Gol. Legend has it that Etsina was finally abandoned when the Ming army dammed back the Etsin Gol and diverted the water, since when the Hei He has never reached as far.

Zhangye television turned up in the morning to our well-kept truck stop lodgings to interview me through my able translator Hua. I understood enough Chinese by now to know he could take the spirit of what I said and turn it into something far more palatable for a Chinese audience. Filming included a riveting shot of me making a cup of instant coffee in the trailer, followed by clips of the horses being fed and tacked up. Bajiu played to the camera and created quite a stir by knocking over his feed bucket, an everyday annoyance to us but the height of entertainment to the film crew. As the three of us rode towards town an extremely energetic young cameraman scampered behind to take shots of us riding through the traffic and under an ornate welcoming Chinese archway. But the civic welcome suggested by the television camera evaporated when we were then quickly diverted round the ring road, no doubt due to an official horror that the horses might leave droppings all over the pristine new town centre. So I never saw the largest reclining Buddha in China, or even the ancient wooden pagoda. Whenever I chatted with other *waiguoren* about various places we had visited in North China, it seemed that while they were lazing in luxury hotels and wafting round fascinating historical sites at the centre of town, I was hanging out at truck stops in the outskirts and tramping through the noisy back streets. But given a choice, I knew which I preferred. I could always come back and do the tourist sights another time.

Soon after we left the city, we crossed a bridge over a strong, deep river running between clearly defined banks. It had to be the Hei He, formerly the Etsin Gol which originally flowed all the way to Khara-Khoto. Zhangye is in the south-east of a large oasis watered by this river and its tributaries. At the time Geil passed through, the local government official reported that 'wheat, peas, beans, melons are all raised in quantities,' and these crops are still evident to this day. Geil also referred to that saviour of the constipated – rhubarb – which apparently grew prolifically and up to ten feet high, 'up the mountainside, on the flats, in the marshes,' near Kanchow as Zhangye was then called. Rhubarb in fact originated from this area, and as Geil put it, 'Yet, be it known, that the Chinese value this, not as the raw material for rhubarb pie, but as a drug.' It was not until about 200 years ago that rhubarb started to be used for culinary rather than purgative purposes in the West, its original value lying in the medicinal and specifically laxative properties of its dried and powdered roots. Like silk, it was an expensive export whose production was for many years confined to specific regions of China. Geil added that the Chinese 'actually thought at the time of the Opium Wars that by ceasing to export it, they could bring the West to terms.' Whether or not it was because they imagined westerners to be blighted by constipation is another question.

Li Jing's continued insistence on pacing ahead on Zorbee was intensely irritating, as apart from the soundness issue, the other horses lost motivation if our pacesetter Zorbee went out of sight. I tackled Li Jing again as politely as I could.

'Please could you go slower on Zorbee and stay just ahead of us. I am worried he will go lame again, and the other horses go so much better if they can see Zorbee. I get tired of pushing Bajiu on all day.'

It was evidently far too much trouble and he paced off again.

'Hua manages to keep Zorbee walking. Perhaps you should swap onto Bajiu,' I ventured the next time he was within earshot. It was very unlikely Li Jing would take up my suggestion, considering how much he loved riding Zorbee, but I hoped a subtle dig at his horsemanship might have an effect. So I was rather taken aback when he agreed, and very soon regretted my rash comment.

In Shajing we stayed in a small friendly home with an elderly couple who ceremoniously presented us with a cardboard box full of apples. The small brick toilet block in a back yard crammed with branches for firewood had separate male and female cubicles with steps leading up to the standard slit in the floor. But taking advantage of the facilities was not an occasion to dawdle as the female cubicle on its throne faced the back door, and the only privacy was an aged hessian curtain which wouldn't pull down.

We set out to Xinhua with Li Jing now on board my faithful Bajiu. Hua returned to Zorbee and I rode Shandan. After our long day's ride to Dong Le I had been worried that Bajiu was a touch unsound behind, and explained this to Li Jing with a request to play safe and keep him to a walk as I had been doing. We were so near to reaching our goal, and the last thing I wanted to do was to mess things up at this late stage. My heart sank as he trotted off. We had a midday stop in the market town of Linze, and once again I gently pleaded with Li Jing to think of Bajiu's welfare and slow his pace. But it was evident that he did not like being told what to do, least of all by a woman and a foreign one at that. He launched into a furious tirade, flinging his arms around and revealing a command of English he had hitherto kept hidden.

'Don't tell me how to manage horses. I know how to manage horses. You don't know how to manage horses.'

A curious crowd began to gather. The spectacle of a tearful elderly female *laowai* being berated by an irate Chinese man with a pony tail was infinitely better entertainment than any martial arts show.

'You don't know how to ride. You can't even gallop. The trouble is you go too slow.'

In the face of such incandescent rage it was not worth listing the endurance races I had won. I retreated to the trailer, followed by a histrionic Li Jing.

'You always want to have your own way.'

It was the final irony and also the final straw in our relationship. Hua and I argued frequently, but it was water off a duck's back and we always remained firm friends. Hua was also susceptible to reason. Li Jing's antagonistic response seemed to result from a total inability to compromise, or even consider any method of approach other than his own whether it was right or wrong. If he did not get his own way he sulked like a sullen teenager. It was making my life a misery and I made up my mind that I could not endure having him as a member of the team the following year. It was unlikely to be an issue with the Beijing sponsors as I was already aware that one of the reasons they had been so keen for Peng to come along was a concern that Li Jing might prove difficult. The only positive part of the whole debacle was that it polarised team sympathies on my side.

Xinhua was a pleasant little town with one-storey buildings on either side of a shady tree-lined main street, and a busy bazaar in full swing. Peng, Li May and I walked round the stalls, Peng cheering me up with a sugar doughnut and helping me negotiate for a pair of toddler's split-bottomed trousers. I had seen some pretty padded waistcoats in embroidered silk hung up outside a tailor's shop, and went in to be measured up for a custom fit by the stout and cheerful female proprietor.

'*Duo shao quian*? How much is it?'

'*Wu shi kuai*. Fifty yuan.'

It was a snip at the equivalent of around £4 sterling, so I immediately ordered another as a Christmas present for my sister. They would take a couple of days to make, but we could pick them up on the drive back to Beijing. There was nothing like a little retail therapy to boost spirits.

The rooms in our small *fandian* were fine, but the yard was too small to accommodate the jeep and trailer. They had to be parked at the side of the road in front, with Zorbee and Shandan tied to the trailer on the walkway side. Li Jing tied Bajiu by himself on a short rope to the front bumper of the jeep. The proprietor of the *fandian* was, like fathers all over the world, excessively proud of his sturdy toddler son, whose chubby face was topped with a soft down of black hair.

'*Ta hui shuo Yingyu*. He can speak English,' he announced grandly, eventually managing to extract a shy 'Hallo,' while the *yingguoren*, or Brit, expressed suitable admiration.

All the way along the Hexi Corridor the local people were friendly and welcoming, calling us over to find out what we were up to, and offering cups of tea, or handfuls of sunflower seeds. But I was a bit nonplussed when a man ran up alongside Bajiu and pushed a couple of onions into my hands.

We were a constant subject of curiosity. Coming into Xinhua as school came out, the long quiet road was striped with the evening shadows of the tall poplars which stood in lines alongside. A trio of school boys on bicycles joined us, chattering confidently to Hua. They all wore identical blue and white tracksuits with '*Nanhuazhongxue*' or 'Nanhua Middle School' on the back.

'*Ni zai xuexiao xue yingyu ma*? Do you learn English at school?' Hua asked.

'*Xue*. We do.'

Hua nodded in my direction.

'*Ta shi Yingguoren. Gen ta shuo Yingyu.* She is British. Speak English to her.'

Wobbling on their bikes, they were covered in confusion and fell silent.

Two more school boys in blue and white tracksuits caught up and joined the gaggle to see what was going on, and then a couple of girls with their long black hair tied back in ponytails. They all crowded after Hua in his matching blue jacket like a flock of brightly-plumaged young birds clinging to their parent, until they lost interest and swooped off down the road.

In Nanhua, Peng found a three-storey hotel with a large empty yard. The spacious rooms had a panoramic view out to the rugged brown foothills on the southern horizon, and when I opened the window the quiet clear air carried in an autumn chill. I took advantage of the washbasin in our room to wash some clothes, before realising just in time that the plug hole emptied straight into a bucket.

With Hua back on Zorbee, we were able to stride out, gossiping and enjoying the scenery while Li Jing did everything he could to provoke me. He now decided to put Bajiu on a weight loss regime, ostensibly because of Bajiu's large belly, but I suspect mainly as a reason to demonstrate his superior horse management skills and try to aggravate me. Bajiu had been thoroughly wormed, given three to four hard feeds a day, and ridden hundreds of miles over the previous ten weeks. As the shine on his coat now testified, he could not have been in better condition, and it was evident that his deep body was just how he was made. Claiming he was trying to get rid of the belly, Li Jing gave Bajiu no water or food from early morning until well after dark apart from a few maize stalks, and incessantly trotted and cantered him everywhere, disappearing ahead as he used to do on Zorbee.

But the stolid Bajiu was not an inexhaustible live wire like Zorbee, and after a few days I noticed that Li Jing was starting to lag behind. In the meantime, Bajiu's belly had not reduced one iota, in spite of being tied up every midday while Zorbee and Shandan grazed, ate and drank their fill. Added to this Li Jing was using his Mongolian saddle. It had a narrow leather strap for a girth which had already caused girth sores on two of the other horses. When I suggested putting my fleecy girth sleeve on it, he flatly refused, and as I feared, after a couple of days I felt lumps appearing in Bajiu's girth area. Thankfully Hua was able to talk sense into him, and the girth sleeve was in place the following morning. But we were so close to the end that I determined to see it out and not to rise to the bait whatever happened. When Li Jing blatantly trotted flat out past me, or tied Bajiu up on a high, short rope in front of me without food or water, I gritted my teeth and ignored him. It was painful to see poor Bajiu gazing dolefully in my direction, but we only had a week to last out, and all Li Jing's behaviour did was further alienate the rest of the team.

It was exasperating, especially as otherwise everything would have been perfect. The weather was glorious and the scenery stunning. After Nanhua, the road swung away from the Hei He valley and the Qilian mountains came back into view to the south, flaunting their gleaming white peaks every day in the brisk autumn air. The oases were interspersed with broad stretches of stony desert where little brown chukar partridges scurried away through the scrub, and wide river beds braided with dry channels swept down from the mountains to the plain. An expanse of pale sand was splashed with bright red piles of chili peppers. In the oasis settlements maize cobs were laid out to dry on concrete surfaces in front of houses, packed together in neat squares and rectangles so they looked like floor mosaics. Wheat, barley and millet had been harvested earlier but we passed a late crop being threshed by the ancient method, an elderly man standing at the centre of a circle of tangled stems, lunging a pair of donkeys round him to trample the stalks and loosen the grain seeds. A little further on a few sheaves of barley had been neatly laid out on the road to let passing traffic do the work. Scattered over the harvested fields, sheep picked on the stubble, and mopeds putted past carrying sheepskins to which swinging feet and tails were still attached.

A few times when crossing a dry watercourse we saw mysterious pieces of folded yellow paper perched on the parapet of the bridge and weighted down with a small stone.

'What are they for, Hua?'

'I don't know. Perhaps it is an offering to the spirit of the water.' Perhaps I will never know.

In the tiny desert oasis of Yuanshanzi, a dust storm blew up as dusk fell and we worried unnecessarily that it might last until morning and hold us up. Rather inconveniently, Li May and I found our solar torches didn't work, and I ended up obeying the call of nature behind a cow on the yard when I couldn't find my way to the toilets in the dust-laden dark. Peng had bought a load of carrots and managed to slip a few to a hungry Bajiu. He usually turned his nose up at them, but now he deigned to eat them for a change. In his usual reliable fashion, Peng was doing a sterling job finding feed for the horses and making it last. The bales of hay that had generously been donated by the Shandan stud turned out to be less nutritious straw, but Peng had managed to track down a couple of bales of real hay to eke out the supply of roughage. For the moment, the horses were chomping on an untidy pile of leafy maize stalks. For their hard feed, he had bought some whole barley, but also whole maize kernels which I had never fed before. Peng assured me he had previously fed whole kernels with no problem, but he also hunted down some ground grain, so between everything we had enough hard feed to take us all the way to Jiayuguan. Hua and I took advantage of any clumps of alfalfa lining the road, stopping to let Zorbee and Shandan gorge on the lush green leaves while Li Jing trotted past on Bajiu. The horses also used their own initiative. In Qing Shui, the jeep and trailer were parked behind our hotel in a large yard with public access. Orange plastic netting sacks of maize cobs were neatly stacked along one side, and a certain miscreant, unfortunately not Bajiu, escaped overnight, ripped open a sack and tucked into the ready meal so I had to fork out 30 yuan compensation the next morning.

It was odd to reflect that the famous Swedish explorer Sven Hedin had seen the New Year in at his camp here while returning from his 1934-35 motor expedition to Xinjiang. I once again felt a sense of awe to be following a path which had been beaten by countless travellers of repute in the past.

The long day in the saddle from Gaoshanbao to Wumianjing two-and-a-half months previously had exhausted both horses and humans, but now we easily covered the forty-seven kilometres from to Qing Shui to Shangba. In a way, it seemed a pity to be heading home when we were all becoming fitter, but it was time for a longer rest, and I was missing my family. Bajiu was not so perky. By the time we reached Jiuquan, formerly known as Suchow or Suzhou, six days after leaving Zhangye, Li Jing was following meekly in the rear and shadowing our movements. Bajiu had obviously run out of steam and Li Jing was finding it easier to get a lead from Zorbee. I felt smugly vindicated. It did not help Bajiu's water situation but at least he was not being chivvied around any more.

Since leaving Beijing we had experienced absolutely no problem with the police, who were unfailingly polite and helpful. More often than not they would already have seen or spoken to Peng as he drove ahead with the jeep and trailer emblazoned with the Beijing to London mission. As we rode along the dual carriageway into Jiuquan a couple of young policemen hailed us to have a chat.

'*Keyi qi nide ma ma?* Can I ride your horse?' one of them asked hesitantly.

From avoiding the police at the start of the Great Wall ride, I now found myself giving them pony rides at the end.

A gaggle of pretty girl reporters turned up, much to the approval of the boys who suddenly became quite animated. We posed for photos by a modern monument on the edge of town, and Hua held Zorbee and Bajiu while the girl reporters scrambled on board their backs. It seemed pony rides were the order of the day. I raised my head to look at the monument rearing up at the top of a wide flight of steps behind the posing group. Four thin silver metal crescents of varying height sliced up into the sky like claws, the tallest one topped by a small globe. About halfway up the tall claw were two leaping golden figures, arms upraised and ribbon-like drapes streaming out behind in a non-existent gale.

I turned to Hua.

'What does this monument mean, Hua?'

'It is a statue of flying to the moon.'

'But who are the people supposed to be?'

'It is the Chinese moon goddess flying to the moon.'

The famous Chinese legend of the goddess Chang'e is associated with the Mid-Autumn or Moon Festival. It comes in many forms, and although they may contain variations and additions, each of them retains some of the same elements. Firstly, she is sent from heaven to live as a mortal. Secondly, she marries the hero archer Houyi. Thirdly, Houyi acquires a pill containing the elixir of life. Fourthly, Chang'e either deliberately or accidentally swallows the pill. And fifthly, she floats up to the heavens. The story sometimes includes additional characters, events, and plotlines but in all of them she ends up on the moon. However, why were there two figures on the monument, one looking decidedly male? Hua explained that the monument of Chang'e Flying to the Moon held a deeper significance for Jiuquan.

At 9am Beijing time on October 15, 2003, almost six years before, the rocket Shenzhou 5 was blasted into space from a secret location deep in the arid wastes of the Gobi Desert, around 200 kilometres north-east of where we were standing. Aboard was Yang Liwei, the first Chinese astronaut or 'taikonaut' to orbit the earth. His trip only lasted 21 hours 23 minutes before he landed safely back in north-west China, within five kilometres of his aim point, but at that moment China officially became the third member of the exclusive club of countries to have launched a man into space. This success was followed by the launch of Shenzou 6, China's first two-man mission in 2005, and Shenzou 7, the first spacewalk mission in 2007. All this activity took place in the isolated Jiuquan Space Launch Centre (JSLC), formed in 1958 and the oldest and most used of four such facilities in China. Ironically it is actually sited in the Ejin Banner of Inner Mongolia, not far over the border with Jiuquan principality, but it is named after the nearest city which just happens to be Jiuquan in Gansu. China had now turned its attention to space exploration, in particular the moon, and the Chinese Lunar Exploration Project was created, known as the Chang'e program after China's pioneering moon goddess. The monument was evidence of the pride Jiuquan civic authorities took in the city's link with the space program, and presumably the inclusion of the male figure of Houyi, who in one version of the Chang'e story flew up to the sun, was a nod to the male astronauts. It was not until three years later, in June 2012, that Liu Yang became the first female astronaut in space when Shenzou 9 roared into space from JSLC on a mission to dock with China's new orbital space station.

If legend is to be believed, Chang'e is still living on the moon to this day, with only a Jade Rabbit for company, (if we set aside the version with a woodcutter). During the Apollo 11 lunar mission in 1969, Houston mission control warned the crew of the possibility of bumping into a pretty girl and a rabbit on the moon.

'OK, we'll keep a close eye for the bunny girl,' responded Michael Collins. Neither Neil Armstrong nor Buzz Aldrin reported a sighting. However, you will now understand why the Chinese called their unmanned moon rover 'Jade Rabbit' when they finally landed spacecraft Chang'e 3 on the moon on 14th December 2013.

The names of some of the places we stayed in the Hexi Corridor reflected the significance of the water supply from the mountains which enabled agriculture to flourish in the oases along its length. Dajing (Big Spring), Shuiquanzi (Water Spring), Qing Shui (Clearwater), and Shajing (Sand Spring) all fell into this category. But the water here apparently came with an added kick, as Jiuquan means 'wine spring', though this would have undoubtedly referred to *baijiu*, made from grain rather than grapes. This goes back to a story involving the great Han general Huo Qubing. Wishing to share the celebration of a victory over the Xiongnu with his troops, in a version of the 'water into wine' bible story he reportedly poured wine into a nearby spring for everyone to enjoy. The spring still flows in Jiuquan Park which was only a short walk from our hotel, but as it no longer contains wine we gave it a miss. A pity, as it would have been great to enjoy a drop of wine, albeit watery, to celebrate our penultimate day. Instead Hua and I went to the police station to extend my visa for a bit longer as it was due to run out by the end of the week, and I had been warned it might take a couple of days. The big boss was rather 'jobsworth', but sorted out my visa there and then.

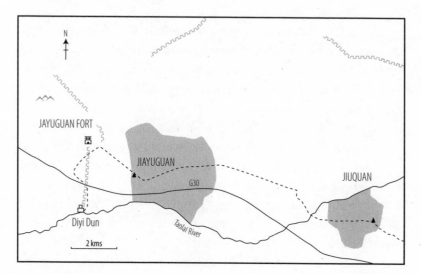

We left Jiuquan on 21 October through the urban sprawl which was rapidly eating up the twenty-four kilometres stretching north-west to Jiayuguan. Snarling guard dogs on chains outside a machinery dealership lunged at us as we passed on a road cluttered with workshops and factories. However before long we were on wide newly constructed roads almost empty of traffic, and as we came into Jiayuguan we found broad avenues divided from pedestrian walkways by belts of greenery and flower beds. Large modern buildings in the modern geometric Chinese architectural style grouped round the crossroads, and here and there high-rise apartments sprouted in clumps like mushrooms, gleaming white against the open blue sky. At the centre of town, we crossed an immense boulevard flanked by street lights hung with great pale light globes. A wide, lawned central reservation stretched away into the distance, and in front of us stood a huge statue of the Flying Horse of Gansu in an enormous bed of red and orange blooms. On the large plinth was a metal plaque engraved with the words 'Top

Tourist City in China'. Jiayuguan's claim to this accolade comes almost entirely from its main attraction, Jiayuguan Fort, and this was where we were headed.

Jiayuguan fort marked the western terminus of the Ming Great Wall, and was strategically located at one of the narrowest points along the Hexi Corridor, between the Hei Shan to the north and the Qilian mountains to the south, and near a spring providing water. It was built during the Ming dynasty as the terminus of the Great Wall defences, and as part of the response to the Tumu disaster. Constructed of earth bricks rather than the stone blocks used at Shanhaigun, it deteriorated over the years but has been subject to more recent restoration. Remnants of the Han dynasty wall can be traced extending further west as far as Yumenguan or 'Jade Gate Pass', but it is Jiayuguan Fort which has traditionally been regarded by the Chinese as the border of civilised China. Beyond it lay the fearful expanses of the Taklamakan and Gobi Deserts, populated by demons and barbarians, and to be exiled outside the wall was regarded as a fate worse than death.

We made our way to our multi-storey *fandian* on the other side of town to settle in and have lunch before tackling the last six kilometres. Peng took over the ride on Zorbee from Hua, and Li Jing continued to skulk behind on Bajiu.

I cannot begin to describe the thrill I felt when Peng and I came over the brow of a railway overpass to see the fort about three kilometres in front of us. The red earth crenellated walls blazed in the late evening sun, and the pagoda style turrets on the great gateways protruded like flared pine cones. In the background the harsh bulk of the Hei Shan or Black Mountains rose abruptly from the plain, and beyond the fort stretched the Sai Wai, or area beyond the Great Wall.

We had arranged to meet a TV crew in the fort, and trotted round to the east gateway, clattering through the outer barbican, under the Rouyan tower and into the central courtyard. Over the years this central space would have been alive with soldiers and travellers, but it was now laid out as a formal park with wide paved pathways leading between trees and neatly clipped hedges. A heading on a billboard in Chinese and English declared, 'Taste Military Culture of the Great Wall,' and below in smaller lettering, 'Welcome you to enjoy the imitation show of ancient military exercises'. We were back in tourist Chinglish Land. Programme items included, 'Changing of the Guard and Be on Duty', the latter part of which promised to be a show-stopper.

On we trotted through three more archways, the last one an echoing tunnel through the fort wall to the west. This was the famous 'Travellers' Gate', sometimes known more ominously as the 'Gate of Sighs', which led out to the desolate and dangerous lands beyond. It was haunting to think of the endless stream of travellers and their animals who had been funnelled through this gate over the centuries since it was built. In particular, I was reminded of Eva and Francesca French and Mildred Cable, British missionaries whose book *The Gobi Desert* I had devoured in my teens. I vividly remember the first time I read their description of setting off in their mule carts through this very gate, and I was exhilarated to think that now I was following in their hoofsteps nearly a hundred years later. We scrambled up the short slope to the plain beyond to pose for photos with the West Gate tower rearing up behind us before retreating to the main courtyard for interviews.

I had always imagined I would feel ecstatic at a moment such as this and want to whoop out loud. I had done it. I had ridden the 3,000 kilometres from Shanhaiguan, covering the entire distance from one end of the Ming Great Wall to the other on horseback. When I was back in Beijing, I contacted Ed Jocelyn to ask Great Wall expert William Lindesay if he knew of anyone else who had done this. Apparently he did not, so it seemed I was officially the first person on record to do so.

But instead of boiling over with excitement, I felt a deep sense of inner calm. Perhaps it was elderly exhaustion. Or perhaps it was just overwhelming relief at having successfully completed the first challenge on the journey in spite of all the many obstacles and setbacks. For the time being I no longer had to worry about lame or injured horses, broken bones, clapped out vehicles or difficult team members.

A final section of 'open wall' ran south from the fort to *Di Yi Dun* or the 'first beacon platform'. This was a watchtower in a spectacular location perched on a cliff overlooking the Taolai river. The next day Hua and I set off quietly on Zorbee and Shandan to ride to the very end of the end of the Great Wall. But it was not as easy as we thought, as within a few hundred yards our path from the fort was blocked by the railway line. Not a problem in itself as we had hopped across railway lines with the horses before, but this time there was a solid fence, no doubt to deter wall followers such as ourselves. We found a floodwater underpass which had just enough headroom to lead the horses through, but immediately came face to face with the expressway. Luckily there was an overpass a little further along, but then Zorbee stubbornly dug in his heels at a level crossing. Hua dismounted and pulled ineffectually on the reins. The Mongols would never have had such difficulties.

At last Zorbee relented and we finally reached the crumbling earth structure of *Di Yi Dun* to peer over the fence at the edge of the gorge. A dizzying eighty-two metre drop down to the Taolai below made me gasp. The river had carved out a deep gorge between two sheer cliffs, and no way could mounted horsemen or even attackers on foot have negotiated such a barrier. It demonstrated forcibly why this tower marked the end of the wall.

An open truck from Shandan turned up to fetch Zorbee and Shandan, backing up to a bank so they could hop on. Back at the hotel, Bajiu was led over and jumped on from a pile of rubble at the side of road. The engine grumbled into life, spurts of dust kicked up from the wheels, and the truck swung onto the road and rattled off to the Shandan stud where we had arranged for the horses to spend the winter. Over the last three months I had spent almost every hour of the day with them, and although it would not be long before we would be together again, I knew I would miss them in the interim.

All the horse equipment and other baggage that would not be needed until the spring was packed into the trailer, which was locked up and stowed away at a sports stadium in Jiayuguan. Li Jing took his leave with little ceremony as the rest of us tucked into noodles in the restaurant. It was a pity that his relationship with the team had soured so badly as in his own way he cared deeply for the horses. I never once saw him strike or even raise his voice to them, and he was endlessly patient with the challenging Hei Feng. But he was his own worst enemy, and his stubborn refusal to consider any way but his own was unproductive in a situation where the horses' welfare should always have come first.

We crossed the Tengger Desert on the three-day drive back to Beijing, and the waterless rocky and sandy landscapes illuminated why the Hexi Corridor formed such a significant finger of fertile land poking out into the inhospitable regions of western China. Arriving in Beijing, Li May and Hua went their separate ways. Hua would not be able to take part the following year but declared his intention of joining me at some point further west on my journey.

Wutzala organised a celebratory Beijing hotpot with Kubi, Harry and Peng, and I was thrilled to find that Guo Sheng had turned up as well. There were smiles all round the table as we toasted the future success of the ride following the resounding achievement of the first stage. Wutzala, Kubi and Harry raised their glasses and confirmed their ongoing commitment. Guo Sheng magnanimously paid for the meal and presented me with a little statuette of the Flying Horse of Gansu, nostrils flaring and foot delicately balanced on a swallow. Our hairy Shandan horses were hardly of the same ilk as this ethereal heavenly horse, but they had plodded valiantly across hills and deserts to bring us safely to our destination in Gansu. It was a fitting memento and I felt a surge of emotion as I held it in my hand and ran my fingers along its smooth flanks. But it was not an occasion for sad goodbyes, as the following spring Peng would be accompanying me across the desolate wastes of the Gobi. It was not an end but a beginning.

～

GLOSSARY

baozi	bao-dze	steamed filled bun
jia	jee-ah	gee up (from an old Chinese word for ride)
jiaozi	jee-ow-dze	meat or vegetable filled dumpling
baijui	buy jee-oh	white spirit (strong alcoholic drink made from grain, usually sorghum)
bajiu	baa jee-oh	eighty-nine
kuai	kwai	spoken term for monetary unit yuan.
lao wai	lao (as in how) why	slang term for foreigner
qi ma	chee mah	to ride a horse
mantou	man-toe	steamed bun (like baozi but no filling)
maotai	mao (as how) tie	a popular brand of baijiu, much loved by Mao Zedong
mei shi	may-sher	no matter
waiguoren	why-gwo-ren	foreigner
wang ba	wahng ba	internet cafe ('*wang*' literally means 'net')
qiezi	chee-eh-dze	aubergine (used instead of 'cheese' when posing for photos)
xiao lu	shee-ow loo	small roads or tracks
xigua	shee-gwah	watermelon
yingyu	ying-yoo	English language
yinguoren	yinguoren	British person, though sometimes inaccurately used to mean English.
yuan	yu-en	commonly used word for RMB (renminbi) unit of currency (kuai)
youtiao	yo-tee-ow	fried breadstick
zhou	joe	watery Asian porridge

Food and Accommodation

There are a bewildering array of names for food and accommodation establishments, which can vary in meaning from place to place. The most common are:

binguan	bin-gwan	a simple hotel or inn
canding	tsan-ding	small eating house or canteen
canguan	tsan-gwan	restaurant
fandian	fun-dee-en	offers both accommodation and food, but can apply to anything from a very basic B&B to a five star hotel
fanguan	fun-gwan	restaurant
jiudian	jee-oh dee-en	hotel and/or restaurant, literally 'wine inn' (as with fandian it can refer to large hotel)
nongjiayuan/ jiayuan	armstay/homestay	generally in tourist area

Many settlement names include the following words for various types of settlement:

cun	tsoon	village
zhen	jehn	town (usually market town size)
xiang	shee-ang	home village or township
cheng	chehng	town or city, probably walled (this also means wall)
shi	sher	city

Equine Terms

canter	slow gallop
cantle	raised part at rear of saddle
cast, to get	when a horse gets cast, this does not refer to a pantomime horse, but when it gets stuck upside-down, usually when it has been rolling, often in a confined stable

compound feed	mixture of concentrates such as oats and barley which may be in pellet form
crupper	strap which goes under the horse's tail to prevent the saddle slipping forward
farrier	blacksmith who specialises in shoeing horses
fodder	non-concentrate feed such as hay, straw, maize stalks
gelding	castrated male horse
girth	belt round horse's belly to keep saddle on
girth gall	sore caused by friction from the girth
gullet	tunnel between saddle panels which keeps saddle seat off horse's spine
hand	measure of height (one hand equals 4 inches)
hard feed	concentrated feeds such as oats, barley, maize etc.
hock	the middle joint of a horse's back leg (although it is sometimes thought of as a backward facing knee, it corresponds to a human ankle)
hogged mane	mane shaved off
napping	when a horse disobeys its rider by spinning, rearing, stopping etc.
pace	gait in which lateral pairs of legs move together
pastern	part of horse's lower leg just above hoof
pommel	raised part at front of saddle
pony	officially a pony is anything under 14.2 hands, but in practice many breeds such as Shandan, Icelandic, Arabian etc. are called horses even when they are pony height
tack	saddles, bridles, harness and other accessories for use with horses
tack up	to put saddle, bridle etc. on horse
trot	gait in which diagonal pairs of legs move together
untack	take off saddle and bridle etc.
withers	top of shoulders (horses are measured to here)

A kilometre is approximately 0.6 miles, and a mile is approximately 1.7 kilometres.

I have expressed distance in kilometres in this book, as it is the standard unit of distance used in China and throughout Eurasia.

SELECTED BIBLIOGRAPHY

Alley, Rewi. *An Autobiography* (Foreign Languages Press 2003)

Alley, Rewi. *Yo Banfa!* (Foreign Languages Press, Beijing 2004)

Bai Shouyi. *An Outline History of China* (Foreign Languages Press 2005)

Barfield, Thomas J. *The Perilous Frontier* (Blackwell 1989)

Bayarsiakhan, Bekhjargal. *Travelling by Mongolian Horse* (Ulaan Baataar, Mongolia 2006)

Becker, Jasper. *Hungry Ghosts* (Henry Holt and Co 1998)

Cable, Mildred and Francesca French. *The Gobi Desert* (Hodder and Stoughton 1942)

Confucius. *The Analects* (Dover Publications 1995)

Deng Rong. *Deng Xiaoping and the Cultural Revolution* (Foreign Languages Press 2002)

Fenby, Jonathan. *The Dragon Throne* (Quercus 2007)

Geil, William Edgar. *The Great Wall of China* (Sturgis and Walton 1909)

Gifford, Rob. *China Road* (Bloomsbury Publishing 2008)

Gray, Nathan Hoturoa. *First Pass Under Heaven* (Penguin Books 2006)

Hanbury-Tenison, Robin. *A Ride Along the Great Wall* (Century Hutchinson 1987)

Hedin, Sven. *The Silk Road* (Macmillan and Co. 1938)

Hessler, Peter. *Country Driving* (Canongate 2010)

Jiang Rong. *Wolf Totem* (Penguin Press 2008)

Jocelyn, Ed and Andy McEwan. *The Long March* (Constable 2006)

Jung Chang. *Empress Dowager Cixi* (Vintage 2014)

Jung Chang and John Halliday. *Mao, The Unknown Story* (Vintage 2006)

Li Zhisui. *The Private Life of Chairman Mao* (Chatto and Windus 1994)

Lindesay, William. *Alone on the Great Wall* (Fulcrum Inc US 1991)

Lindesay, William and Michael Yamashita. *The Great Wall From Beginning to End* (2007)

Lindesay, William. *The Great Wall in 50 Objects* (Penguin Random House 2015)

Lindesay, William. *The Great Wall Revisited* (China Intercontinental Press 2007)

Lovell, Julia. *The Great Wall* (Grove Press 2007)

Ma Jian. *Red Dust* (Vintage 2002)

Man, John. *Genghis Khan* (Bantam Press 2005)

Man, John. *The Great Wall* (Bantam Press 2009)

McManus, James. *Ocean Devil* (Harper Perennial 2008)

Paludan, Ann. *Chronicle of the Chinese Emperors*
(Thames and Hudson 1998)

Shepard, Wade. *Ghost Cities of China* (Asian Arguments 2015)

Sima Qian. *Records of the Grand Historian*
(Columbia University Press 2007)

Shwartz, Daniel. *The Great Wall of China* (Thomas and Hudson 2001)

Steinhardt, Nancy. *The Tangut Royal Tombs near Yinchuan*
(In Muquarna Vol X. Leiden 1993)

Tolstoy, Alexandra. *Last Secrets of the Silk Road* (Profile Books 2004)

Waldron, Arthur. *The Great Wall of China*
(Cambridge University Press 1990)

Wei Yuqing. *Tales of Ming Emperors and Empresses*
(Foreign Languages Press 2007)

Wood, Frances. *Did Marco Polo go to China?* (Secker and Warburg 1995)

Zhang Xianliang. *Grass Soup* (Minerva 1995)

Panoramic China Series (Foreign Languages Press)

Hebei: The Great Wall Legacy

Inner Mongolia: The Horseback People.

Ningxia: A Land Blessed by the Yellow River

Megan Knoyle Lewis has never led a conventional life. During her childhood living in Malaya (now Malaysia) she travelled in South-East Asia and Australia. She attended school in both Kuala Lumpur and London, and holds an MA in South-East Asian Studies from the School of Oriental and African Studies. Megan is the first and only person to have ridden round the world on horseback, covering such iconic routes as the Pony Express Trail in the United States of America and, during her epic trek from Beijing to London, parts of the Silk Road. When not travelling the world, Megan can be found at home on her Cwrtycadno stud in Pumpsaint, Carmarthenshire, where she breeds award-winning Welsh Section B ponies.